BREAKTHROUGHS

in Science

DEVELOPING READING IN THE CONTENT AREA

Nancy F. Knapp

JAMESTOWN PUBLISHERS

a division of NTC/CONTEMPORARY PUBLISHING GROUP
Lincolnwood, Illinois USA

Cover and interior design: Michael Kelly
Cover images: Image Bank; Stock Imagery

ISBN: 0-89061-810-0

Published by Jamestown Publishers,
a division of NTC/Contemporary Publishing Group, Inc.,
4255 West Touhy Avenue,
Lincolnwood (Chicago), Illinois 60712-1975 U.S.A.

Manufactured in the United States of America.

7 8 9 10 11 12 13 14 15 16 113 09 08 07 06 05 04 03 02

CONTENTS

TO THE INSTRUCTOR

This *Breakthroughs in Science* text is designed to help students develop the critical-reading and thinking skills they need to read and apply scientific information.

Most chapters are divided into two parts: The first covers a reading skill, and the second covers a science topic. While students may already have mastered some of the reading skills, we recommend that they work through *all* of the science topics in order to assure a solid grounding in key science concepts.

Some special features to note are the pre-test and post-test, the chapter reviews, and the answer key.

- **Pre-Test** and **Post-Test**. These tests are in multiple-choice format, similar to that found on many tests. Questions are drawn from the entire range of skills and content in the book. Evaluation charts correlated to the chapters help you identify strong and weak areas for each student.
- **Chapter Reviews**. These tests, also in multiple-choice format, are brief reviews of the skills taught in a chapter. Some questions also test skills taught in previous chapters.
- **Answer Keys**. A full answer key is located in the back of the text. Students should be encouraged to check their answers as soon as they complete each exercise.

Some exercises in this book ask students to write short answers in their own words. They should make every effort to complete these written exercises. Writing has been shown to be one of the most effective demonstrations of comprehension and thinking skills. When coaching your students in writing tasks, focus on their ideas and how they can be expressed clearly rather than on spelling, grammar, or handwriting.

Finally, encourage your students to learn more about science and help them find appropriate materials. You may want to discuss science issues in class. Try to help students feel comfortable with science and help them overcome any perceptions of it as a foreign and inaccessible subject. Your students will be much better prepared not only to tackle science topics but also to deal with science in their everyday lives.

TO THE STUDENT

Welcome to *Breakthroughs in Science*. In this book, you'll learn how to study reading passages as well as illustrations such as diagrams, charts, and graphs. You'll also study many of the basic ideas that are important in science.

Most of the chapters are divided into two parts. The first part of the chapter covers a reading skill, while the second part covers a science topic.

As you read through this text, do not try to memorize every fact. Instead, try to get a good understanding of the main ideas in each section. Pay special attention to the words that are printed in ***boldface type***. These are words that you will need to know when you are reading or talking about science.

You'll find answers to all the exercises at the back of the book. Be sure to check your work at the end of each exercise before you move on. And when an exercise asks you to write, answer fully in your own words.

Finally, try to learn more about science issues in your daily life. Read science articles in newspapers and magazines. Look for science programs on your local radio and television stations. Science awareness will help you not only in school but also in your everyday life.

Good luck!

PRE-TEST

Because of your life experience, there are many facts about science that you already know. Surprised? Remember, *science* just means the organized study of the world around you and everything in it. Every time you try to figure out how something works or why something happens, you are thinking scientifically.

Directions: You can use this pre-test to test your science reading skills. Read each passage carefully. Look closely at any illustrations that accompany it. Then choose the *one best answer* for each of the questions that follow. Don't worry if you find many of these questions difficult. You will learn how to answer questions like these as you work through this text.

Questions 1 and 2 are based on the following passage.

> Everyone knows what a cold is, and many of us have had one recently. But did you know that a "common cold" can be caused by any one of more than a hundred different viruses? Or that women tend to catch more colds than men, but baby girls actually catch fewer colds than baby boys?
>
> A few people (about 5% of the population) seem to be immune to colds. They rarely, if ever, catch one. But that doesn't mean they are the lucky ones. Scientists in West Germany have discovered that people who catch less than one cold per year are six times more likely to develop cancer. Maybe having a cold isn't all that bad!

1. What is the best title for this passage?
   (1) Avoid Cancer by Catching a Cold
   (2) Men Catch More Colds
   (3) How to Cure the Common Cold
   (4) Odd Facts About the Common Cold
   (5) The Lucky 5%

2. The "common cold" is probably called "common" because
   (1) many ordinary doctors can cure it
   (2) it is caused by one very common virus
   (3) most people catch one fairly often
   (4) famous people don't catch cold as often as ordinary, "common" people do
   (5) it is unusual in men

Questions 3 and 4 are based on the following passage and chart.

Hunting laws and regulations have two main purposes: to let game animals reproduce without being disturbed by hunters and to prevent overhunting of the rarer animals. The chart below shows some rules from the *1987 Wisconsin Hunting Regulations* booklet.

Small Game Hunting Seasons*

Species	Daily Limit	Open Season
Gray & Fox Squirrel	5	Sept. 12 to Jan. 31
Woodcock	5	Sept. 12 to Nov. 15
Jackrabbit	3	Oct. 17 to Nov. 15
Bobwhite Quail	5	Oct. 17 (noon) to Dec. 9
Hungarian Partridge	3	Oct. 17 (noon) to Dec. 9
Bobcat	1 *per season*	Oct. 17 to Dec. 31 (north of Hwy. 64 *only*)
Snowshoe Hare	Unlimited	Year-round

* *Only selected portions of the chart have been reproduced here. Those seeking complete information should obtain a copy of the original booklet.*

3. On which of the following dates could a person in northern Wisconsin legally hunt all of the seven animals listed?
   (1) September 9
   (2) October 16
   (3) November 11
   (4) December 4
   (5) February 28

4. From the information in the chart, which of these animals would you infer is the most common?
   (1) gray squirrel
   (2) jackrabbit
   (3) bobwhite quail
   (4) bobcat
   (5) snowshoe hare

Questions 5–7 are based on the following passage and diagram.

Keeping the proper amount of air pressure in your automobile tires is important. Incorrect tire pressure can cause extra tire wear. It can also cause accidents. Underinflation can cause a tire to heat up, possibly leading to a blowout on the highway. Overinflation prevents tire tread from fully gripping the road, making the car more likely to skid.

UNDERINFLATED

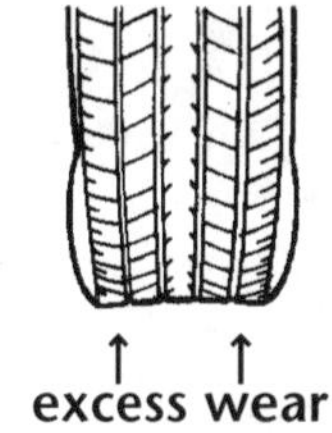

OVERINFLATED

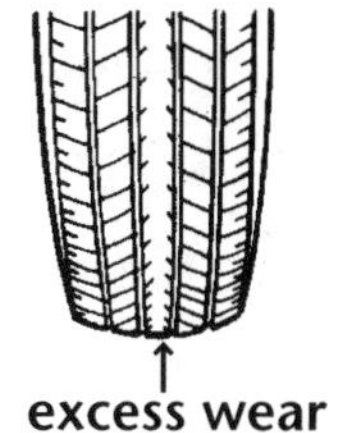

5. An "overinflated" tire means a tire that
   (1) costs too much
   (2) has too little pressure in it
   (3) is badly worn
   (4) has too much air in it
   (5) requires 50 pounds of pressure

6. From this passage you can conclude that
   (1) too much heat causes rubber to weaken
   (2) most people do not use correct tire pressure
   (3) cold weather makes tires swell up
   (4) all tires require the same air pressure
   (5) only an expert can check tire pressure

7. This passage is most likely to be from which of the following books?
   (1) *Cooking Great Meals on the Road*
   (2) *1,001 Ways to Save Money*
   (3) *Choosing the Right Automobile*
   (4) *Safe Travel in the Air*
   (5) *Tips for New Car Owners*

Questions 8 and 9 are based on the following passage.

People have been making glass for thousands of years, using some of the same methods we use today. Ordinary window glass is made from a mixture of sand (SiO_2), soda (Na_2CO_3), and lime (CaO). This mixture is heated until the different chemicals fuse together into a thick semiliquid, which can be blown or pressed or stretched into different shapes before it cools and hardens.

Depending on how it has been mixed and shaped, glass can be used for windows, cups and dishes, lenses in eyeglasses and telescopes, airtight containers for foods and medicines, glass bricks for building, and many other purposes. Glass can even be drawn into a fine thread called fiberglass, which can be used for insulation and filters, or woven into a handsome fabric for curtains and drapes.

8. Which of the following statements is true, according to the passage?
   (1) Sand, soda, and lime are heated separately and then mixed to make glass.
   (2) Glass must be cool before it can be shaped.
   (3) The basic materials in glass fuse together after they are heated.
   (4) After the glass is shaped, it is heated to make it strong.
   (5) After it hardens, glass is carved into the desired shape.

9. Oxygen is an element present in sand, soda, and lime. The chemical symbol for oxygen must be
   (1) Si
   (2) O
   (3) Na
   (4) C
   (5) Ca

Questions 10–12 are based on the following graph.

Weather forecasters use an anemometer to measure the speed of the wind. On the next page is a graph showing one day's anemometer readings at a certain weather station.

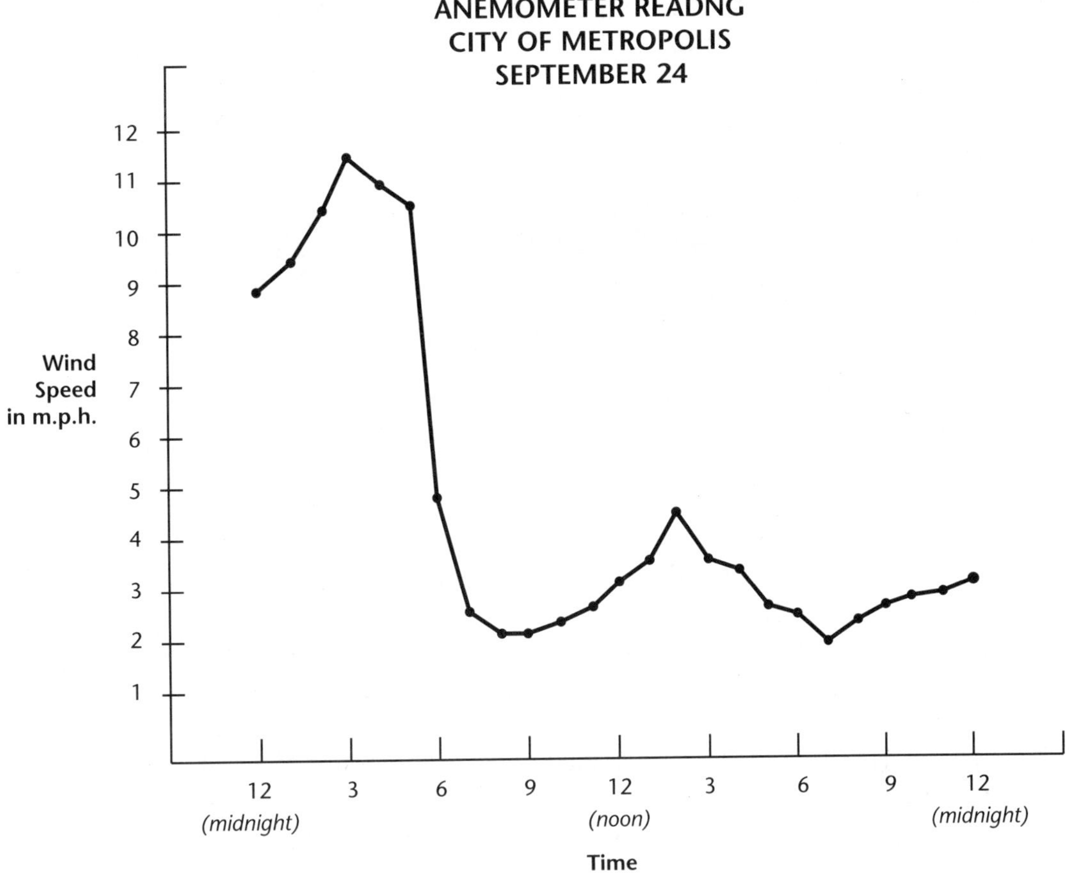

10. Considering that both light and wind are needed to fly a kite successfully, what was the best time to fly a kite in Metropolis on September 24?

(1) 2 A.M.
(2) 3 A.M.
(3) 10 A.M.
(4) 2 P.M.
(5) 6 P.M.

11. Using the graph, what can you predict about the wind on September 25?

(1) There will be a lot of wind.
(2) There will be less wind than there was on September 23.
(3) The wind will get lower as the day goes on.
(4) The wind will be strongest in the afternoon.
(5) Nothing about September 25 can be predicted from this graph.

12. Since a *thermometer* measures temperature, and an *anemometer* is used to measure wind speed, an *altimeter* is probably used to

(1) breathe at high altitudes
(2) hold things attached to tall buildings
(3) measure altitude in airplanes
(4) teach women to sing alto music
(5) plan alternative methods of driving

Questions 13–15 are based on the following passage.

When a human being is enjoying something, certain cells in the brain release a chemical called dopamine. When the dopamine travels to other brain cells, called receptors, the person feels pleasure. After a short time, the dopamine is absorbed back into the cells that produced it, so it can be used again.

New research indicates that the drug cocaine gets in the way of this process. Cocaine keeps dopamine from being absorbed back into the producer cells. Instead, the dopamine stays near the receptor cells, causing the cocaine user to feel intense pleasure for several minutes. But after 15 or 20 minutes, the dopamine has broken up. The user has to take cocaine again in order to feel that "rush" of pleasure.

Every dose of cocaine uses up more of the brain's supply of dopamine. Soon there is very little left. Then the user must have bigger and bigger doses to feel the same "rush." Also, the brain can no longer release dopamine in response to ordinary enjoyment, like food or music. The cocaine user gets pleasure only from cocaine.

Obviously, cocaine is not the "harmless" drug that people used to say it was. In fact, cocaine addiction is one of the hardest drug habits to break. Fortunately, this new research doesn't just point out the dangers of cocaine. It also points the way toward new medical treatments that may help users break the cocaine habit.

13. This passage mainly discusses

(1) the effects of cocaine on the body
(2) the reasons people decide to take cocaine
(3) the treatments available to cocaine addicts
(4) the effects of cocaine on the brain
(5) the different ways people feel pleasure

14. According to the passage, cocaine causes pleasure because it

(1) causes more dopamine to be produced
(2) keeps dopamine from being reabsorbed
(3) substitutes for dopamine in the brain
(4) allows users to manufacture dopamine in a lab
(5) destroys dopamine over a period of time

15. The author of this passage would be most likely to vote for
(1) more government money to pay for drug-related research
(2) harsher prison sentences for convicted drug users
(3) cuts in funding for drug-education programs
(4) government programs to supply addicts with dopamine
(5) shorter prison sentences for drug dealers

Questions 16 and 17 are based on the following passage and diagram.

There are two main scales used to measure temperature today. The Fahrenheit scale is used by most people in the United States. The Celsius, or centigrade, scale is used by the people of most other countries as well as by scientists all over the world. Use this diagram comparing the two scales to answer the following questions.

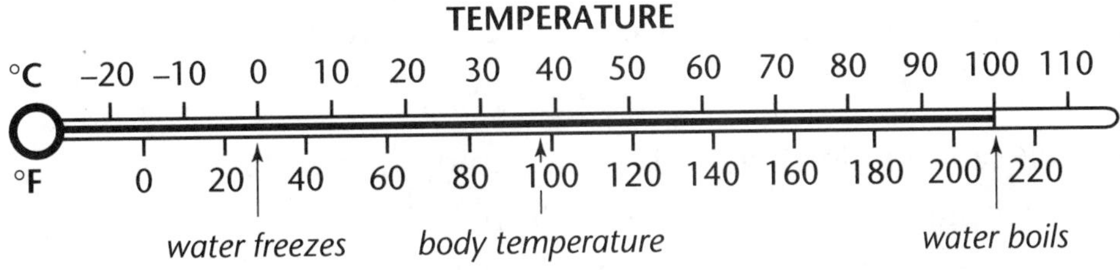

16. What is the boiling point of water on the Celsius scale?
(1) 0°C
(2) 60°C
(3) 98.6°C
(4) 100°C
(5) 212°C

17. Which statement correctly reflects the information in the diagram?
(1) When the temperature outside is 35°C, most people would want to turn on the air conditioner.
(2) The weather is warmer in the United States than in other countries.
(3) The Celsius scale is harder for most people to understand.
(4) Water freezes at a lower temperature in centigrade than it does in Fahrenheit.
(5) 70°F is warmer than 25°C.

Questions 18 and 19 are based on the following passage.

Yellowstone National Park in the western United States was the first national park established in the world. Little was known about this beautiful area, famous for its hot springs, geysers, and spectacular scenery, until after the Civil War, when two different groups of men set out to explore the region.

Judge Cornelius Hedges was a member of one of the expeditions. Around the campfire one night he suggested to his friends that, instead of claiming the land for private profit, they should find a way to preserve the amazing landscape for all the American people to enjoy. Because of their efforts, in 1872 Congress passed the Yellowstone Act, a law that required everything in the park to be preserved in its natural condition. No one would be allowed to cut down trees or to spoil the park in any way. This law was the foundation for the entire system of national parks in the United States, preserving millions of acres of land.

18. From the passage you can tell that

(1) no one had ever seen the Yellowstone area before 1865
(2) the president did not want to sign the Yellowstone Act
(3) Judge Hedges and his friends acted unselfishly
(4) other countries had national parks before the U.S. did
(5) all the most beautiful places in the U.S. are preserved in national parks

19. Which of the following is a fact, not an opinion?

(1) Campfires should never be built in forests.
(2) Natural beauty is more important than private profit.
(3) The Yellowstone area is famous for its scenery.
(4) Yellowstone National Park is the most beautiful park in the world.
(5) Everyone should spend some time in a national park.

Questions 20–22 are based on the following passage and diagram.

When you cut a tree, you can read its life history by counting the number of tree rings in its trunk. Each ring is one year's growth. The inside rings are the earliest, while the outside rings show the tree's most recent growth. Tree rings are easiest to read in deciduous trees, because these trees have a period of almost no growth each winter after their leaves fall.

In a good year, with plenty of water and sunshine, a tree grows a lot, leaving a wide ring as a record of that year. In a bad year, the tree grows only a little, leaving a thin ring. If the tree is attacked by fire or disease, this evidence, too, will show in the tree rings.

20. In the diagram on page 8, the tree ring indicated with an arrow is a record of

(1) a good year followed by another good year
(2) a bad year followed by a good year
(3) two bad years in a row
(4) the first year the tree was alive
(5) a good year followed by a bad year

21. From the passage, you can tell that deciduous trees are trees that

(1) live only in warm climates
(2) lose their leaves in the fall
(3) grow very tall
(4) are very young
(5) stay green all year

22. Which of the following would be most likely to cause a conflict of values for a tree lover who had a job studying tree rings?

(1) He would have to cut down trees to study their rings.
(2) He would feel wrong using trees to study human history.
(3) He would feel wrong getting paid to study trees.
(4) He would not really be interested in his work.
(5) He would not want other people to study tree rings.

Questions 23–25 are based on the following passage.

One type of psychotherapy that is becoming more and more popular is family therapy. In family therapy, all the members of a family work together with a counselor. They learn to communicate better and to untangle the relationships among family members. Working with the whole family makes sense when dealing with problems like incest, child abuse, marriage trouble, or teen runaways.

Family therapists believe that many other psychological prob-lems, such as alcoholism, drug abuse, depression, and even school problems, may be caused at least partly by unbalanced family relationships. They believe that one person's problems can affect the whole family. If an individual works with a therapist to "cure" his problem, but then goes back into the same family situation, the problems may start all over again. Family therapy helps build a healthy family, which in turn helps each individual family member.

23. According to the information in the passage, which of these people would be *least* likely to be helped by family therapy?

(1) a couple thinking about getting a divorce
(2) a sixteen-year-old with a drug problem
(3) a depressed housewife
(4) a six-year-old afraid to go to school
(5) a forty-year-old who is afraid of elevators

24. A family therapist would most probably agree with which of the following statements?

(1) Medical doctors are the best-qualified people to treat psychological problems.
(2) It is important to be open and honest in your communication.
(3) Every person is the main cause of his or her own problems.
(4) It is not necessary to treat an entire family if just one family member has a psychological problem.
(5) Too much time and money is spent trying to help people with psychological problems.

25. You could infer that one common problem with family therapy is that

(1) it is not as good as other therapies
(2) schools won't tell parents about students' problems
(3) it takes a very long time
(4) some family members may be unwilling to come to therapy
(5) it can be done only by a counselor who has a large family

Answers and explanations start on page 11.

PRE-TEST ANSWER KEY

1. (4) Choice (4) is the best summary of the ideas in the passage. Choice (1) does not cover the entire passage, only the very end. Choice (3) is not included in the passage at all. Choices (2) and (5) disagree with the information in the passage.

2. (3) Having a cold is a familiar experience for almost everyone. Choice (2) is untrue, according to the passage. Choices (1) and (4) are not mentioned at all in the passage.

3. (3) November 11 is the only date that is open season for all animals listed. Choice (4) is wrong because the jackrabbit and woodcock cannot be hunted then.

4. (5) The snowshoe hare is probably the most common animal because the law allows hunters to shoot any number of hares at any time during the year. All the other animals can be shot only at certain times and in certain numbers.

5. (4) This meaning can be figured out from the drawing of an overinflated tire and from the meaning of the prefix *over-*, meaning "too much."

6. (1) You can tell this is true from the line in the passage that says, "Underinflation can cause a tire to heat up, possibly leading to a blowout." Choices (2), (3), and (5) are not indicated in the passage.

7. (5) The paragraph gives helpful information for car owners. Choice (3) is wrong because the passage does not discuss how to choose an automobile, only how to take care of one. Choice (2) is wrong because the passage talks more about safety than about saving money on tire wear.

8. (3) See the first paragraph for the answer. All the other choices are untrue, according to the passage.

9. (2) O is the only symbol contained in all three chemical formulas.

10. (4) You need daylight and wind to fly a kite successfully. Choices (1) and (2) are wrong because it is dark out at those times. Choices (3) and (5) are not right because the graph shows less wind at those times.

11. (5) No record of wind today can tell you what the wind will be like tomorrow.

12. (3) The two examples, *thermometer* and *anemometer*, show you that the suffix *meter* indicates something used to measure with.

13. (4) The passage describes how cocaine affects the dopamine supply in the brain. None of the other topics is actually mentioned in the passage.

14. (2) Cocaine keeps dopamine from being absorbed back into producer cells. Choices (1) and (3) are untrue, according to the passage. Choice (5) is true, but it is not the reason given that cocaine causes pleasure.

15. (1) The author would vote for choice (1) because the more we know about drugs, the better prepared we'll be to deal with them.

16. (4) The arrow pointing to "water boils" is at 100°C.

17. (1) According to the diagram, 35°C is nearly equal to 100°F, a temperature at which most people would want to turn on their air conditioning. Choices (2) and (3) may or may not be true, but they are not shown by the diagram. Choice (4) is impossible. Choice (5) is untrue, according to the diagram.

18. (3) The passage says the team of explorers wanted the land for all the people, instead of just for themselves. Choices (1) and (4) are untrue, according to the passage. Choice (2) is not mentioned at all. Choice (5) is wrong because you could not assume that *all* the beautiful spots are in parks.

19. (3) This fact is mentioned in the first paragraph of the passage. All the other statements are opinions.

20. (5) The indicated ring is wide, showing that it records a good year. The ring next to it toward the outside is narrow, showing a bad year that followed.

21. (2) This is shown by the phrase "each winter after their leaves fall."

22. (1) The values in conflict would be his desire to preserve trees and his desire to study their history as required by his job.

23. (5) There is no indication in the passage that family therapy can help people with problems like fear of elevators. All the other answers are situations that the passage specifically mentions can be helped by family therapy.

24. (2) This is mentioned as one of the things that family therapists teach people to do. Choices (3) and (4) are directly opposite the ideas in the passage. A family therapist would not agree with choice (1) because he feels that he himself is best qualified to help people with psychological problems. He would not agree with choice (5) because this is his life's work.

25. (4) The passage says therapy is best done with all members of the family.

PRE-TEST EVALUATION CHART

Use the answer key on pages 11–12 to check your answers. Then, on the chart on the next page, circle the number of each question that you missed. If you missed many of the questions that correspond to a certain reading skill, you will want to pay special attention to that skill as you work through this book.

While this test is used to focus on particular reading skills, you will notice that each chapter covers science topics as well as reading skills. Even if you do well on the reading skills in a particular chapter, be sure to go through *all* of the science topics in this book.

	Scientific Method pages 14–27	Understanding What You Read pages 28–36	Understanding Illustrations pages 57–72	Analyzing Ideas pages 96–106	Building Vocabulary pages 129–37	Evaluating Ideas pages 160–66
Plant and Animal Biology			3, **20**	**4**	21	22
Human Biology		1		**23, 25**	2	24
Physics			**16**	**6,** 17	**5**	7
Chemistry		13, 14		8	9	15
Earth Science	**11,** 19	18	**10**		12	
NUMBER CORRECT:	_____ / 2	_____ / 4	_____ / 4	_____ / 6	_____ / 5	_____ / 4

The numbers in **boldface print** are questions based on illustrations.

_____ / 25 TOTAL

CHAPTER 1

READING SKILL

THE SCIENTIFIC METHOD

THE HIGGENBOTTOM MYSTERY

Clarence R. Higgenbottom, well-known British millionaire, is found dead on the floor of his library at 7:00 P.M. Saturday night. He has been shot through the heart. Inspector Stokes of Scotland Yard is called in to solve the mystery. He discovers the following facts:

- Higgenbottom was shot with a Ruger .22 pistol. The pistol is not in the library now.
- The butler heard a shot at 4:40 P.M. He thought it was just somebody shooting rabbits outside.
- The police doctor, who looked at the body at about 8:00 P.M., said Higgenbottom had been dead for three to four hours at that time.
- Two people recently threatened Higgenbottom. John James Percy hated him because Higgenbottom was ruining his business. Bob Jones, who used to be Higgenbottom's gardener, was fired on Friday. Friday night Jones was down at the local tavern, yelling that "people like Higgenbottom ought to be shot!"

- J. J. Percy says he was at a meeting with his banker from 2:00 P.M. until 5:00 P.M. Saturday afternoon.
- Bob Jones ran into a telephone pole at 3:30 A.M. Saturday. He has been in the hospital ever since with a bad concussion.
- Percy's banker says that Percy left the meeting early, about 4:30, because of a doctor's appointment.
- Percy's regular doctor says that Percy had no appointment with him on Saturday.

From these facts, Inspector Stokes guesses that Percy killed Higgenbottom. He gets a search warrant and searches Percy's big house. He finds a Ruger .22 pistol hidden under the front staircase. In a police lab test, the gun fires a bullet marked exactly like the one found in Higgenbottom's body. Percy is arrested for the murder, and another case is solved successfully by the famous Inspector Stokes.

What is a detective story doing in a science book? Well, detectives and scientists have a lot in common. They both have to figure out mysteries, and they do it mostly the same way. First a detective or scientist has to decide what problem he is going to work on. Then he collects all the facts he can. Next, he makes a careful guess, based on those facts, about what is really happening. Then he tests his guess by doing an experiment. Finally, he draws a conclusion from his experiment and decides whether his guess was right or not. This way of solving problems is called the ***scientific method***.

Here's a summary of the five steps Stokes followed in solving the crime. You can see how solving a mystery is a lot like using the scientific method.

Solving the Mystery	The Scientific Method
1. Inspector Stokes is assigned to find out "Who killed Higgenbottom?"	**1.** What's the question?
2. Stokes collects facts to find out what happened.	**2.** Finding the facts
3. Stokes guesses that Percy killed Higgenbottom.	**3.** Forming a hypothesis
4. Stokes searches Percy's house and finds the murder weapon.	**4.** Testing the hypothesis
5. Stokes concludes that his guess is right: Percy is guilty.	**5.** Deciding on a theory

FIRST STEP: WHAT'S THE QUESTION?

Scientists can often decide what problems they want to work on; there are thousands of questions in our universe waiting for answers. Detectives, on the other hand, are usually assigned a question; they don't have much choice. Like detectives, students are usually assigned the questions they need to answer.

It is important to read a question very carefully before you try to answer it. Many people give wrong answers because they don't take the time to figure out what the question is really asking. Let's read through a sample question and figure out what kind of answer the writer is looking for.

Question 1. What is the average yearly rainfall in Nebraska?

▶ Will the answer to this question be a word, a number, a place, or somebody's name? ______________________

(The answer will be a *number*.)

▶ What unit of measure (inches, feet, miles, or whatever) will this answer probably be in? ______________________

(From listening to the radio weather reports, we know that rainfall is usually measured in *inches*.)

▶ Where do you think you are expected to find the answer to this question?

____

(If this were a question on a test, you would probably be able to get the information you needed to answer the question from a reading passage, graph, or chart. This is not the kind of information you would be expected to have in your own head. Nobody memorizes the average rainfall in all fifty states!)

Let's look at another question.

Question 2. What would probably happen to people if all the green plants on Earth died?

▶ Will this answer probably be in words or numbers?______________

(The answer will probably be in *words*. The question doesn't ask for a number or anything that would show that a number is called for.)

▶ Where are you expected to find the answer to this question?

____

(If you have studied science, you know how important green plants are, so you should be able to figure out the answer. There might also be something in a reading passage to help you decide the answer to the question.)

As you can see, reading a question carefully can give you lots of information about the answer. The more information you have, the better chance you have of answering the question correctly.

SECOND STEP: FINDING THE FACTS

A ***fact*** in science is something that can be proven by ***observation*** (watching something with your own eyes) or ***measurement*** (using a tool like a ruler or a scale to find differences you can't see very easily). Many things we read and hear every day seem to be facts but may not be.

Often, we confuse opinions with facts. ***Opinions*** are usually statements that depend upon a person's ***values*** (the things someone likes or considers important), so they cannot be proven. Our values matter to us very much, but because each of us likes different things and believes different things are important, values cannot be used to prove facts.

Here are some examples of opinions:

- Broccoli tastes horrible.
- Women should work in any field that interests them.
- Blue is the prettiest color.
- School is fun.

You may agree or disagree strongly with some of these opinions, but no one can prove them right or wrong. In life, as well as in science, you need to recognize what is a fact and what is an opinion.

Fact vs. Opinion Tip

Phrases like *I think*, *I believe*, and *we should* tell you that an opinion is being expressed.

EXERCISE 1: FACT AND OPINION

Directions: Write *F* before the statements that are facts (that you could prove by observation or measurement) and *O* before the statements that are opinions (that depend on your values). Then write three examples of strong opinions that you have.

________ **1.** Robert Larson is 5 feet, 10 inches tall.

________ **2.** Susan Anderson is beautiful.

________ **3.** Denver is a nicer place to live than Chicago.

________ **4.** New York is 92 miles away from Philadelphia.

________ **5.** Everyone should try to earn a high school diploma or GED.

________ **6.** Eighty percent of employers surveyed said they had hired a job applicant with a diploma or GED over an applicant without one.

________ 7. Listening to music played very loudly can damage a person'sears.

________ 8. Rock music is not good for people to listen to.

________ 9. Nuclear power plants ought to be shut down for the next five years.

________ 10. There have been several accidents at nuclear power plants in the last five years.

11. Now write three opinions you feel strongly about.

Answers and explanations start on page 209.

Answer Key Tip

After you finish each exercise in this book, check your answers in the Answer Key section at the back of the book. Carefully read the explanations for any questions you miss or that you are unsure about. If you are still puzzled, ask your teacher for help.

You may feel that reading the explanation is a waste of time, but making mistakes and correcting them is actually one of the best ways to learn. Once you understand your mistake and correct it, you probably won't make the same sort of mistake on a test.

THIRD STEP: MAKING A HYPOTHESIS

After scientists have collected all the facts they can find out about a particular problem, they use these facts to make a careful guess about the solution. This guess is called a ***hypothesis*** (plural—***hypotheses***).

Scientists are not the only people who make hypotheses. We all make careful guesses (hypotheses) about things everyday. For instance, if your child comes home from school soaking wet, you might ***hypothesize*** (make a good guess) that it is raining outside. Of course, not all hypotheses turn out to be right. It is possible your child walked through a sprinkler or got into a water fight on the way home. But each hypothesis is the best guess that can be made at the time based on all the facts that are available.

▶ Try making a hypothesis for this situation: Your washing machine won't go on and neither will the light over your laundry table. What do you think has happened?

____

▶ Should you guess that your washing machine is broken? ___________

(No, because that doesn't explain why the light won't go on either. Your first hypothesis could be that *something is wrong with the electricity*.)

EXERCISE 2: EVERYDAY HYPOTHESES

Directions: Practice making hypotheses with these everyday situations. Write your hypothesis in the space provided.

1. It is just before dinner, and you see spaghetti sauce cooking on the stove.

   Your hypothesis:

2. During a big thunderstorm, your lights go off suddenly.

   Your hypothesis:

3. Bill, who works for you, has been asking for time off during hunting season, but you have had to turn him down. On the first day of the season, Bill's wife calls and says that Bill is too sick to come to work.

   Your hypothesis:

4. Just before Christmas, your parents spend a lot of time in the basement workshop. They tell you not to come down without warning them.

   Your hypothesis:

5. Your crew leader at work has left his job, and you have a good chance to be promoted to his position. Your boss calls you into her office, saying she has some good news for you.

   Your hypothesis:

Answers start on page 209.

Fitting All the Facts

Of course, most scientific hypotheses are based on more than one or two facts. When you go to the doctor, she bases her ***diagnosis*** (her hypothesis about why you are sick) on many facts. She considers many things, including your temperature, your appearance, any pains or other symptoms you talk about, and your ***medical history*** (the sicknesses you and your family have had before).

Like any other scientist, a doctor needs as many facts as possible to make a good hypothesis. That is why you need to tell her everything you can about your illness.

A good hypothesis must fit all the facts available. A careful scientist never ignores a fact just because it doesn't fit her first ideas. Instead, she changes her ideas to fit all the facts. You can do this in everyday life, too. For example, if you saw a woman on Main Street wearing a black dress and pointed hat and carrying a broom, you might hypothesize that she was really strange. Later, if you found out she was going to a costume party, you would probably change your hypothesis.

EXERCISE 3: CHOOSING HYPOTHESES

Directions: After carefully reading about these situations, choose the number of the hypothesis that best fits each set of facts.

1. This is a well-known experiment with green plants. A scientist had twelve plants. All the plants were the same kind and about the same size. He put three plants on a window sill inside a room. He put another three plants in a closet without a light. He put three more plants outside on the ground. He put the last three plants outside, too, but covered them with paper bags that had holes punched in them for air.

All the plants were given good soil and enough water. The plants on the window sill and the plants outside in the open grew well. The plants outside in the bags turned yellow and grew very badly. The plants in the closet died. What was learned from this experiment with green plants?

(1) Green plants turn yellow due to disease.
(2) Green plants don't live for very long.
(3) Green plants need light to grow.
(4) Green plants cannot grow inside.
(5) Green plants grow well in closets.

2. Louis Pasteur, a famous scientist who lived over 100 years ago, made an important hypothesis about certain germs called *bacteria.* He noticed that bacteria grew quickly in open jars of liquid, like chicken soup. Bacteria also grew in jars of soup that were sealed tightly so that no air could get in. However, they didn't grow in soup that was sealed tightly in a jar, then boiled and kept sealed after it cooled. What was Pasteur's correct hypothesis?

(1) Bacteria cannot grow in jars.
(2) Bacteria must have air to survive.
(3) Bacteria grow only in chicken soup.
(4) Bacteria can be killed by boiling.
(5) Bacteria can live in boiling liquids.

3. Janet kept track of the weather outside and the fuel she burned for the first five months in her new house. She made this chart showing the facts that she found.

Month	Average Temperature	Weather	Oil Used
September	45	Mostly rainy	60 gal.
October	39	Sunny, some snow	90 gal.
November	23	Rainy and snowy	140 gal.
December	26	Mostly snowy	125 gal.
January	20	Mostly sunny	160 gal.

What did Janet discover about the amount of oil she burned?

(1) More oil was burned when it was not sunny.
(2) More oil was burned when temperatures were lower.
(3) More oil was burned each month as winter went on.
(4) More oil was burned whenever it snowed.
(5) More oil was burned during the holidays.

Answers and explanations start on page 209.

Hypothesis Tip

One thing to remember about hypotheses in science is that they are only good guesses. They are often proven wrong by new facts or careful testing. In fact, scientists working on a difficult problem, like curing a disease, will usually try many hypotheses that prove to be wrong before they find one that works. Their wrong hypotheses aren't a waste of time, though. Every time they test a hypothesis, they find out new facts to make a better hypothesis.

EXERCISE 4: MAKING HYPOTHESES

Directions: Write your own scientific hypotheses to fit the following situations.

1. A water tester checks the water in a certain river. It is polluted with lead, mercury, and detergent. He walks upstream and passes a small town. He tests the water again and finds lead and mercury, but no detergent. He keeps walking and passes a factory. When he tests the water again, it is clean and not polluted.

   Knowing that water flows downstream, what is the tester's hypothesis about where the detergent is coming from?

2. A veterinarian sees a large dog that seems very sick. It keeps choking as if it were going to throw up. The owner says that both of her dogs ate the last of an old bag of dog food that morning. Then they played inside with their toys. One toy, the squeaky rubber mouse, is missing. Her other dog seems to be fine. What is the vet's hypothesis about the dog's problem?

3. Carl had a two-inch magnet. He did an experiment to see what it would pick up. The items it would pick up are in List A. The items it would not pick up are in List B.

List A	List B
1-inch steel paper clip	pile of pepper
wet iron nail	1-inch goldfish
tiny iron filings	2-inch copper wire
3-inch steel wire	wet dollar bill

What kind of things can Carl's magnet pick up?

Answers start on page 209.

FOURTH STEP: CHECKING IT OUT

Once a scientist has made a hypothesis, he tries to test it—to check it out. This is the fourth step of the scientific method. The most common way for a scientist to check a hypothesis is to do an ***experiment***.

In an experiment, a scientist takes groups of things, called ***subjects***. He puts them in an artificial situation where everything is the same except the ***variable***, the one thing he wants to test. He usually leaves at least one subject in its natural state. This natural subject is called his ***control***. Then he records the results of his experiment and checks to see if the results prove his hypothesis correct or not. It's easier to understand these parts of an experiment when we look at an example from everyday life.

> Let's say a house painter has just found out about a new type of paint. He hypothesizes that it will keep its color better than the paint he is regularly using.
>
> He takes ten pieces of wood to test. These are his subjects. He paints five pieces of wood with the new paint and five with the old paint. The new paint is the variable. The pieces of wood with the old paint are the control group.
>
> The painter leaves all of the boards together in his backyard for a month. When he brings the boards back in, he notices that the boards painted with the old paint have faded more than the boards with the new paint. These are the results of the experiment. The painter's hypothesis is correct: the new paint fades less.
>
> In order to really prove his hypothesis, the painter must repeat the experiment with two new sets of boards to see if it comes out the same way again. It would be even better if he had someone else repeat the experiment. Scientists will not accept the results of an experiment unless it is ***reproducible***, that is, unless it can be repeated with the same results. This shows that the first results were not just a coincidence.

The chart below shows the parts of the painter's experiment.

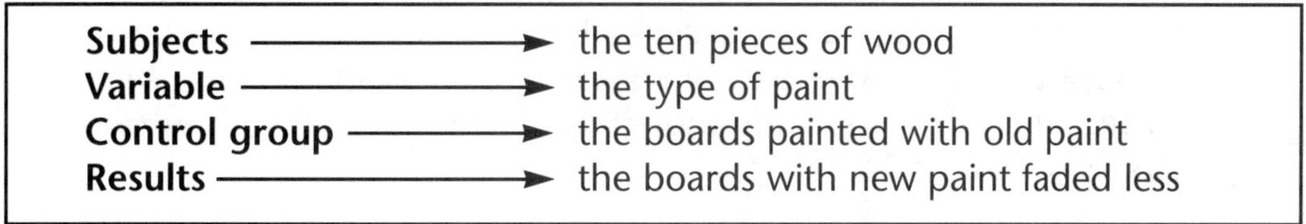

Here is a list of the requirements that we have discussed for a good experiment:

- The subjects need to be similar, and there should be more than one subject in each group.
- All the conditions of the experiment should be the same, except for the one variable being tested.
- There should be a control group.
- The results should be reproducible.

If an experiment does not meet these requirements, the results are not ***valid*** (reliable and true), so the experiment is not very useful. You can see this for yourself by looking at the following experiment. Can you figure out what is wrong with it?

> A chef wanted to find out if egg whites could make his pie crust more tender. He made five pies using egg whites in the crusts and five pies without egg whites. As they baked, he noticed that the pies with the egg whites browned more quickly, so he took them out ten minutes early, leaving the other pies in the regular amount of time. When he served the pies, everyone said that the first five were more tender. The chef has decided that using egg whites will make his pie crusts better.

▶ What's wrong? ______________________________

____

The problem with the chef's experiment is that *he didn't keep all the conditions the same*. The variable he wanted to test was the use of egg whites, but he also used different cooking times for the two groups. Maybe it was the egg whites that made the first group of pies more tender; maybe it was the shorter cooking time. He can't be sure, so his experiment is not good.

Now try this one:

> A teacher wanted to find out whether teaching for a short time worked better than teaching long classes. He cut all his classes from 50 minutes to 30 minutes long. Most of his students passed at the end of the semester, so he decided that shorter classes were better for teaching.

▶ What's wrong? ______________________________

____

If you said that the teacher had *no control group,* you were right! He doesn't know how many of his students would have passed with the usual 50-minute classes, so how can he say that 30-minute classes worked better? He should have kept half his classes at 50 minutes and changed half to 30 minutes. Then he would have been able to tell which length of class was better by comparing the results of each class at the end of the semester.

EXERCISE 5: ERRORS IN EXPERIMENTS

Directions: Tell what is wrong with each of these experiments. Choose from the list below.

- not enough subjects
- subjects were not similar
- conditions of experiment not kept the same
- the experiment was not reproduced

1. A gardener wanted to know if XYZ fertilizer would be good for his vegetables. He fertilized all his bean plants with XYZ but didn't put any fertilizer on his pepper plants. His beans didn't do well at all, but he got a good crop of peppers. He concluded that XYZ fertilizer was no good.

2. Alice Larsen wanted to see if a new premium gasoline would give her more miles to the gallon. She filled her car with the new gas and went on a long trip. When she figured her mileage, she discovered that she had gone 20 miles farther on this tank of gas than she went on a tank of regular gas when she was driving around town as usual. She decided to buy the premium gas from then on to get better mileage.

3. A molding machine in a factory was not working very well. About a third of the time, the plastic squirt guns that it was making came out with a flaw in the handle. The repair mechanic adjusted the stamping pressure. Then she ran one gun through. It came out just fine, so the mechanic figured she had solved the problem.

Answers and explanations start on page 209.

FIFTH STEP: DECIDING ON A THEORY

Nothing Is Certain!

After a scientist has chosen a problem, collected facts, formed a hypothesis, and checked it out with several experiments, he is ready to decide if his correct hypothesis is a theory. A ***scientific theory*** is an idea or explanation based on the available facts and experimentation. Scientists are never absolutely sure about any of their theories because new facts are always coming up that contradict the old theories.

For example, seventy-five years ago scientists had "proven" that the atom was one solid particle that could not be split. Then Einstein and others discovered that atoms could be split, and they discovered atomic energy. Forty years ago, chemical companies had "proven" that DDT was perfectly safe. Now DDT is forbidden for use in this country because it turned out to be so deadly to fish, birds, and even people. Scientists today have "proven" that nothing can travel faster than the speed of light, but don't be surprised if by the year 2020 somebody finds a way to do it!

Making Decisions

You can use the scientific method to help solve problems in everyday life, too. When you have to make an important decision, you collect all the facts you can about your decision. Then you look at possible solutions. These are your hypotheses.

You try out these solutions one by one. Sometimes you just try them out in your head, saying to yourself, "What would probably happen if I did this? Or this? Or maybe that?" You might ask some friends for their opinions. If you can, you try out a solution in real life, just to see what will happen. Finally, you make your decision, but you can't tell right away whether you have decided correctly. Just as in science, in real life there are very few guarantees.

When you are taking a test, you can use some of this process to help you choose good answers. You are given the question. You read the passage and any illustrations carefully; this is collecting your facts. Then you look at all the possible answers, checking them out in your head to see which ones make sense. Many people miss questions because they do not read all the answers.

EXERCISE 6: REVIEW OF THE SCIENTIFIC METHOD

Directions: As you read through this real-life example of the scientific method, answer each question as you come to it.

> Smallpox is a terrible disease that once killed thousands of people every year. Today doctors think smallpox may be totally gone from the world. This is mostly because of the work of an English doctor named Edward Jenner, who lived from 1749 to 1853.
>
> When Jenner was a young doctor, an epidemic (a situation in which many people catch a certain disease) of smallpox broke out. He worked hard to save his patients, but many of them died. He noticed that milkmaids—the women who milked the cows on dairy farms—didn't seem to catch the disease. He decided to find out why.

1. As the first step in his process, what question did Jenner ask himself?

____

He talked to many milkmaids and discovered that the women often caught a disease called cowpox from the cows. This disease caused spots like smallpox, but the spots were only on the women's hands, and the disease wasn't very serious; no one ever died of cowpox. The remarkable thing was that no one who had had cowpox ever seemed to catch smallpox.

2. What hypothesis would you make if you were Jenner?

____

Jenner guessed that having cowpox somehow protected people against smallpox for the rest of their lives.

3. How do you think Jenner decided to test his guess?

____

Jenner decided to check his hypothesis by taking cowpox germs on a needle and deliberately injecting them into people. After these people got over the cowpox, he watched to see if any of them got smallpox. He did this to several people, and none of them got smallpox.

Jenner's idea of deliberately giving someone a mild disease to protect him from a serious disease was the beginning of all our modern vaccinations. At the time, though, many people did not like Jenner's idea. They were afraid to catch any disease. Some people said that what Jenner was doing was "against Nature." Others even accused him of witchcraft! But after a while, when it became clear that many lives were being saved, more and more people came to get vaccinated, and Jenner became famous.

Answers start on page 209.

CHAPTER 2

READING SKILL

UNDERSTANDING WHAT YOU READ

"I can read OK, but I just can't seem to understand what I read." Have you ever heard this? Many people have trouble understanding technical writing like the kind found in science textbooks. This chapter covers three special reading techniques that can help you understand what you read: restating facts, summarizing, and finding the main idea.

RESTATING FACTS:
Say It Again, Sam

One way to show that you understand something you have read is to ***restate*** it—to say the same thing in different words. You will often be asked to do this on tests. For example, a sentence from a reading passage could say, "Studies show that eating fish oil could help protect you against heart disease." Suppose that a test question asked you to choose a restatement of the information in that sentence. The correct answer to the question might read, "Researchers have found that your chances of getting heart disease may be lower if you consume fish oil."

Notice that the answer means the same thing as the sentence from the passage, but it does not use exactly the same words. When test writers write this type of question, they usually do not use exactly the same words in the answer as they did in the passage. Therefore, you should look for an answer with the same *meaning* as the sentence in the passage.

▶ To see if you've got the idea, try this. Write the numbers from Group One before their restatements in Group Two.

Group One	Group Two
1. Luther Burbank was a very famous plant breeder.	_____ Burbank lived a long and happy life doing his work.
2. He was one of the first people to breed hybrid plants.	_____ His plants helped to improve many people's diets.
3. He developed many of the plants that farmers grow today.	_____ He was one of the most well-known plant breeders around.
4. Burbank enjoyed developing new plants right up to the end of his long life.	_____ Many important food plants were bred by Luther Burbank.
5. Many people eat better today because of Luther Burbank.	_____ He was one of the discoverers of hybrid plants.

The correct answers are 4, 5, 1, 3, 2.

EXERCISE 1: RESTATING FACTS

Directions: Restate each of the following facts. Write a new sentence that says the same thing in different words.

1. If you don't smoke, you have less chance of getting lung cancer.

   ____

2. Many GED graduates are successful businessmen and businesswomen.

   ____

3. Nuclear energy is a powerful tool and a dangerous weapon.

   ____

4. Learning is often easier as you get older because you have more experience.

____

5. Never feed honey to babies under twelve months because it can give them botulism (a deadly disease from food).

____

Answers start on page 209.

SUMMARIZING: Putting It All Together

Another type of test question might ask you to summarize a passage. To ***summarize*** something is to put all the important points together in one short statement. Look at these facts.

- John decided to start his science experiment.
- He spilled the chemicals he was mixing.
- The Bunsen burner wouldn't light.
- When he finally turned in his results, they were all wrong.

One way to summarize these facts would be to say, "Everything went wrong for John when he tried to do the science experiment."

▶ Now you try it. Choose the statement that best summarizes these facts.

- Most snakes are not poisonous.
- The old stories about snakes milking cows and strangling babies are not true.
- Snakes eat many insects, mice, and rats that otherwise would destroy farmers' crops.
- We need snakes, just as we need most other living things, to keep the natural balance of our world.

▶ What is the best summary of these facts?

(1) Snakes eat insects, mice, and rats.
(2) Most snakes do more good than harm.
(3) Snakes drink milk and strangle babies.
(4) Only farmers need snakes.
(5) Some snakes are poisonous.

Did you choose the right summary? Answer (2) is the best because it covers all of the facts. Answers (3) and (4) are not true according to the facts listed. Answers (1) and (5) are true, but they each deal with only one fact. If you had trouble with this example, read this section again or discuss it with your teacher before trying the next exercise.

EXERCISE 2: SUMMARIZING

Directions: Read these groups of facts carefully. Circle the number of the correct answer.

- Florence Nightingale was one of the first people to see that nursing had to be a professional job.
- When she went to nurse soldiers wounded in the Crimean War, she was shocked by the poor conditions.
- Most of the "nurses" had no training.
- They didn't even know enough to keep the bandages and the hospital rooms clean.
- Florence Nightingale taught them basic ideas of cleanliness and nursing.
- Later she went on to start one of the first real nursing schools.

1. What is the best summary of these facts?
   (1) Crimean War nurses had little training.
   (2) Soldiers need the best nursing care.
   (3) Florence Nightingale was a famous woman.
   (4) Crimean War hospitals were very bad.
   (5) Florence Nightingale made a big improvement in nursing.

- Aspirin is a medicine that has been around for a long time, but it is not at all old-fashioned.
- Everyone knows that aspirin can help stop minor pains like headaches and backaches.
- Aspirin reduces the swelling in joint injuries like sprains and even arthritis.
- Because aspirin makes blood less likely to clot, it can also sometimes be used to prevent heart attacks and strokes.

2. What is the best summary of these facts?
   (1) Aspirin has been used for a long time.
   (2) Everyone should use more aspirin.
   (3) Aspirin has many uses in modern medicine.
   (4) Aspirin is good for headaches.
   (5) Aspirin can prevent all heart attacks.

Answers and explanations start on page 210.

THE MAIN IDEA: Getting the Point

How many times have you read something and said to yourself, "What's this guy talking about? What's the point?" What you're looking for is the author's ***main idea***, the main thought he is trying to get across.

A ***paragraph*** is a group of related sentences. Every paragraph should have one main idea. The rest of the paragraph is filled with ***details*** that explain or prove the main idea. Here is an example.

MAIN IDEA

Albert Einstein was a "slow learner" who turned out to be a real genius. He didn't learn to talk until he was almost three. Later, he did very poorly in school, especially in mathematics. One teacher even said he was retarded! But when he was grown up, he developed the Theory of Relativity, which is the main scientific theory about nuclear energy. He became known as one of the greatest scientists of our time.

The main idea of this paragraph is in the first sentence: *Albert Einstein was a "slow learner" who turned out to be a real genius.* The rest of the paragraph contains the details that show you how this happened.

Many paragraphs have the main idea in the first sentence, but others do not. Sometimes the author builds up the details and then puts the main idea at the end. Look at this example.

Nancy Simmons kept watching the clock, but it never seemed to move. She hated the smell of the alcohol. Looking at the pieces of the cut-up worm she was supposed to be studying was making her sick. **Nancy could hardly wait for biology class to end.**

MAIN IDEA

This time the main idea was in the last sentence.

Other times, the main idea is somewhere in the middle of the paragraph, as in the example below.

Women are working as doctors, veterinarians, and laboratory technicians. Some of the most respected science professors at large universities are women. **More and more women are working at scientific jobs that people used to think were only for men.** Several women have even become astronauts and flown in space.

MAIN IDEA

Probably the most difficult type of paragraph is one in which the main idea is never really stated. The author just ***implies*** (hints at) an idea by using details.

> She held her breath as the top of the skull came into sight. Very carefully she brushed away the sand until she could lift it out. It must be over two million years old! Her hands trembled as she realized that she was holding the oldest human bone she had ever seen.

The main idea of this paragraph is that *the woman is very excited about the old skull that she has found.* The author never really says it, but all the details about the way the woman held her breath and how her hands trembled show you how excited she was.

When you are asked to find the main idea, don't make the common mistake of picking one of the supporting details. The supporting details are all true, but they are not the main idea. Remember, the main idea is the idea that covers the whole paragraph, not just one part of it.

▶ Now you try it. Underline the main idea in the paragraph below.

> It was swimming around the aquarium when Tom first saw it. It was a sort of mud-brown and covered with warts that were black and a sick shade of blue. Its mouth was huge, and its cloudy eyes bulged out and never seemed to focus. Little shreds and strings of flesh hung from its skin, making it look like something that had died but didn't know enough to stop moving. It had to be the ugliest fish he had ever seen.

Did you spot the main idea? It was the last sentence: *It had to be the ugliest fish he had ever seen.* If you had trouble finding this main idea, reread this section before going on to the next exercise.

EXERCISE 3: FINDING THE MAIN IDEA OF A PARAGRAPH

Directions: In the next three paragraphs, underline the sentence that contains the main idea.

1. Cactuses are remarkable plants, made to live in one of nature's harshest environments. In place of regular leaves, they have needles that also serve as a good defense against hungry animals. Their stems are full of hollow cells that can store enough water to last for months. They can survive the great heat of the desert sun at noon and the bitter cold of the desert night.

2. Henry Ford's first car had only one cylinder in the engine and ran on bicycle wheels. It was steered with a stick that connected directly to the front wheels. In the 1960s, cars had up to eight cylinders, power steering, power brakes, and even power windows. Cars just seem to get more and more complicated. Present-day cars have electronic ignition, catalytic converters, cruise control devices, and some even have special on-board computers.

3. Allen Cramer has red eyes and a runny nose. He is sneezing and coughing, and his skin is all broken out in big, red, itchy patches. Does Allen have some horrible disease? No. In fact, Allen doesn't have any disease at all. He has an allergy. When you have an allergy, your body's defenses react strongly to something normally harmless, like dog hair or ragweed pollen. Allergies can be mild or very serious. Some people have even died of severe allergic reactions. Even though it is only a reaction of your own body, an allergy can really make you miserable!

Answers and explanations start on page 210.

The Main Idea of a Passage

Test questions often ask you to find the main idea of a passage. Questions that ask you what a passage "mainly says" or what it is "mainly about" are really asking for the main idea. So are questions that ask you for the "best title" for a passage.

Many passages are longer than one paragraph, but you can use the same skills to find the main idea. In a paragraph, each detail supports the main idea of the paragraph. In a longer passage, each paragraph supports the main idea of the passage. To find the main idea of the passage, first look at the main ideas of the paragraphs. These ideas should all be related and point toward one major main idea for the passage.

Try this method to find the main idea of the following passage. Beneath each paragraph, write the main idea of that paragraph.

Where would you be if you saw a wallaby? How about a spiny anteater or a duck-billed platypus? If I say a kangaroo, I'll bet you know—you would be in Australia!

MAIN IDEA: ______________________________

Many animals in Australia, like those listed above, belong to a very old group of animals called marsupials. Marsupials raise their young differently than ordinary animals do. Most marsupials give birth when their young are still very undeveloped. These tiny babies are often blind and hairless. They do not have fully developed arms or legs. They must live in their mother's pouch until they are ready to survive in the outside world.

MAIN IDEA: ______________________________

This way of raising young is not as safe as that of other mammals, where the baby is carried inside the mother until it is ready to be born. These old-fashioned animals still survive in Australia only because they didn't have much competition from animals that came into being more recently. Long ago, Australia got cut off from the main part of Asia by a big piece of the Pacific Ocean. Animals that developed after this couldn't get to Australia since it was too far to swim to.

MAIN IDEA: ____

In recent times, many new animals, like rabbits and sheep, have been brought to Australia. These animals are pushing out the marsupials. If we do not take action to save the marsupials, we may lose some of these interesting animals forever.

MAIN IDEA: ____

The main idea of the first paragraph is that *some very unusual animals live in Australia.* The second paragraph explains that *these animals, called marsupials, raise their young from very undeveloped babies.* The third paragraph says that, *because of this, most marsupials survived only in Australia,* where more highly developed animals could not go. The main idea of the last paragraph is that the *marsupials are now threatened by animals brought in by man.*

▶ Now put all these ideas together and choose the sentence that tells the main idea of the whole passage.

(1) All unusual animals need to be protected.
(2) Marsupials are unique because of the way they raise their young.
(3) Many people want to save the marsupials.
(4) The marsupials can survive without any help from us.
(5) The marsupials, a unique group of animals, are now in danger.

If you chose sentence (5), you were correct! This sentence covers all of the ideas in the passage. Sentence (1) is too broad; the passage is not about all unusual animals, just marsupials. Sentence (2) is too narrow; the passage does say that marsupials raise their young in an unusual way, but that is not all it says. Sentence (3) is probably true, but it is not mentioned in the passage. Sentence (4) is false, according to the passage.

EXERCISE 4: FINDING THE MAIN IDEA OF A PASSAGE

Directions: Practice choosing the main idea of this passage. Circle the number of the best answer. Be careful not to choose an answer that is too broad or one that covers only part of the passage.

One of the most important things that parents buy for a new baby is a crib. Babies spend a lot of time in their cribs, but many parents spend more time shopping for cute clothes than they do for a crib.

Any crib for a new baby, whether it is bought new or borrowed from friends or relatives, should have several safety features. First, the spaces between the bars must not be more than $2^3/_8$ inches wide. Many old cribs have more widely spaced bars. Today we know that if the spaces are any wider, a young baby might slip through the bars, catching his head and strangling himself. The same thing can happen if there are fancy designs in the ends of the crib with holes big enough for a baby to catch his head in.

Next, the crib mattress must fit tightly so that the baby cannot get caught between the mattress and the sides. The crib must also be built strongly. The bottom springs must not slip out when the child jumps up and down. The side catches must be strong enough to hold the weight of a child without giving way. Finally, the paint or varnish must be lead-free, so the baby can teethe on it without getting lead poisoning.

1. This passage is mainly about
   (1) problems babies have during teething
   (2) advantages of buying a brand-new crib
   (3) fancy designs on cribs
   (4) safety features of a crib
   (5) safety features of a crib mattress

2. The best title for this passage would be
   (1) Keeping Your Baby Safe
   (2) Only $2^3/_8$ Inches Apart
   (3) Choosing a Safe Crib
   (4) How to Buy Baby Clothes
   (5) Choosing an Inexpensive Crib

Answers and explanations start on page 210.

SCIENCE TOPIC

PLANTS AND ANIMALS

We share the Earth with millions of other living things, from the smallest bacteria to the huge blue whale. Many of these creatures affect our lives directly. All of them have some of the same needs as human beings: to find food, to escape enemies, and to reproduce. When we learn about other living things, we also learn something about ourselves.

CELLS:
Life Comes in Small Packages

Did you know that you are made up of millions of tiny units called ***cells***? You are! In fact, every living thing is made up of cells. Cells are so small that you can see them only through a microscope; there are thousands of cells in just your little finger. Some cells, like the ones in you, are part of larger, many-celled beings. Other cells live on their own as one-celled creatures.

There are lots of different types of cells. A nerve cell in your brain is very different from a muscle cell in your arm and even more different from a cell in the trunk of an oak tree. Still, there are some things that are alike in all cells.

Animal Cells

Look at the diagram of an animal cell to see the major cell parts. Every cell has a ***nucleus***, which is a dark spot, usually near the center of the cell. The nucleus is like the "brain" of the cell. It controls most of what happens inside the cell. The ***chromosomes*** inside the nucleus carry the directions (similar to blueprints) for making new cells.

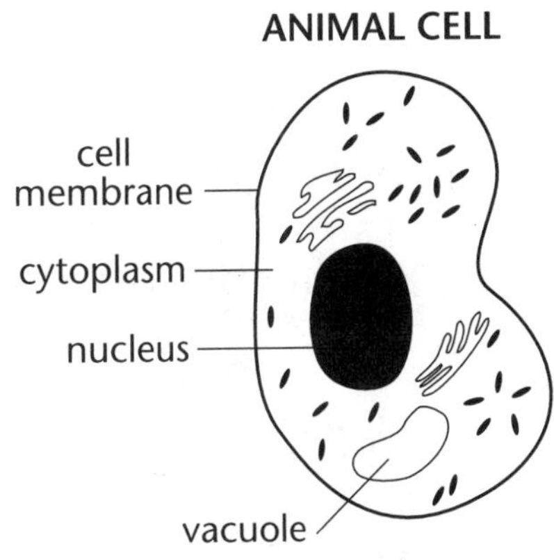

The ***cell membrane*** is a thin wrapping around the outside that holds the cell together. It keeps out many things that could harm the cell, while letting in things the cell needs, like oxygen and food. The inside of the cell is filled with ***cytoplasm***, a clear, jellylike liquid. The space you see in the cytoplasm is called a ***vacuole***. Vacuoles store water and food for the cell.

Plant Cells

Now look at the diagram of a plant cell. It is mostly the same as an animal cell, but there are some differences. In plant cells, a large vacuole often takes up much of the space inside the cell. All plant cells have a ***cell wall*** around the outside of the membrane. This wall is made of a stiff material called ***cellulose***.

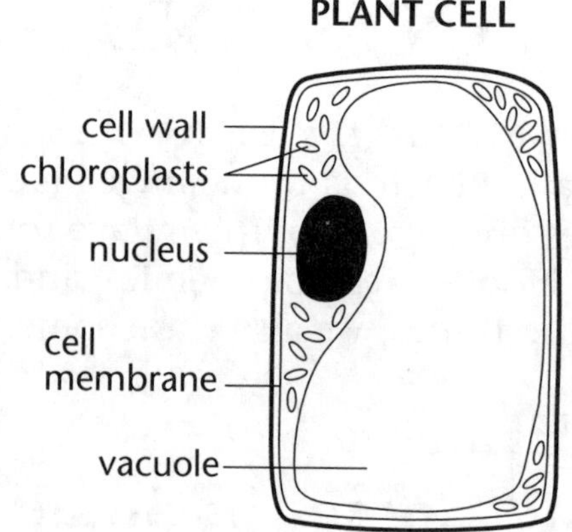

In most plant cells there are also small oval objects called ***chloroplasts***. These chloroplasts contain a green chemical called ***chlorophyll***. Chlorophyll is the chemical that helps green plants make their own food. No animal cells have cell walls or chloroplasts, and no animal can make its own food.

EXERCISE 5: CELLS

Directions: Match the word with its definition.

______ **1.** Cell membrane	**a.** Contain chlorophyll
______ **2.** Cell wall	**b.** Jellylike liquid inside cells
______ **3.** Cellulose	**c.** Carry "blueprints" for new cells
______ **4.** Chloroplasts	**d.** Directs most cell activities
______ **5.** Chlorophyll	**e.** Stores food and water for the cell
______ **6.** Chromosomes	**f.** Holds animal cells together
______ **7.** Cytoplasm	**g.** Stiff material in cell walls
______ **8.** Nucleus	**h.** Chemical that helps plants make food
______ **9.** Vacuole	**i.** Stiff structure around plant cells

Directions: Circle the number of the best answer.

10. What is the main topic of this passage?

(1) what is inside an animal cell
(2) what a cell wall is made of
(3) which is the most important part of a cell
(4) what cells are and what is inside them
(5) how a cell makes new cells

11. One difference between plant and animal cells is that
    (1) plant cells have cell walls; animal cells don't
    (2) plant cells can't move; animal cells can
    (3) plant cells live in water; animal cells don't
    (4) plant cells have a nucleus; animal cells don't
    (5) plant cells have vacuoles; animal cells don't

Answers and explanations start on page 210.

GERMS: The Smallest Enemy

If you get sick, it can be a big problem for you. But that big problem can be caused by something very small, so small you can't even see it without a microscope.

Infectious diseases (diseases you can catch from someone else) are caused by ***germs***, tiny one-celled living things that invade your body and make you sick. Viruses are the smallest of the three main types of germs. A ***virus*** lives by getting inside a cell in your body and forcing that cell to make hundreds of copies of the virus. Eventually, all the copies burst out of the cell and go looking for other cells to invade. Colds, the flu, and the measles are a few diseases caused by different types of viruses. Some scientists think that viruses may even cause some kinds of cancer.

One problem with viruses is that they are not killed by antibiotics or other medicines. If you go to the doctor with a bad cold, he can't give you an antibiotic to make it go away faster. You usually just have to get through it.

Bacteria are another kind of germ. Different kinds of bacteria cause different diseases, such as strep throat, tetanus, and tuberculosis. Luckily for us, many bacteria can be killed by penicillin and other antibiotics, so many diseases that were once very serious can now be cured.

Bacteria under a microscope

Not all bacteria cause diseases, though. Some bacteria are actually helpful. Bacteria are needed to break down dead plants and animals in nature. There is even one kind of bacterium that lives in your intestines and helps your body produce certain vitamins.

Other diseases are caused by protozoans. ***Protozoans*** are larger than bacteria, but they are still single-celled creatures. If you have ever looked at a drop of pond water through a microscope, you have probably seen protozoans swimming around in it. Although most protozoans are harmless, malaria and some forms of diarrhea are caused by types of protozoans. One type of protozoan, the ameba, is shown at right.

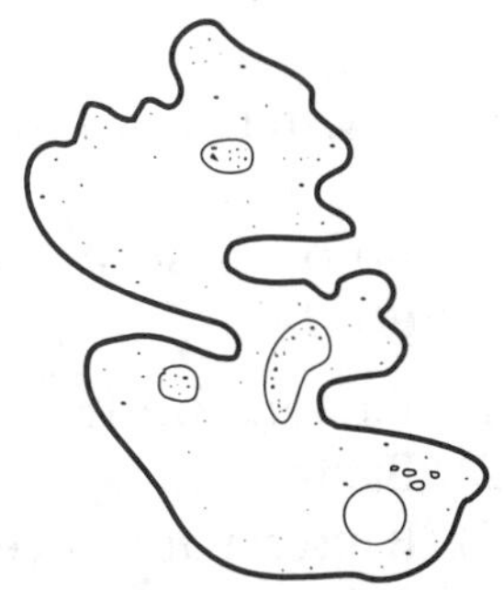

Ameba under a microscope

Viruses, bacteria, and protozoans are all around us, so why aren't we sick all the time? One reason is that a person's body creates defenses against germs it has fought before. We call this building immunity to a disease. One way to build immunity to a disease is to catch it. A better way is to get a shot, called an ***immunization*** or a ***vaccination***, from your doctor. The doctor puts a small number of dead or weakened germs into you. This makes your body create the same defenses it would if you had had the real disease, but you don't really get sick.

Immunizations are available for only some diseases. Some immunizations last all through your life, while others have to be repeated every five or ten years. Most immunizations should first be given to people when they are babies.

It is very important to make sure children get all of their immunization shots because those shots protect them from many serious, even deadly, diseases. However, some vaccines can cause some bad side effects. It is wise to ask your doctor about all the risks and benefits of an immunization. Immunizations are available from doctors as well as county public health departments.

EXERCISE 6: GERMS

Directions: Write the best word in each blank to complete the review of this passage.

1. Diseases can be caused by problems inside your body or by

 ____________________ (a) invading from outside of your body. Three types of germs are ____________________ (b), ____________________ (c), and ____________________ (d). Your body builds up some protection, called ____________________ (e), to diseases it has fought before. A shot that causes your body to build immunity is called an

 ____________________ (f) or a ____________________ (g). Most of these shots should first be given to people when they are

 ____________________ (h). Children should get all their shots to

 ____________________ (i) them against many serious diseases.

Directions: Circle the number of the best answer.

2. Which of these statements best summarizes all the functions of bacteria?

 (1) Bacteria both help and harm us.
 (2) Bacteria make us sick.
 (3) Bacteria are never useful.
 (4) Bacteria help us make vitamins.
 (5) Bacteria cannot be killed by antibiotics.

3. What is the main idea of the last paragraph in this passage?
   (1) Doctors have medicines to cure disease.
   (2) Immunizations can be given by doctors or clinics.
   (3) Most diseases can be prevented.
   (4) People should get immunized to protect themselves.
   (5) Immunizations are given only to babies.

Answers and explanations start on page 210.

PLANTS AND PHOTOSYNTHESIS:
Food Factories

Unlike animals, plants have the ability to make their own food. Without plants, there would be no food on the Earth. Since animals cannot make their own food, they must eat plants or other animals to survive.

Plants make food using a process called ***photosynthesis***. They use energy from the sun to combine carbon dioxide, water, and minerals into food. Carbon dioxide is a gas in the air, while water and minerals come from the soil. Plants carrying out photosynthesis also give off oxygen, which all animals, including people, need to breathe.

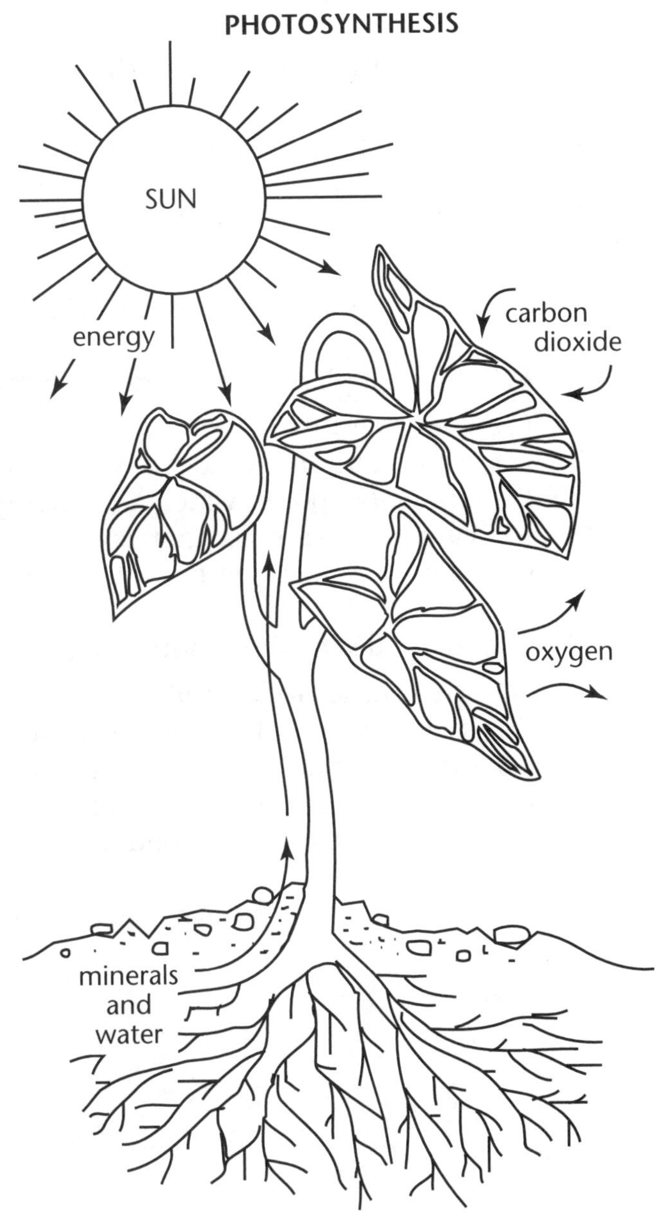

Photosynthesis can take place only in plant cells that have ***chlorophyll***. (Chlorophyll is the green chemical first mentioned on page 38.) Scientists have not been able to figure out how to perform photosynthesis in a laboratory. It takes place only in living green plants, so you can see why plants are so important to us.

The most advanced plants are members of either the fern family or the seed-bearing plant family. Plants of both of these families use chlorophyll to make their own food.

The less advanced plants found in the ***fungus*** family are not able to make their own food. Fungi cannot make their own food because they have no chlorophyll in their cells. They must live off other living things, often things that are dead or decaying. Molds, mildews, and mushrooms are all types of fungi. Some fungi are helpful to people, like the yeast that makes bread rise. Other fungi are harmful, like the fungus that causes athlete's foot or the molds that spoil food.

The simplest plants have only one cell, like the bacteria we discussed in the last passage and like certain kinds of ***algae*** (green or brown plants that grow in water). Surprisingly, many of these plants do contain chlorophyll.

EXERCISE 7: FOOD FACTORIES

Directions: Read the following statements. Circle *T* if the statement is true or *F* if the statement is false.

T F **1.** All fungi are harmful to people.

T F **2.** Fungi cannot make their own food.

T F **3.** All plant cells have chlorophyll.

T F **4.** Oxygen is given off during photosynthesis.

Directions: Choose the best answer for each question.

5. What does a plant that contains chlorophyll need to make food?
(1) energy, water, carbon dioxide, and minerals
(2) water, carbon dioxide, oxygen, and minerals
(3) minerals, spores, water, and energy
(4) carbon dioxide, oxygen, spores, and energy
(5) oxygen, water, energy, and minerals

6. The main idea of this reading passage is
(1) what makes food spoil
(2) how different plants get or make their food
(3) different types of one-celled plants
(4) the way animals get their food
(5) pollution created by food factories

Answers and explanations start on page 210.

EVOLUTION AND CLASSIFICATION: From the Beginning. . .

Imagine finding a footprint over a million years old! How about a piece of petrified wood from a forest 100 million years old or the skeleton of a fish that died 500 million years ago! These ***fossils***, the remains of ancient animals and plants, help scientists discover the story of ***evolution***, how life developed on Earth.

Millions of years ago, fossils were made when living things left traces, like footprints or bones, in mud or sand. Over the centuries the mud or sand turned to rock, and the remains were preserved. Other fossils were preserved in tar or in amber, which is ancient tree sap that has turned to stone. When the Earth was formed, it was a ball of hot, molten (melted) rock and poisonous gases. As it began to cool, clouds formed and the first rain fell. The low spots on the cooling Earth filled with water and became oceans. Life began in the oceans, probably about $3^1/_2$ billion years ago.

The first living things were very simple beings like viruses and bacteria. About 3 billion years ago the first true plants developed. These were one-celled algae that could carry out photosynthesis. Much later, about 1 billion years ago, simple one-celled animals developed and fed on the plants.

Gradually these single-celled creatures grouped together in colonies. These became the first many-celled plants and animals.

Early Animals

The first many-celled animals lived in the sea. They were all ***invertebrates***—animals without skeletons or backbones. There are many invertebrates still living today, such as insects, worms, crabs, and jellyfish. The first ***vertebrates*** (animals with backbones) were the fish, which appeared about 550 million years ago. All other vertebrates, including humans, are descended from the fish.

About 400 million years ago, the first descendants of the fish crawled out on land. These were early ***amphibians***. The amphibians had to stay close to the water because they laid their eggs in water. The eggs hatched into tiny creatures that swam with fins and breathed underwater with gills just like fish. When they grew older, these creatures lost their fins and gills, grew legs and lungs, and went out onto the land. You can watch the same thing happening in present-day amphibians, when tadpoles change into toads or frogs.

The next animals to develop, over 250 million years ago, were the ***reptiles***. Snakes, turtles, and alligators are all reptiles that are alive today. Reptiles look similar to amphibians, but they have scales instead of smooth skin, and they lay their eggs on land rather than in water. A reptile ***embryo*** (the not-yet-born form of an animal) goes through its gill-breathing stage inside the egg, which has a tough outer covering to preserve moisture. Some reptiles developed into some of the most amazing animals that ever lived, the giant ***dinosaurs***.

Birds and Mammals

During the last part of the Age of Reptiles, while dinosaurs were still everywhere, two new types of animals began to be seen. ***Birds*** developed from some of the smaller two-legged dinosaurs. ***Mammals*** were small mouselike creatures that came from reptiles that lived before the dinosaurs. Birds and mammals had an advantage over the reptiles; they were ***warm-blooded***. This meant that their bodies stayed at a constant temperature. To help them do this, birds developed feathers, while mammals developed hair. Both of these are much better insulators than scales. This meant that birds and mammals could survive in a colder climate than reptiles.

Birds and mammals also improved on the reptiles' way of having young. Birds lay eggs with shells that are tougher than those of reptile eggs. Mammals developed a whole new way of reproducing. The female mammal carries the embryo inside her body until it is grown enough to survive in the outside world. Then she feeds her young on milk that she makes in her own body. This way of reproducing is safer than egg-laying because the young are better protected.

About 70 million years ago, the dinosaurs and most of their relatives suddenly died out. No one knows why this happened. Some scientists think the cause was a change to cooler, drier weather over most of the Earth. At any rate, only a few families of reptiles survived, and the Age of Mammals began.

The small, furry mammals changed and developed into many of the animals we see today. Dogs, cats, horses, bears, and every animal that bears its young alive and gives milk are members of the class of mammals.

The final part of the story (so far) begins only about 2 million years ago with the coming of the first human. Humans are mammals, since we bear our young alive and feed them with milk. We belong to the primate order in the class of mammals, along with our cousins, the monkeys and apes. To understand better how humans are related to other animals, look at the part of our "family tree" on page 45.

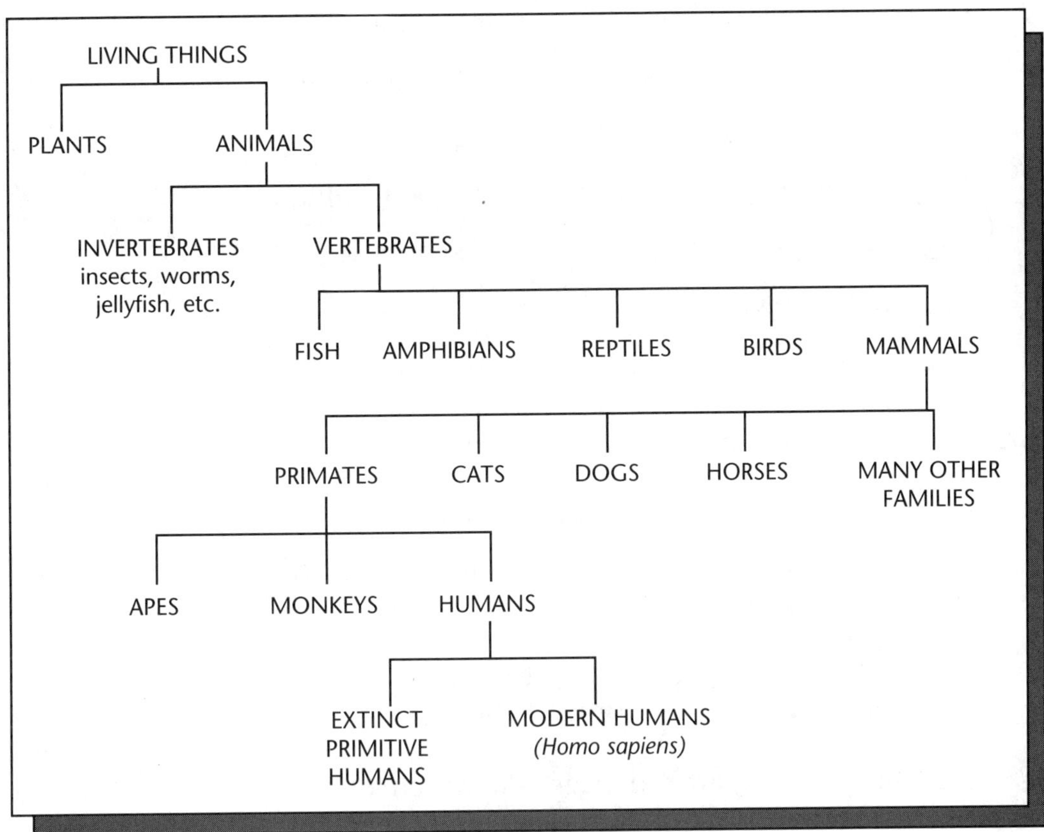

EXERCISE 8: TYPES OF ANIMALS

Directions: Next to each word in the left column, place the number of the matching answer in the right column.

1. Match each word with its definition.

_____ **a.** invertebrates	(1) animals that feed their young with milk
_____ **b.** vertebrates	(2) animals that live first in water, then on land
_____ **c.** fish	(3) animals without backbones
_____ **d.** amphibians	(4) animals with scales that lay eggs on land
_____ **e.** reptiles	(5) animals that breathe with gills
_____ **f.** birds	(6) animals with backbones
_____ **g.** mammals	(7) animals with feathers

2. Match each animal with the group it belongs to.

_____ a. cow	(1) invertebrate
_____ b. rattlesnake	(2) fish
_____ c. robin	(3) amphibian
_____ d. guppy	(4) reptile
_____ e. bumblebee	(5) bird
_____ f. bullfrog	(6) mammal

Directions: Choose the best answer for each question below.

3. This passage describes the process of evolution. Evolution is
   (1) development from simple to complex living things
   (2) a very fast process
   (3) the growth of an embryo
   (4) an animal with gills instead of lungs
   (5) a process scientists no longer believe in

4. Based on the diagram on page 45, which of these animals is *not* a mammal?
   (1) human
   (2) ape
   (3) dog
   (4) bird
   (5) horse

Answers and explanations start on page 210.

ANIMALS HELPING PEOPLE:
Animal Partners

You have probably heard of seeing-eye dogs, the dogs that guide blind people, but how about hearing-ear dogs? Have you heard of therapeutic horseback riding or pet therapy? These are all programs in which animals are used to help people.

Probably the best-known animal partners are seeing-eye dogs. They are carefully chosen and trained to work with blind people. Seeing-eye dogs can lead their blind masters wherever they want to go. They can help blind people cross streets and avoid running into things in unfamiliar territory. Blind people with seeing-eye dogs can be more independent because they don't need other people to lead them around.

Dogs can be just as much help to deaf people. A hearing-ear dog can be trained to tell a deaf person when the telephone or doorbell is ringing. It can wake its master up when an alarm clock goes off. If a fire or smoke alarm sounds, a hearing-ear dog will pull its master to safety. Dogs owned by young parents learn to fetch the mother or father whenever their baby cries. Dogs can even be trained to tell deaf drivers about sirens or railroad signals by putting a paw on their shoulders.

Dogs are not the only animals that work well with handicapped people. Horses can help people in something called ***therapeutic riding***. Children and adults who cannot walk can often learn to ride, because riding takes much less strength in the lower body and legs. Riding is good exercise for them. It strengthens their muscles and improves their balance and coordination.

Any animal that can show affection can be used to help people who need affection and interest in their lives. Children who have been abused and neglected are often afraid of other people, but they will open up to a dog or cat. Lonely people in nursing homes welcome a visit from a cuddly puppy or kitten. Some prisons are even experimenting with letting the prisoners have pets.

EXERCISE 9: ANIMAL PARTNERS

Directions: On a separate piece of paper, write short answers to these questions.

1. List some kinds of people who can be helped by animals.
2. What are some of the things a hearing-ear dog can be trained to do?
3. Why is it good for some handicapped people to learn to ride horses?
4. Why do you think a hospital might have a dog in the children's ward?

Answers and explanations start on page 210.

GENETICS:
It's in the Genes

"Oh, he's got his mother's eyes!"

"I just hope he doesn't have his father's nose!"

How many times have you heard things like this when people are looking at babies? We all know that children tend to look like their parents, but why? The science that studies this question is called ***genetics***, the study of how things are ***inherited*** (passed along) from parents to children.

Every cell in your body contains a kind of "blueprint" of the plans for your whole body. Inside the nucleus of each cell are tiny threadlike things called ***chromosomes***. The chromosomes are made of ***genes*** strung together like beads. Each pair of genes carries the code for a certain ***trait***: things like the color of your hair or eyes and your size and general shape.

Inside the cells of every creature are chromosomes carrying the genes for that creature. It is these genes that are passed on to the next generation.

The simplest one-celled plants and animals ***reproduce*** by splitting. For example, each chromosome in a bacterium's nucleus splits into two identical copies. Then the nucleus splits, with one copy of each chromosome going into each new nucleus. Finally, the whole cell splits into two bacteria, which both start growing again until each of them is the same size as the original cell.

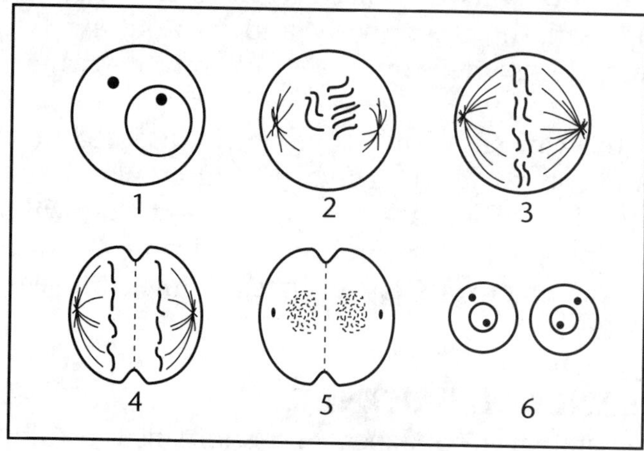

A cell splitting

More advanced plants and animals reproduce sexually. A male cell and a female cell must combine to form the first cell of the new being. This new being gets half its chromosomes from each parent. This way of reproducing allows for more variety, because the new being will inherit characteristics from both its father and its mother. It will not be an exact copy of either.

Let's look at an example from an experiment done by Gregor Mendel, a monk who first investigated the basic facts of genetics. He crossed a tall pea plant with a dwarf pea plant. Each of the ***offspring*** (the new plants) got a gene for tallness from one parent and a gene for shortness from the other. Plants with mixed parents like this are called ***hybrid*** plants.

The next diagram shows the results of Mendel's experiment.

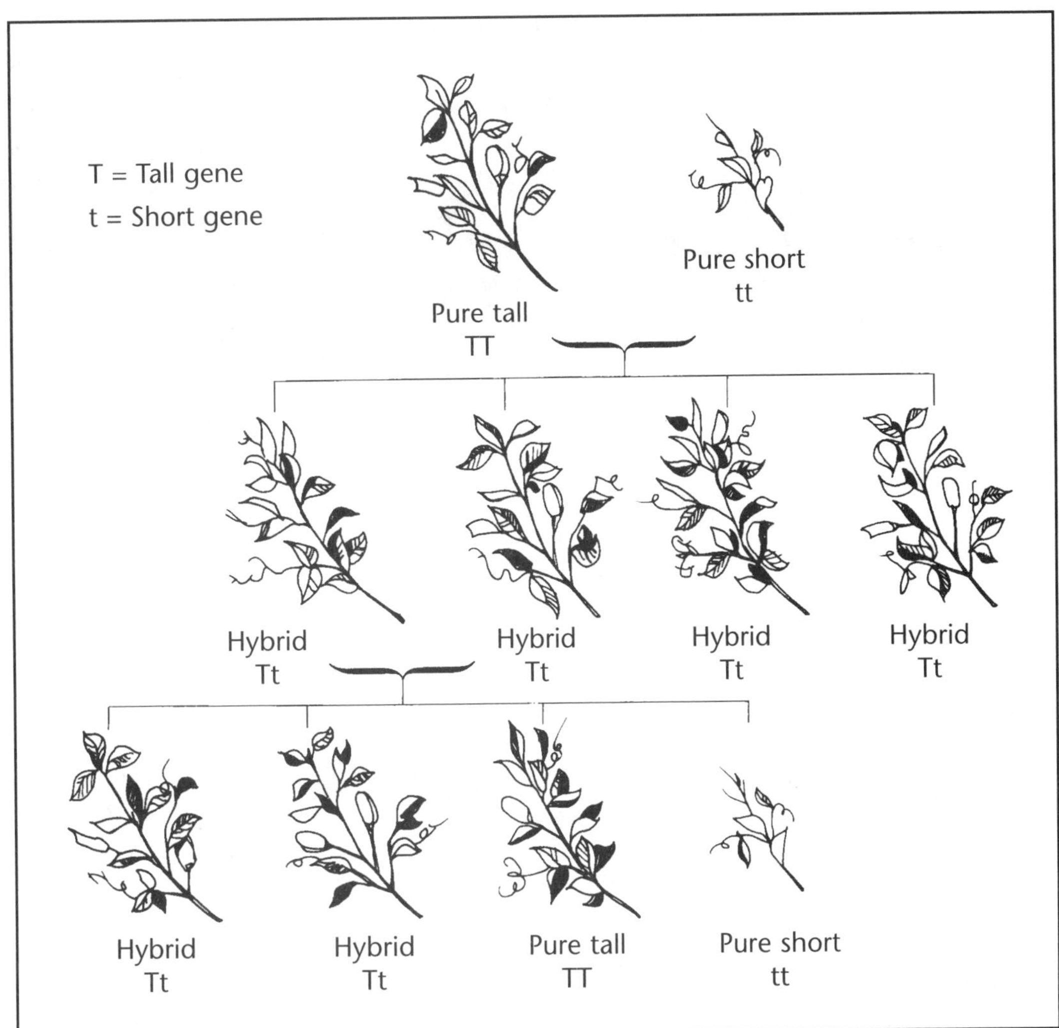

Strangely enough, all the first generation of new plants looked tall, even though they each had one gene for shortness. The gene for tallness is ***dominant***, which means that the gene for tallness will always override the gene for shortness. The gene that is not dominant, in this case the gene for shortness, is called ***recessive***.

As you can see in the diagram above, if two of these hybrid plants are crossed, one-quarter of the offspring will be short, because they have inherited two genes for shortness, one from each parent. Half of the offspring will be tall but carry a hidden gene for shortness. The last quarter will be pure tall plants, plants that carry both genes for tallness.

Inheritance in people works the same way, though it can be more complicated. Sometimes more than one set of genes controls a certain trait, as in skin color.

In humans, many inherited diseases, like juvenile diabetes and Tay-Sachs disease, are the result of recessive genes. This means that a person could be healthy yet be carrying a dangerous gene. If that person marries another person with the same recessive gene, their children could get both recessive genes and therefore have the disease. People whose families show any of these diseases often have their genes checked before they have children. This is called ***genetic counseling***.

EXERCISE 10: GENETICS

Directions: In hamsters, dark eye color is dominant and light eye color is recessive. First, fill in the following gene chart showing what happens when a dark-eyed hamster with two *DD* genes mates with a light-eyed hamster with two *dd* genes. Then answer the questions that follow.

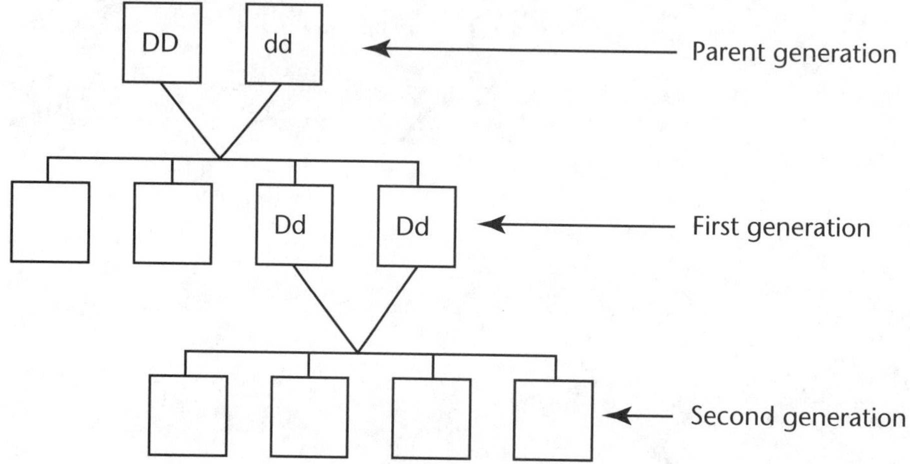

1. In the first generation of hamsters, how many would probably have dark eyes?
2. In the first generation, how many hamsters would carry one recessive gene for light eyes?
3. Two of the first-generation hamsters mate with each other. How many of the offspring out of every four would probably have light eyes and how many would have dark eyes?
4. Three out of four of the second-generation hamsters have dark eyes because they carry the dominant gene (D). How many of these dark-eyed hamsters would probably carry a gene for light eyes?

Directions: Choose the best answer for this question.

5. In hamsters, brown fur is dominant over white fur. Therefore, any hamster with white fur must have both genes for white fur. If a brown hamster and a white hamster mate, and some of their offspring are white, what can you tell about the brown parent hamster?
   (1) It had only genes for brown fur.
   (2) It had only genes for white fur.
   (3) It had one gene for brown fur and one gene for white fur.
   (4) It didn't have any genes for fur color.
   (5) You can't tell anything about its genes for fur color.

Answers and explanations start on page 211.

SCIENTIST IN THE SPOTLIGHT:

Dr. George Washington Carver

"Start where you are with what you have. Make something of it. Never be satisfied." These are the words of Dr. George Washington Carver, and he followed them throughout his life. He started with almost every strike against him but went on to become a scientist famous for his genius and his concern for his fellow man.

Born in Missouri of slave parents in 1864, George was a small and sickly baby. His parents couldn't live together because they belonged to different owners. Soon after he was born, George's mother was stolen by slave raiders, and he never saw her again. George was taken in by the Carvers, a German farmer and his wife who had no children of their own.

Because of damage done to his vocal cords by the slave raiders, George couldn't talk until he was about eight. He was a quick worker, though, and he had a real gift with plants.

Once George learned to talk, he never stopped asking questions. He wanted to know everything. The nearest school for black people was in a town called Neosho in the next county. So at the age of ten, George set out to earn his own living and go to school.

The first year was very hard. Since George had never learned to read, he started out far behind his class. The other students laughed at his ragged clothes and at the funny way he talked. He had no money, so he slept in a barn and often had little to eat. But he learned quickly!

Soon George had learned everything he could at the small-town school. There was no high school near Neosho that would take black students. So George set out on his own again, this time to Kansas, where there were high schools that would take both black and white students.

After finishing high school, George Carver applied to several colleges. He was overjoyed when he was awarded a scholarship to Highland University. However, when he went to register, the man behind the desk told him that there had been a mistake. Highland University did not accept black students. Later Carver discovered that because his high school record was so good, the college officials had simply assumed he was white.

Carver was so disappointed that he gave up the idea of going to college. He spent several years traveling out west, farming and doing whatever work he could get. This hard work gave him an understanding of the common man's problems that he never forgot.

Finally, he tried again and was accepted first at Simpson College and then at Iowa State University. Carver graduated from Iowa State in 1894 and was immediately hired to teach in the university's well-known biology and agriculture department. He made a good salary and was granted a master's degree two years later. Then he received a letter that changed his life.

The letter was from Booker T. Washington. Washington was trying to start a school, called Tuskegee Institute, for poor black students. He wanted to help black people out of poverty by showing them how to farm better and make a decent life for themselves. He asked George Washington Carver to head his department of agriculture. At the age of thirty-two, Carver left his safe job with its good salary and many opportunities, and he went to Tuskegee.

He stayed at Tuskegee for the rest of his life. When he arrived, there was no laboratory equipment. Carver had his students go out and ask for old bottles and pans to make laboratory equipment. Carver believed that an educated man should know how to work with his hands and make do with whatever materials were available.

Carver made many of his great discoveries because he was looking for a way to help poor people, who often came to him with their problems. For instance, he figured out how to make paint out of the sticky Alabama clay so that poor people could afford to paint their small shacks and churches. When the boll weevil came and wiped out the cotton crop, he taught southern farmers how to grow peanuts. Then, when the market for peanuts was flooded, he shut himself in his lab for a week and discovered over two dozen new products that could be made from peanuts, including ice cream, face powder, ink, and dandruff cure. He was the father of modern ***synthetic*** chemistry, the science that today gives us so many different products from simple plants and minerals.

Carver worked until he died, at the age of seventy-nine. His accomplishments were enormous. He discovered over 300 products that could be made from peanuts and 118 from sweet potatoes. He found good uses for waste products like wood shavings, straw, and peanut hulls. He raised thousands of dollars that helped make Tuskegee Institute one of the best schools for black people in the South. But perhaps most importantly, he taught and helped hundreds of students. Many of students went on to become well-known scientists and teachers themselves.

EXERCISE 11: GEORGE WASHINGTON CARVER

Directions: Write short answers to these questions.

1. How did being black make Carver's early life more difficult?

2. How did learning to read change Carver's life? What do you think his life would have been like if he hadn't learned to read?

3. Why do you think Carver left a good job at Iowa State to go to Tuskegee? Do you think it was a good decision?

4. George Washington Carver was loved as well as respected. Why do you think people thought so highly of him?

Answers and explanations start on page 211.

EXERCISE 12: CHAPTER 2 REVIEW

Directions: Read each passage carefully. Then circle the number of the one best answer to each question.

Questions 1–3 are based on the following passage.

Vaccines play an important role in keeping children healthy. However, some people are questioning whether the pertussis (whooping cough) vaccine, which is part of the standard DPT shot given to babies, is being used safely. A group called Dissatisfied Parents Together claims that too many children are permanently hurt by reactions to this shot. The American Medical Association admits that pertussis vaccine can cause bad reactions, but it says that the risk of a bad reaction is very small. Many people would like to see the government investigate this problem. In fact, some drug companies are working to make a safer vaccine. In the meantime, some doctors say that if a child has a severe reaction to a DPT shot, the child probably shouldn't be given any more pertussis vaccinations.

1. What is one *opinion* discussed in this passage?
   (1) DPT shots are commonly given to babies.
   (2) Pertussis vaccine can cause bad reactions.
   (3) Whooping cough is a dangerous disease.
   (4) The government may investigate this problem.
   (5) The American Medical Association is always right.

2. One safe and effective way the government could investigate this problem would be to
   (1) test the vaccine on different groups of babies
   (2) ask the companies that make the vaccine if it is safe
   (3) require doctors to keep records of all reactions to the vaccine
   (4) stop the shots and see how many children get sick
   (5) take an opinion poll to see how many people think the shots are dangerous

3. If a child has a bad reaction to a DPT shot, some doctors recommend that the child should
   (1) get his next shot later
   (2) not get any more pertussis vaccine
   (3) get his next shot earlier
   (4) stop all shots of any kind
   (5) continue the shots on schedule

Questions 4–6 are based on the following passage.

The word *dinosaur* comes from two Greek words, *deinos* ("terrible") and *sauros* ("lizard"). During the long Age of Reptiles, from 225 to 70 million years ago, dinosaurs dominated the Earth. There were dinosaurs that lived in swamps and ate plants. One of these, the huge apatosaurus, was over 90 feet long and weighed 70,000 pounds. There were terrifying meat-eating dinosaurs, such as the allosaurus (50 feet long, 16,000 pounds) and its even larger cousin, the tyrannosaurus rex (50 feet long, 20,000 pounds). There were dinosaurs that glided through the air, like the pterosaurs, and dinosaurs that swam in the ocean. There were even small three-foot-long dinosaurs that ran around on two legs. They probably lived by eating the eggs of their larger relations.

4. The largest dinosaur mentioned in this passage is the

(1) apatosaurus
(2) allosaurus
(3) tyrannosaurus rex
(4) pterosaur
(5) archaeopteryx

5. This passage is mainly about

(1) reptiles
(2) dinosaurs
(3) pterosaurs
(4) eggs
(5) relations

6. Which of the following is *not* true according to the passage?

(1) Dinosaurs were reptiles.
(2) Dinosaurs lived 70 million years ago.
(3) Some dinosaurs could swim.
(4) Some dinosaurs were smaller than people.
(5) Dinosaurs ate only meat.

Questions 7–9 are based on the following passage.

Some genetic problems are caused by mutations. A mutation happens when radiation, chemicals, or chance causes a sudden change in a gene. The offspring that has that gene will be different from its parents in some way. Some mutations are harmful, like the one that causes some horses to be born with one short leg. When a mutation is life-threatening, the mutated creature will probably not survive to breed, so the damaged gene will not be passed on. Once in a while, a mutation is helpful; for example, a mutation that made one hen lay stronger eggshells than normal. A helpful mutation makes a creature more likely to survive and have offspring who will inherit the new gene. This is called natural selection, and it is one of the ways evolution happens.

7. A mutation is

(1) a change in a gene
(2) made by human beings
(3) always harmful
(4) usually helpful
(5) something stronger

8. A harmful mutation is not usually passed on in animals because the mutated animal

(1) doesn't want to pass it on
(2) lays stronger eggs
(3) has a shorter leg
(4) is chosen by natural selection
(5) probably will not survive to breed

9. The idea that successful creatures will have more offspring and pass on their good genes is called

(1) mutation
(2) radiation
(3) survival
(4) natural selection
(5) evolution

Questions 10–12 are based on the following passage.

Gardening is a hobby that can be enjoyed by people of all ages. Small children love to plant seeds and will wait impatiently for the first signs of the new plants. Energetic teenagers can get a good tan and a good workout while digging the ground or hoeing the weeds. Parents can share this hobby with their children and stretch the food budget with fresh, home-grown vegetables. Even very elderly people can pick flowers and enjoy the fresh air while sitting out in the garden.

10. The main idea of this passage is that

(1) gardening is a hobby
(2) children like gardening
(3) people of different ages can enjoy gardening
(4) gardening saves money
(5) older people can't enjoy gardens

11. What is one opinion stated in this passage?

(1) Older people can pick flowers.
(2) Home-grown vegetables help the food budget.
(3) Gardening is an enjoyable hobby.
(4) Small children shouldn't work in gardens.
(5) Digging requires energy.

12. How many different age groups are discussed in this passage?

(1) one
(2) two
(3) three
(4) four
(5) five

Answers and explanations start on page 211.

CHAPTER 3

READING SKILL

UNDERSTANDING ILLUSTRATIONS

"A picture is worth a thousand words." That old saying can be true even when you're reading a textbook. Sometimes a picture can give you information more quickly and easily than any number of words. Many textbooks and tests use special pictures called diagrams, charts, and graphs. Understanding these special illustrations is a very important "reading" skill.

DIAGRAMS:
Getting the Picture

The science topics in this chapter are about your body—about some of its many parts and how they work. Many of the articles will have ***diagrams*** to go with them. A diagram is a drawing that shows the parts of something or how a process works.

Look at the diagram below.

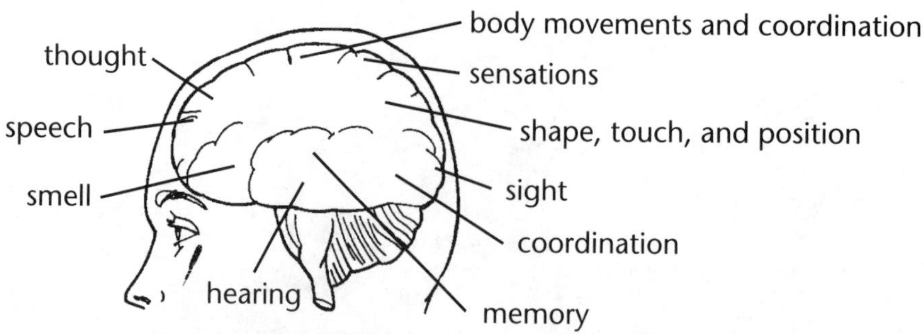

Always look at the ***title*** of a diagram first. The title tells you what the diagram is about. The title of this diagram is "Areas of the Brain." This title tells you that the diagram is showing you different parts of the brain.

Now look at the drawing. It is a drawing of the inside of a person's head. It is not a realistic drawing. Like most diagrams, this drawing has been simplified to get the main point across.

Finally, look at the ***labels***. The labels are words identifying important parts of the drawing. In this diagram, the words are telling which parts of the brain are used to do different things. For example, the part that gets messages from the eyes is at the back of the brain. If a woman were injured at the back of her head, she might lose her sight. The part that directs body movements is at the top of the brain. A person injured here might not be able to move well.

▶ You can use the diagram to figure things out. For instance, what might happen to a man injured at the forehead?

____

If you said *he might have trouble speaking,* you were right. You got that information from the diagram.

Diagram Reading Tip

In order to understand a diagram, first read the title. Next, look at the drawing itself. Finally, read all the labels.

EXERCISE 1: DIAGRAMS

Directions: Look at the diagram below and answer the questions.

PARTS OF THE EYE

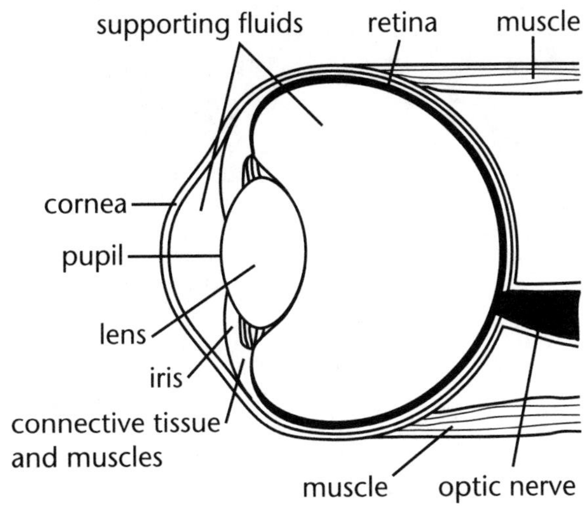

1. What is the title of the diagram? ______________________

2. Is the eye perfectly round? ______________________

3. What is the opening in front of the lens called? ______________

4. What is the inside of the eye filled with? ______________

5. What is the screen on the back of the eyeball called? ___________

6. What is the name of the nerve that runs out of the back of the eye?

   ____

7. When a person gets a cataract, the cornea of the eye gets clouded over. Why would this make it hard to see?

   ____

Answers and explanations start on page 211.

COMPARING DIAGRAMS

Sometimes a diagram will have more than one drawing. You should carefully compare the drawings. Look to see how they are alike and how they are different.

Let's look at this diagram with three drawings. Try to answer the questions that follow. Then read on to see if your answers were correct.

▶ Read the title. What is this diagram about? ______________________

____

▶ What is shown in each drawing? ______________________

____

▶ What is the difference in shape between the normal eye and the nearsighted one?

____

____

▶ What is the difference in shape between the normal eye and the farsighted one?

____

____

VISION AND EYE SHAPE

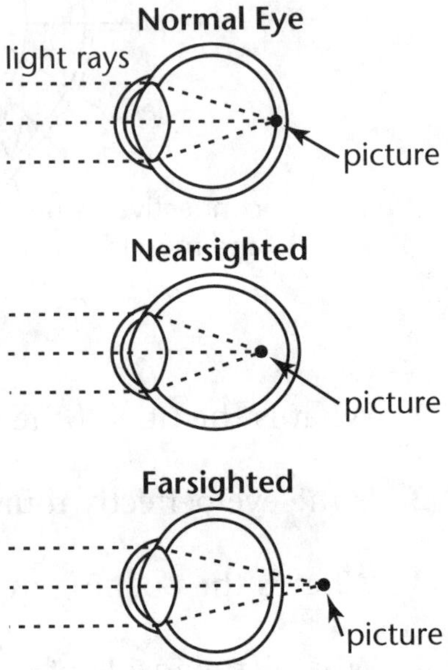

The title tells us that this diagram is about *the relationship between vision and eye shape*. There are three drawings of *eyeballs*. The *nearsighted* eyeball is *longer* than the normal one; the *farsighted* eyeball is *shorter*.

When you see something, a picture forms where the light rays focus (come together) in your eye. In a normal eye, the pictures form on the retina.

▶ Where does a picture form in a nearsighted eye? ______________________

▶ Where does a picture form in a farsighted eye? ______________________

▶ Why do you think that nearsighted and farsighted people have trouble seeing clearly? ______________________

Because a nearsighted eye is longer, the light rays focus on the picture *ahead of the retina*. In a farsighted eye, they focus *behind the retina*. In both cases, the picture is blurry because *the light rays are not focused exactly on the retina*.

EXERCISE 2: COMPARING DIAGRAMS

Directions: Look at this diagram. Then answer the following questions.

GROWTH OF THE FETUS DURING EARLY PREGNANCY

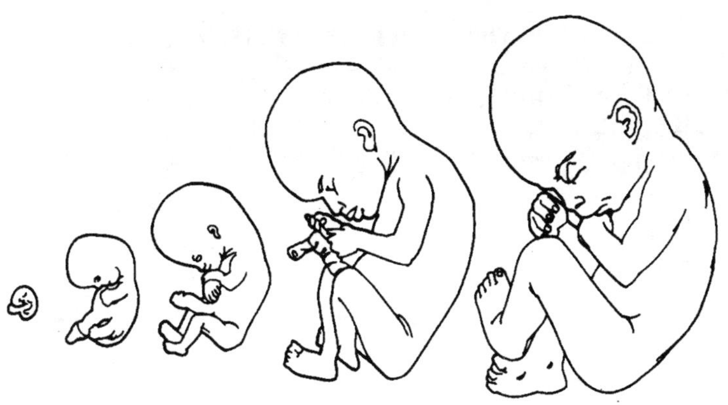

1 month 2 months 3 months 4 months 5 months

1. What does this diagram show? ______________________________

2. What happens to the fetus as time goes on? ____________________

3. When does the fetus first show toes? _________________________

4. From the title and the diagram, what do you think the word *fetus* means? (Circle the best answer.)
   (1) a baby
   (2) a deformed head
   (3) a young boy
   (4) an unborn child
   (5) a new drug

Answers and explanations start on page 211.

CHARTS

Another way to get information is from charts. Charts are very useful for organizing information. Here is an example.

Blood Types and Transfusions		
Blood Type	**Can Take Blood from**	**Can Give Blood to**
O	O	O, A, B, AB
A	O, A	A, AB
B	O, B	B, AB
AB	O, A, B, AB	AB

To understand this chart, you have to know that different people have different ***blood types***. There are four main blood types, called *O*, *A*, *B*, and *AB*. If a person gets blood from someone else in a ***transfusion***, it has to be the right blood type. The wrong type of blood could kill someone.

First look at the title of this chart. This chart tells what types of blood are safe to use in transfusions between people with different blood types. Notice that the information in charts is organized in vertical ***columns***. Each column has a ***heading***. The three headings on this chart are "Blood Type," "Can Take Blood from," and "Can Give Blood to." These headings tell you what information each column holds.

Now read the chart across in rows. For example, look at the first blood type, "O." Look to the right. In the second column, under "Can Take Blood from," the chart lists only "O" again. This means that a person with type O blood can take blood only from another person with type O. Look right again, under "Can Give Blood to." The chart lists types O, A, B, and AB. This means that a person with type O blood can safely give blood to people with any of the four blood types.

Now you try it. Look on the chart for blood type B.

▶ A person with blood type B can take blood from what types? ________

▶ Type B people can give blood to what types? ____________________

According to the chart, type B people can take *type O* or *type B* blood. They can give blood to *type B* or *type AB*. If these were your answers, you read the chart well.

Chart Reading Tip

When reading a chart, first look at the title of the chart. Then read the headings on each of the columns and rows. Do not try to get specific information from the chart until you understand what the chart is about.

EXERCISE 3: CHARTS

Directions: Use this chart to answer the following questions.

Vitamins		
Vitamin	**Source**	**Use in the Body**
A	Fish, butter, eggs, liver, yellow vegetables	Keeps eyes and skin healthy. Helps digestion and breathing.
C	Leafy vegetables, tomatoes. Citrus fruits like lemons and oranges.	Prevents a disease called *scurvy.*
D	Sunshine, fish oils, liver	Helps to build strong bones and teeth.
E	Vegetable and animal oils	Protects the nervous system and the reproductive system.
B Group		
B_1 (thiamine)	Yeast, liver, nuts, grains, lean pork	Protects the nervous system. Prevents a disease called *beriberi.*
B_2 (riboflavin)	Yeast, wheat germ, liver, meat, eggs	Affects entire body. Prevents skin and mouth diseases.
Niacin	Vegetables, meat, yeast, beer	Prevents skin disorders like pellagra.
B_{12}	Vegetables and liver	Prevents anemia.

1. What is this chart about? ______________________________

2. What eight vitamins does this chart cover? ______________________________

3. What disease does vitamin C prevent? ______________________________

4. What two vitamins are found in fish? ______________________________

5. What three vitamins might a doctor recommend for a skin problem?

____

Answers and explanations start on page 212.

LINE GRAPHS

Sometimes a chart is not the best way to show information. This is what Jack Johnson discovered.

Many people like to grow tomatoes. Jack Johnson was very proud of his tomatoes. He was always looking for a way to grow more of them and to make them grow bigger. One year, he did an experiment to see how fertilizer affected the way his tomatoes grew. He put a different amount of fertilizer on each row of plants. Then he kept track of how many pounds of tomatoes he picked from each row. He put his results in a chart.

Fertilizer	Tomatoes	Fertilizer	Tomatoes	Fertilizer	Tomatoes
2 oz.	4 lb.	8 oz.	20 lb.	14 oz.	28 lb.
4 oz.	10 lb.	10 oz.	23 lb.	16 oz.	20 lb.
6 oz.	16 lb.	12 oz.	26 lb.	18 oz.	13 lb.

Set up in a chart like this, Jack's information was a little difficult to read and understand, so Jack decided to make a graph. People use graphs because graphs show some kinds of information more clearly and easily than written words or charts. There are many types of graphs. Jack decided to draw the ***line graph*** shown on page 65.

A line graph has four parts:

- the title,
- the horizontal axis,
- the vertical axis, and
- the graph line.

First look at the title of this graph. Like the title of a diagram or a chart, this tells you what the graph will be about. Many people make the mistake of ignoring the titles of diagrams, charts, and graphs, but titles can be important clues to the information you will be expected to find.

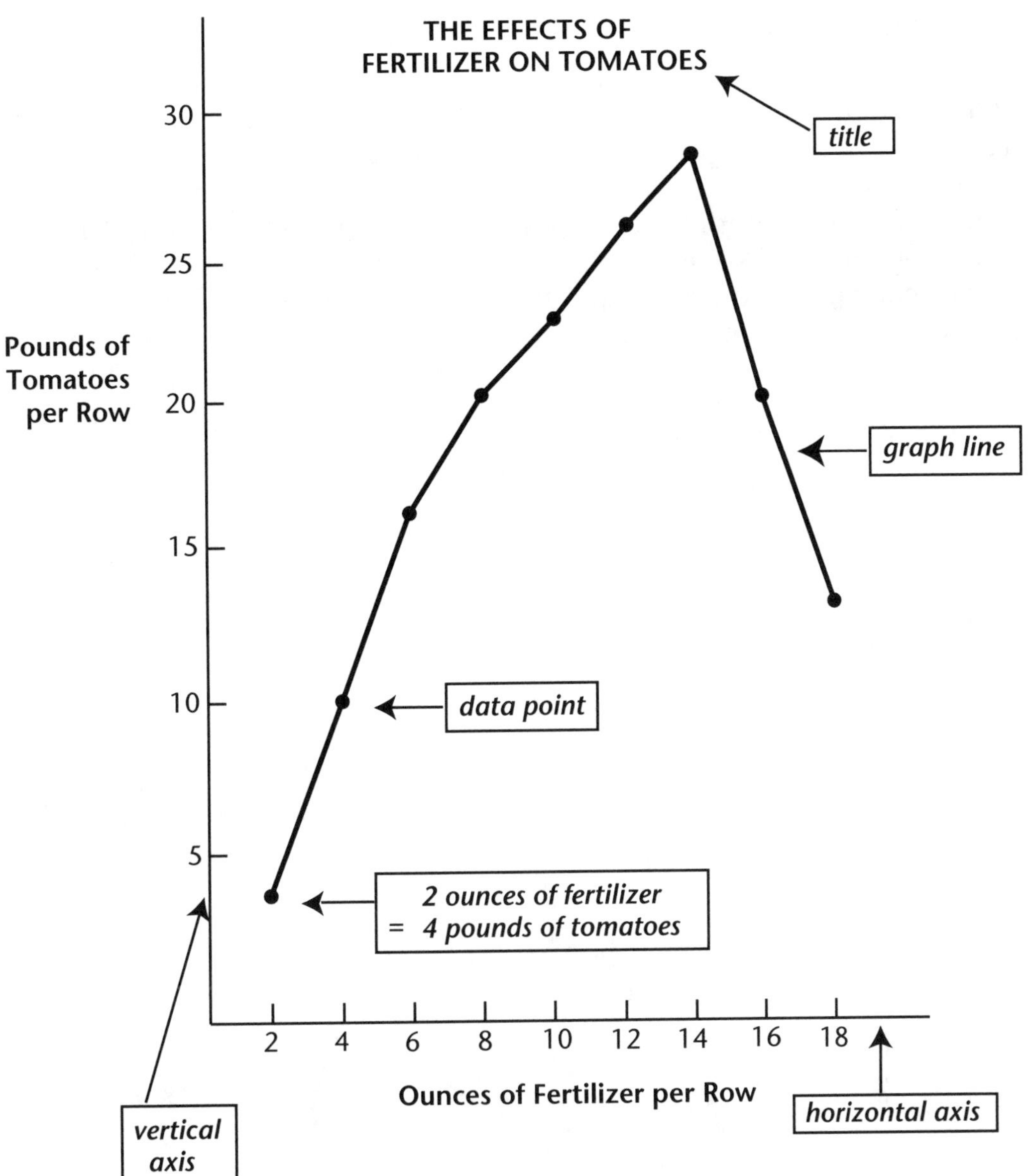

Reading Each Axis

Next look at the two axes. The axis that runs across the paper from left to right is called the ***horizontal axis***. The axis that runs up and down is called the ***vertical axis***. Each axis has a scale of numbers or measurements on it and a label to tell you what the axis is recording. For instance, in this graph the horizontal axis records the ounces of fertilizer Jack used in each row. The vertical axis records the pounds of tomatoes that were picked.

Always read the scales and labels of each axis carefully. Notice that each step on an axis can be more than one unit. In this graph, each step on the vertical axis is equal to five pounds. If Jack had drawn each step as one pound, he wouldn't have been able to fit the whole graph on a sheet of notebook paper.

The Graph Line

Only after reading the title and the axis labels should you look at the ***graph line*** itself. You can find specific pieces of information using the graph line. On Jack's graph, for example, you can find the amount of tomatoes that grew with only two ounces of fertilizer (4 pounds). You can also find the maximum amount of tomatoes that grew in one row (28 pounds).

Many graph lines have dots on them, called ***data points***, to help you find particular points on the graph. If a point lies between two steps on the scale, you must ***estimate*** the measurement for that point. If you can't tell just where a certain point on the line falls, use something straight, like the edge of a piece of paper or a ruler, to line up the point with the scale on the axis. The graph below shows how to read an *exact* and an *estimated* data point.

The overall shape, or ***trend***, of the graph line can help you draw conclusions about the graph's subject. For example, the shape of Jack's graph line shows that more fertilizer is not always better for tomatoes. Jack will probably decide to use 14 ounces of fertilizer on each row of his tomatoes next year.

Let's look at another example of a line graph. As you read, try to answer each question.

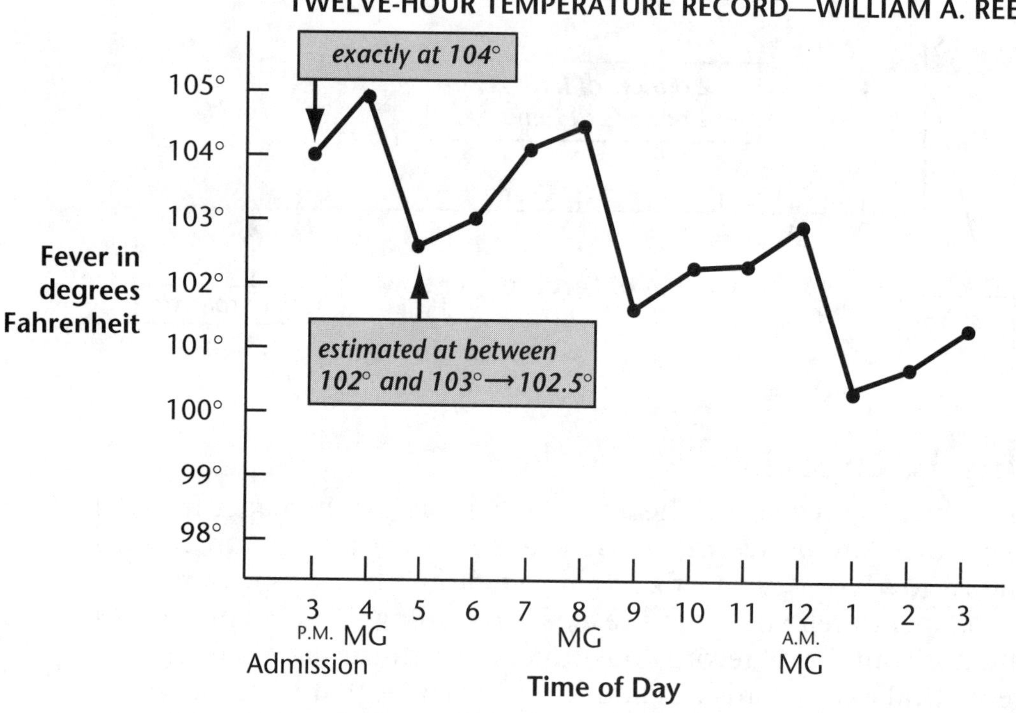

Note: MG = medication given

▶ What is the title of this graph? ______________________________

The title is *Twelve-Hour Temperature Record—William A. Rees*. From this title, we might guess that Mr. Rees is sick, because someone is keeping careful track of his temperature.

▶ What does the horizontal axis measure? ______________________

It measures *time*, in hours.

▶ What does the vertical axis measure? ________________________

It measures *Mr. Rees's fever* on the Fahrenheit scale. The scale (named after Gabriel Fahrenheit, the man who invented it about A.D. 1726) is the same temperature scale we usually use in our daily lives. Scientists and people in other countries often use a different scale, called the Celsius or centigrade scale.

▶ Now look at the graph line and answer these questions.

1. When was Mr. Rees admitted?_______________
2. When was his temperature highest?_______________
3. What was his temperature at 6:00 P.M.?_______________
4. For what two hours did his fever remain the same?_______________
5. What happened every time Mr. Rees was given medicine?

   ____
6. On the whole, does Mr. Rees seem to be getting better? Why or why not?

   ____

Here are the correct answers: (1) 3:00 P.M. (2) 4:00 P.M. (3) 103°F (4) 10:00 P.M. and 11:00 P.M. (5) Every time he was given medicine, his fever would drop. (6) On the whole, he seems to be getting better because his fever is getting lower with each cycle of medication.

Line Graph Tip

When a data point on a graph falls between two values, you need to estimate. For example, in the line graph on page 66, the data point for 5 P.M. falls about halfway in between 102° and 103° on the vertical scale. We estimate that the data point is at 102.5°.

EXERCISE 4: LINE GRAPHS

Directions: Sarah Burns was prying rocks out of the lawn at her cabin in the mountains. She noticed that she had to use different-sized crowbars to move different rocks. She did some experimenting with this idea, and this graph shows her results.

Look at the graph carefully. Then circle the best answer for each of the following questions.

CROWBARS AND ROCKS

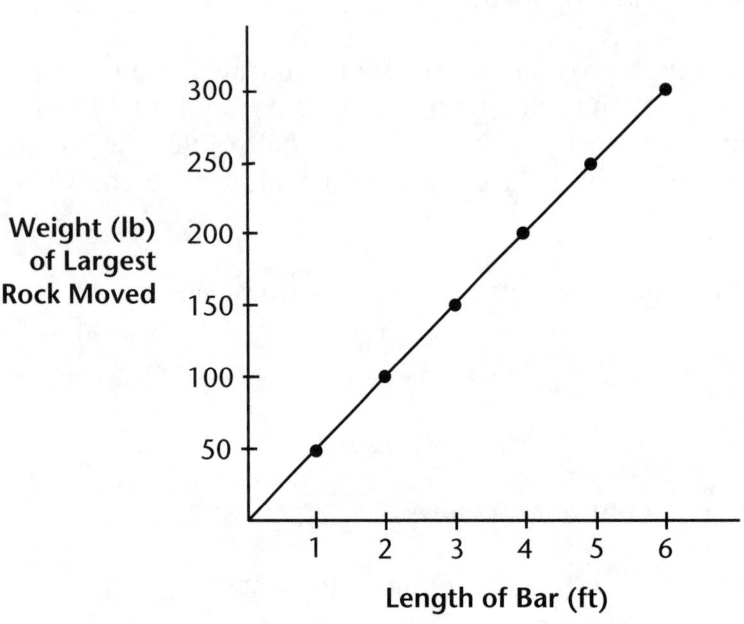

1. What was the weight of the heaviest rock Sarah could lift with a 2-foot crowbar?
   (1) 25 pounds
   (2) 50 pounds
   (3) 100 pounds
   (4) 150 pounds
   (5) 250 pounds

2. What length crowbar helped her move the heaviest rock?
   (1) 2 feet
   (2) 3 feet
   (3) 4 feet
   (4) 5 feet
   (5) 6 feet

3. Which hypothesis could be based on this graph?
   (1) Sarah is an extremely strong person.
   (2) To move a heavy rock, you should use a thick crowbar.
   (3) There were no rocks under 50 pounds on Sarah's lawn.
   (4) The longer the crowbar, the heavier the rock that can be moved.
   (5) Everyone needs a five-foot crowbar to move a 250-pound rock.

4. "Crowbars and Rocks" is not a very accurate title for this graph. Which of the following would be the best title?
   (1) Lengths of Crowbars Needed to Move Different Rocks
   (2) How Sarah Cleared Her Cabin Lawn
   (3) Weights of Rocks That Can Be Moved
   (4) Lengths of Crowbars Commonly Available
   (5) Weights of Rocks on a Mountain Cabin Lawn

5. What is the heaviest rock that Sarah could move with a 4-foot crowbar?
   (1) 175 pounds
   (2) 200 pounds
   (3) 225 pounds
   (4) 250 pounds
   (5) 275 pounds

Answers and explanations start on page 212.

BAR GRAPHS

Another type of graph is a ***bar graph***. As you might guess, a bar graph uses bars instead of lines to show pieces of information. The bars usually come up from the horizontal axis. You read the graph by seeing how high the bars go on the vertical scale. Look at the example on page 70.

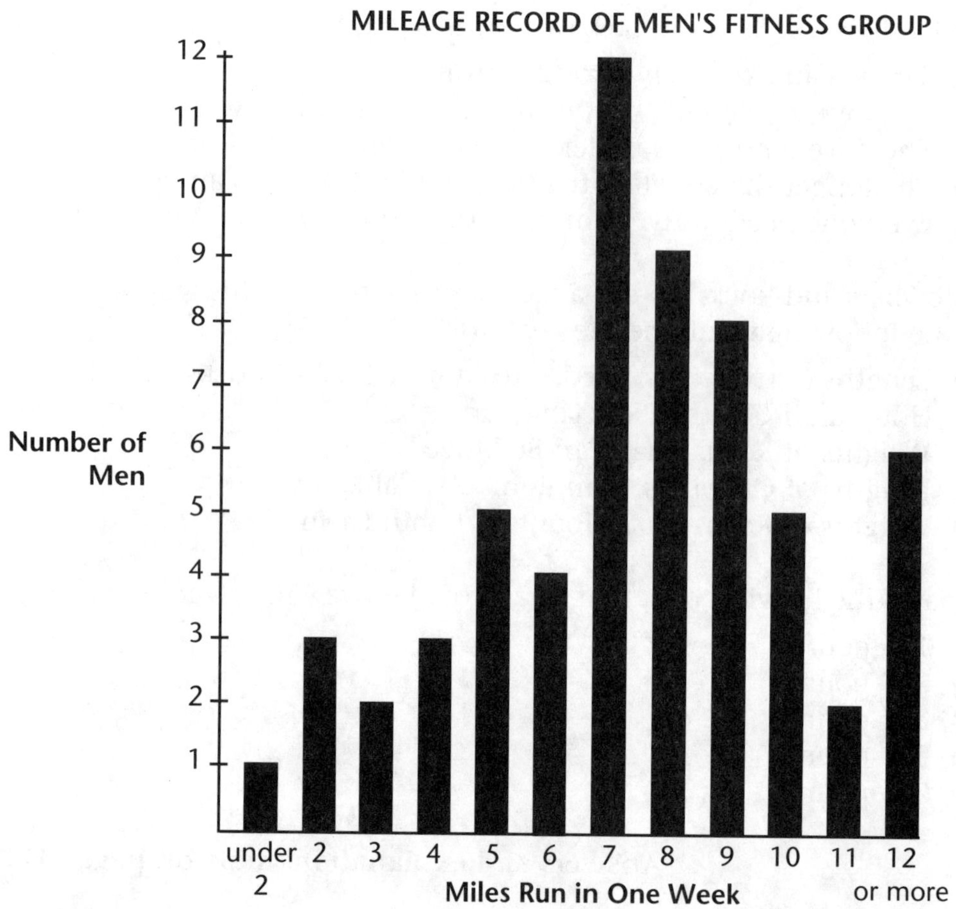

To read this graph, look at the bars coming up from the horizontal axis. Try answering these questions. If you have trouble telling where the top of the bar falls on the vertical scale, use a straight edge like a piece of paper to line them up.

- ▶ How many men ran just two miles? ________________
- ▶ What distance was run by exactly eight men? ________________
- ▶ What exact distance was run by the greatest number of men? ________

Your answers should be as follows: *three men*, *nine miles*, and *seven miles*.

Bar Graph Tip

On some bar graphs, the bars come out from the vertical axis. To read this type of bar graph, read down from the bar to the value given on the horizontal axis.

EXERCISE 5: BAR GRAPHS

Directions: Look at this bar graph carefully. Then answer each of the following questions.

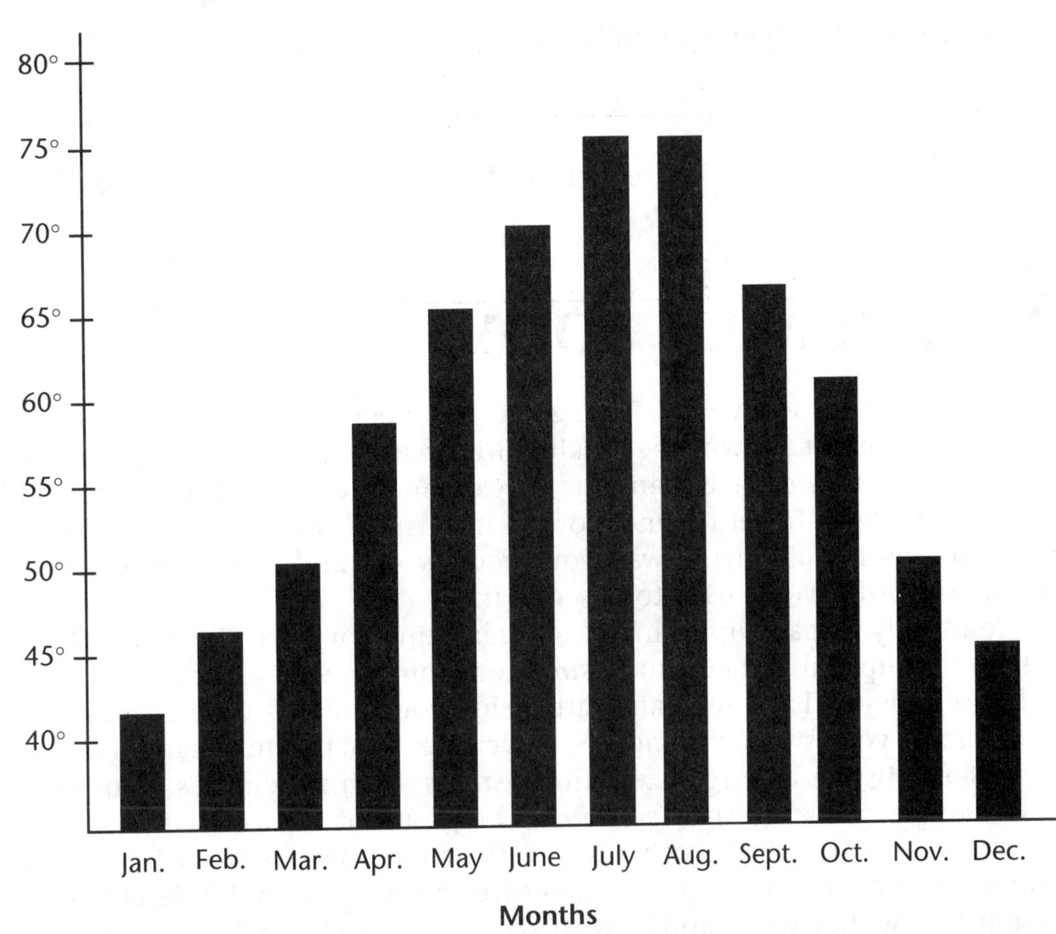

1. Looking at the title, what information do you expect to find on this graph? ______________________________
2. What does the horizontal axis show? ______________________________
3. What does the vertical axis measure? ______________________________
4. How big is each step on the vertical axis? ______________________________
5. What is the average high temperature in November? ______________________________
6. Which month is the coldest? ______________________________
7. Which two months are the warmest? ______________________________

8. Do you think it often gets below freezing in Vancouver? Why or why not? ______________________________

9. Do you think you could grow tropical plants in your yard in Vancouver? Why or why not? ______________________________

____

Answers and explanations start on page 212.

SCIENCE TOPIC
THE HUMAN BODY

It happens to everybody. You go to the doctor, and when he starts talking, he might as well be talking in Greek. Or you end up in the hospital, and you can't get anyone to explain in clear, simple terms just what is going on. To get the most out of modern medical care, you need to know something about the way your body works and about some of the special scientific words used to describe it.

Your body is made up of many different kinds of cells. Similar kinds of cells are grouped together into ***tissues***; for example, we talk of nerve tissue or muscle tissue. Each separate part inside your body is called an ***organ***. Your brain, your stomach, and your liver are all separate organs. Finally, organs and tissues are organized into ***systems***. Each system has a purpose. For example, your ***digestive system*** is the group of organs that help you digest your food. It includes your mouth, your stomach, your intestines, and many other organs. In this chapter we will study several different body systems, how they work, and how to keep them healthy.

BONES AND MUSCLES:
The Strong Stuff

All the strength in your body comes from two systems: the ***skeletal system***, containing the bones and their connecting tissues, and the ***muscular system***, which is all the muscles in your body.

The Skeletal System

There are 206 separate bones in your body! Some are large, like the bones in your legs. Others are small, like the delicate bones in your hands. The diagram of a skeleton on page 73 shows some of the most important bones.

Your bones do three important things for you. First, they support your body. Without your skeleton, you would be a shapeless blob, like a jellyfish. You wouldn't be able to move or breathe or even live. Second, some bones protect different parts of your body. Your hard skull bones protect your brain. Your ribs protect your heart, stomach, and lungs.

You might not guess the third thing your bones do. Inside some of your bones there is a soft substance called ***marrow***. If you've ever gotten soup bones from a store, you might have seen the marrow inside them. The bone marrow is where most of your blood cells are made.

Besides your bones, the skeletal system contains two other kinds of tissue, called cartilage and ligaments. ***Cartilage*** is a stiff kind of tissue, but it is softer than bone. Your nose and the outside of your ears are made of cartilage. People often say that children's bones are "soft." What they mean is that young children's bones have much more cartilage in them. The cartilage hardens up into real bone as they get older. This is why children should eat well and avoid certain sports that might bend or break their growing bones.

A ***joint*** is a place where two bones come together. Most joints are padded with cartilage. Bones are held together at the joints by very tough bands of tissue called ***ligaments***. When a doctor says that you have sprained something, like your ankle, she means you have stretched or torn some ligaments. This is usually caused by a sudden bending or twisting of a joint in the wrong direction.

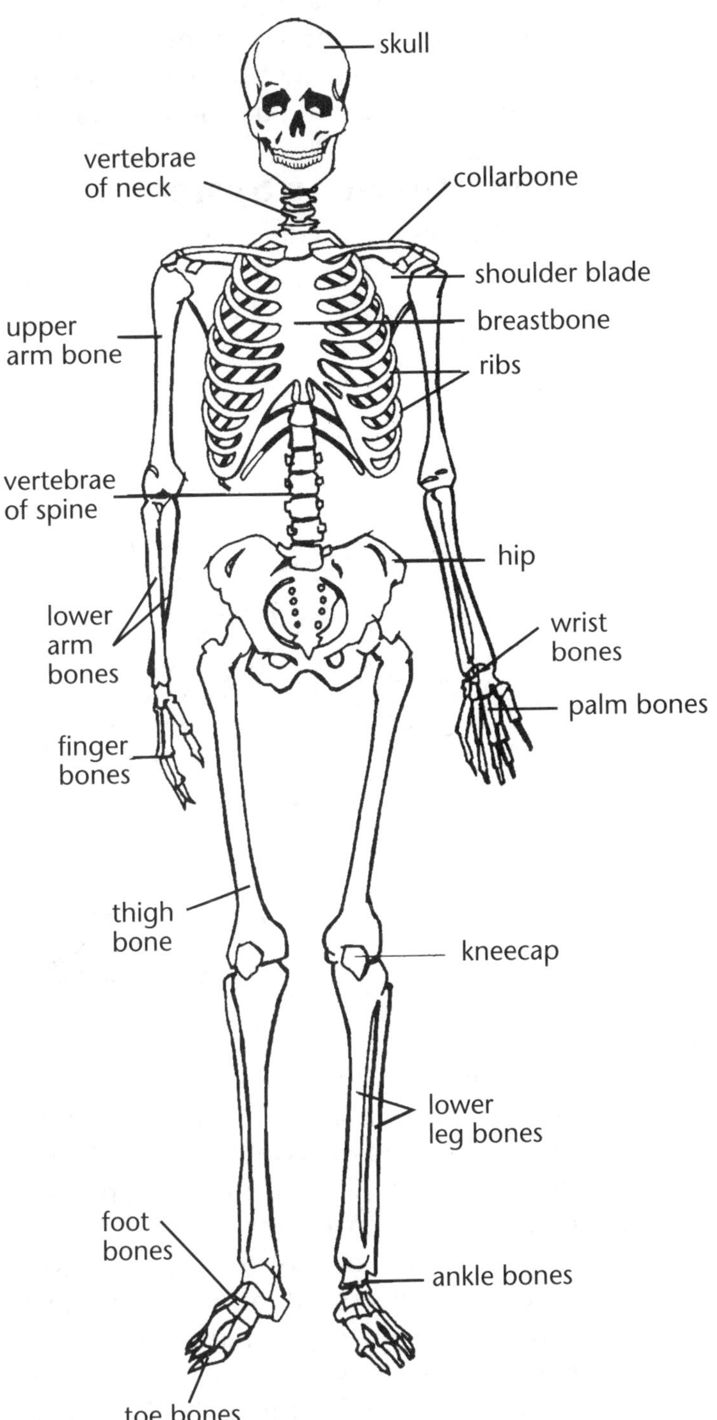

A common problem with the skeleton is ***osteoporosis***, which makes a person's bones become very brittle and breakable. It has many causes. One cause is not having enough calcium in the diet. Osteoporosis is particularly common among older women, which is why women should get lots of calcium all through their lives, either from foods like milk and cheese or from vitamin and mineral pills.

The Muscular System

Muscles are made of special cells that contract to get shorter and relax to get longer. That is how muscles move. Look at this diagram of an arm.

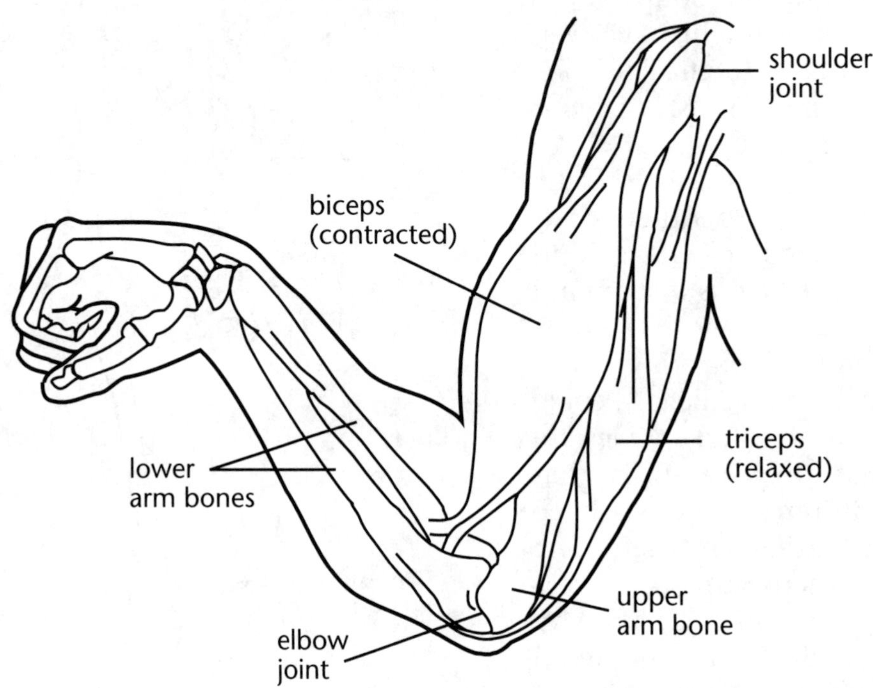

When you tighten your arm muscle, every little cell in that muscle contracts. Your ***skeletal muscles*** are attached to your bones by ***tendons***. When your muscle contracts, it pulls on the tendon, which pulls your arm bone up. Your skeletal muscles are ***voluntary***, which means that you can control their movement.

Two other kinds of muscles are mostly ***involuntary***—not controlled by your conscious mind. ***Smooth muscles*** are the kind in your stomach and intestines. They expand and contract in rhythm to help digest your food and keep it moving through your digestive tract. ***Cardiac muscles*** are especially strong and reliable. They are found only in your heart, which is the most important muscle in your body.

EXERCISE 6: BONES AND MUSCLES

Directions: Circle *T* if the statement is true and *F* if it is false.

T F 1. There are over 200 bones in your body.

T F 2. Bones support and protect your body.

T F 3. Few of your blood cells are made in your bone marrow.

T F 4. Cartilage is harder than bone.

T F 5. Ligaments attach one bone to another.

T F 6. Osteoporosis is caused partly by lack of calcium.

T F 7. Muscles move by contracting.

T F 8. Voluntary muscles are not under your control.

T F 9. There are four different types of muscle.

T F 10. Your heart is a muscle.

Directions: Circle the best answer.

11. Look at the diagram of a skeleton in this article. What are the bones in your backbone and neck called?
    (1) ribs
    (2) palm bones
    (3) collarbones
    (4) vertebrae
    (5) mandibles

Answers and explanations start on page 212.

RESPIRATION AND CIRCULATION:
In and Out; Round and Round

(A man lies unconscious on the sidewalk. Two paramedics arrive on the scene in an ambulance.)

"Is he breathing?"

"No."

"What about a pulse?"

"I can't find any pulse. I'm checking his heart. (Pause) No heartbeat."

"We'd better start artificial respiration and CPR immediately. This guy's in real trouble!"

Scenes like this, on TV and in real life, tell us just how important our breathing and blood systems are. We can live for days without food and carry on even with a broken bone, but if our breathing or blood circulation stops, we can live for only about four to six minutes.

Breathing

Your ***lungs*** are the main organs in your ***respiratory system*** (your breathing system). Look at this diagram to see how your lungs work.

THE RESPIRATORY SYSTEM

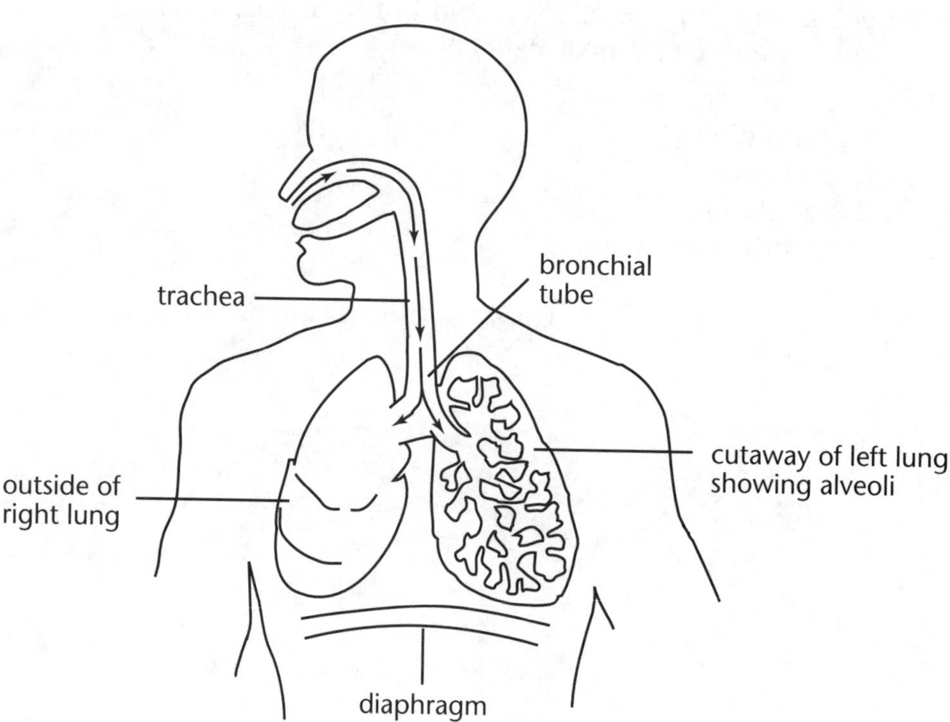

When you breathe in, your ***diaphragm***, a thin, flat muscle that lies under your lungs, pulls down. Your chest muscles pull up and out. This causes suction inside your chest, which makes your lungs expand and pull in air. The air enters through your nose or mouth. It comes down your ***trachea*** (your windpipe). Then it splits and goes down your two ***bronchial tubes*** into your lungs.

Inside your lungs are all kinds of little tubes running to groups of tiny air sacs called ***alveoli***. These sacs get filled with air. Surrounding these sacs are small blood vessels. Some of the oxygen in the air passes into these blood vessels. Carbon dioxide, which is a waste material in our bodies, moves from the blood vessels into the small air sacs.

Then your diaphragm and your chest muscles relax, putting pressure on your lungs. The air in the alveoli makes the return trip back through the little tubes, into your bronchial tubes, up your trachea, and back out your nose or mouth. Then you are ready to start all over again.

It sounds complicated, but you have been doing it twelve to twenty times a minute since the moment you were born, usually without thinking about it.

One activity that can really damage your respiratory system is regular smoking. Tars and other chemicals in smoke build up in the alveoli. If you smoke enough, these air sacs may get stiff. Then they can't pull air in or push it out easily anymore. We call this disease ***emphysema***. A person with emphysema cannot breathe deeply or exercise. Eventually, he cannot breathe at all.

The Circulatory System

The ***circulatory system*** is the body's transport system. It carries food, chemicals, oxygen, and waste materials from place to place in your body.

The center of your circulatory system is your heart. Your heart is an amazing muscle that contracts and relaxes 60 to 80 times every minute of every day of your life. It pumps the blood around and around, through miles of ***blood vessels*** throughout your body.

We have already seen how blood vessels get rid of carbon dioxide by carrying it to your lungs and how they pick up oxygen there to take back to your heart. Other blood vessels take oxygen and food out to all the parts of your body. Blood vessels going away from your heart are called ***arteries***, while blood vessels going toward your heart are called ***veins***. The veins take waste materials away from the cells.

Blood contains three different types of cells. Each kind of cell has a different purpose. The ***red blood cells*** carry oxygen to your body cells. The ***white blood cells*** fight disease by attacking harmful bacteria and viruses in your body. And whenever a blood vessel gets torn, small blood cells called ***platelets*** break along the edge of the wound and release a chemical that causes your blood to clot so that you don't lose too much blood.

You can do a lot to keep your heart and circulatory system healthy. Not smoking, staying reasonably thin, getting regular exercise, and learning to manage tension—all these things will help you avoid high blood pressure and heart attacks, two of the most common killers in America.

EXERCISE 7: HEART, BLOOD, AND LUNGS

Directions: To summarize this article, fill in the blanks in these paragraphs.

1. Your ______________ (a) are the main organs in your respiratory system. Air comes in your ______________ (b) or ______________ (c), goes down your ______________ (d), into your two ______________ ______________ (e), then into small tubes in your lungs that lead to tiny air sacs called ______________ (f). Tiny blood vessels collect ______________ (g) from the air in these sacs and get rid of ______________ ______________ (h).

   ______________ ______________ ______________ (i) in your blood carry oxygen to your body cells. ______________ ______________ (j), ______________ help your body fight disease. ______________ (k) carry a chemical that helps your blood clot.

Directions: Circle the best answer.

2. A person with AIDS has trouble fighting off ordinary illnesses. There is something wrong with the person's
   (1) red blood cells
   (2) plasma
   (3) platelets
   (4) heart muscle
   (5) white blood cells

Answers and explanations start on page 212.

NUTRITION:
You Are What You Eat!

"Be sure to eat all your spinach!" This is the introduction most of us had to nutrition, the study of the foods, or ***nutrients***, our bodies need. With that kind of introduction, no wonder nutrition is not always a popular subject.

Poor nutrition can be a real problem. It can cause severe depression, high blood pressure, premature births, and many other serious health problems. It can also weaken us so we are more likely to catch other illnesses.

Your body needs six types of nutrients: protein, carbohydrates, fats, vitamins, minerals, and water. The following chart shows why you need these nutrients and gives examples of some typical foods containing them.

Nutrients		
Nutrient	**What It Does**	**Some Good Food Sources**
protein	• provides building material for new cells	meat, fish, eggs, tofu, milk products, beans, soybeans, peanuts
carbohydrates (starches and sugars)	• provides energy	whole-grain bread, tortillas, rice, corn, pasta, desserts
fats	• provides concentrated energy • needed for body chemistry	meat, butter, whole milk, olives, avocado, vegetable oils
vitamins	• needed for enzymes and other body chemistry	fruits, vegetables, liver, whole grains, cod liver oil
minerals	• makes strong bones and teeth • iron needed for blood • needed for body chemistry	milk products, green leafy vegetables, seafood, liver, kelp
water	• needed by *all* parts of the body. Your body is about 70% water.	water, milk, fruit juices

Nutritionists (people who study nutrition) have set up a food guide pyramid that shows what people should eat to get all the nutrients they need. It is important to eat a variety of different foods. Listed below are the average adult's daily requirements. Children, teenagers, pregnant or nursing women, and athletes have slightly different needs.

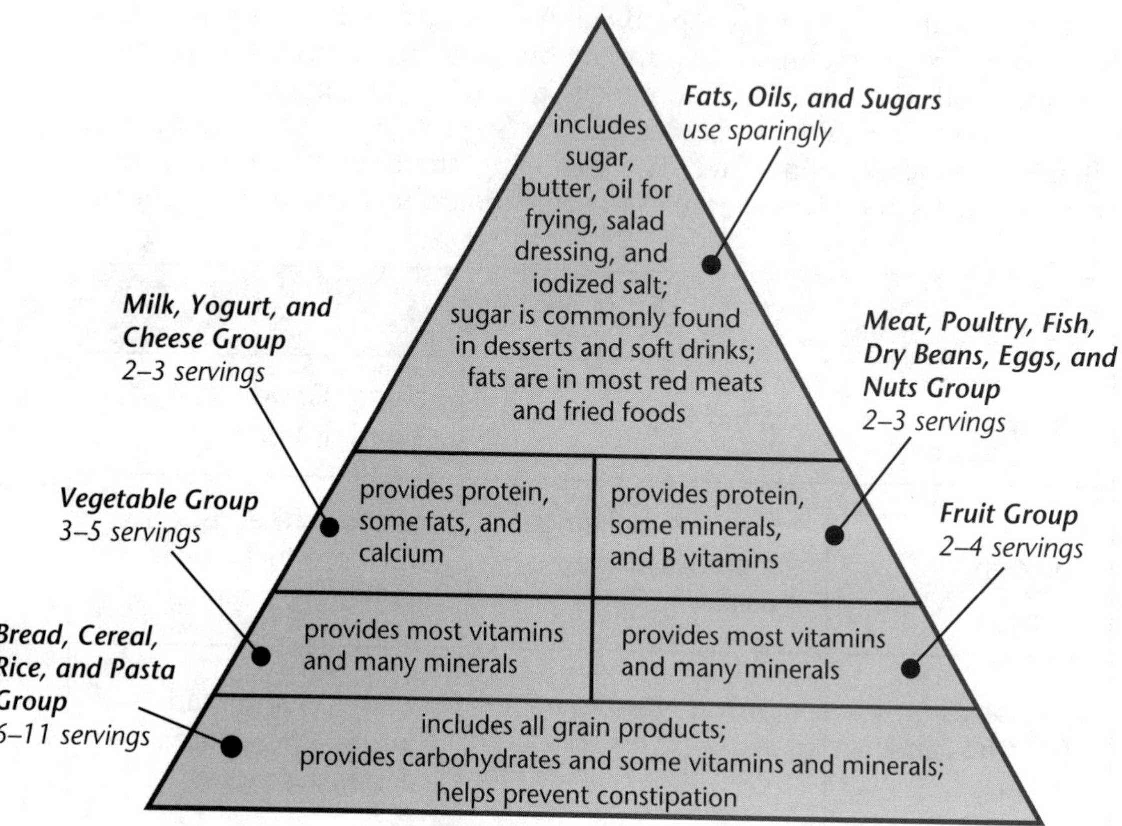

EXERCISE 8: NUTRITION

Directions: Many of us have trouble finding time to cook and eat balanced meals every day, although we know we'd probably feel better if we did. But you can balance your diet with ordinary foods.

Choose from this list to make up a sample menu for one day with the recommended number of servings from each of the six groups. As you write the name of the food on the menu, check off the group it belongs in on the checklist. An example has been done for you. Remember that you can sometimes use more than one serving of a particular food (like bread or milk).

Foods

eggs	hamburger patty	bean soup	apple
lettuce	whole wheat bread	milk shake	corn
tomatoes	chicken breast	baked potato	milk
orange	peanut butter	green beans	✓cereal
butter	cheddar cheese	brown rice	

Balanced Menu

1. Breakfast:
   cereal
   ______
   ______
   ______
   ______

2. Lunch:
   ______
   ______
   ______
   ______
   ______

3. Dinner:
   ______
   ______
   ______
   ______
   ______

Checklist

Bread, Cereal, Rice, and Pasta
4–6 servings
☑ ☐ ☐ ☐ ☐ ☐

Fruits
2–4 servings
☐ ☐ ☐ ☐

Vegetables
3–5 servings
☐ ☐ ☐ ☐ ☐

Meat, Poultry, Fish, Dry Beans, Eggs, and Nuts
2–3 servings
☐ ☐ ☐

Milk, Yogurt, and Cheese
2–3 servings
☐ ☐ ☐

Fats, Oils, and Sweets
(use sparingly)

Directions: Circle the best answer.

4. According to the chart on page 79, the main purpose of carbohydrates is to
   (1) build new cells
   (2) provide energy
   (3) make enzymes
   (4) provide liquid
   (5) keep bones healthy

5. Which of the following is an opinion, not a fact?
   (1) It is important to eat a variety of foods.
   (2) Some vitamins are destroyed by cooking.
   (3) Poor nutrition can cause health problems.
   (4) Everyone should take vitamin pills.
   (5) Cheese and meat provide protein.

Answers and explanations start on page 212.

THE DIGESTIVE TRACT:
The Food System

The food you eat goes through a long journey and many changes before it is ready to be used by your body. The process of breaking down food into simpler chemicals that the body can use is called ***digestion***. The place where this process happens is called the ***digestive tract***.

THE DIGESTIVE SYSTEM

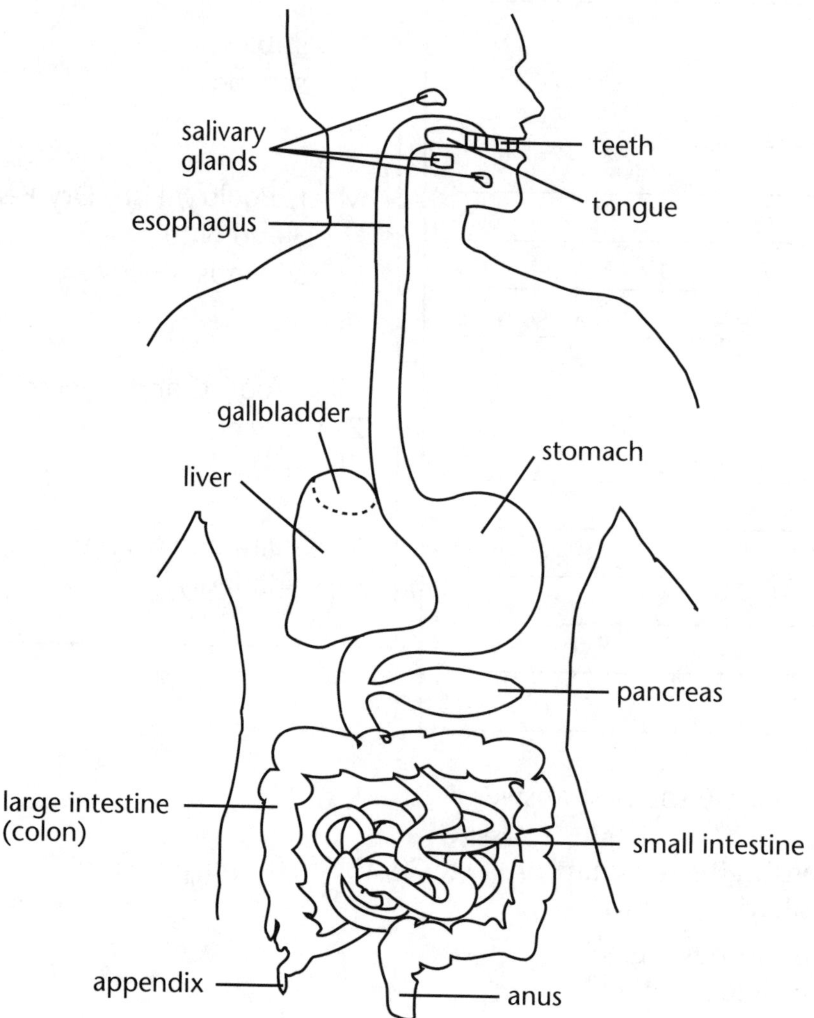

Your digestive tract begins with your mouth. Here food is taken in and ground down into small pieces by your teeth. It is mixed with ***saliva***, which is produced by salivary glands that lie next to your mouth. Saliva moistens the food so that it slides easily down the long tube of your ***esophagus*** into your stomach. The stomach is a muscular sac that turns and squeezes the food, mixing it with a little acid and some enzymes. ***Enzymes*** are special chemicals that help you break down foods. An enzyme in saliva breaks down starches, and two enzymes in your stomach break down proteins.

After the food is mixed and mashed into liquid in your stomach, it goes into your ***small intestine***. The small intestine is over twenty feet long. At its beginning, more enzymes that come from your liver, gallbladder, and pancreas are mixed with the food. These enzymes help you digest fats and complete the digestion of proteins. As the digested food moves along, the nutrients you need are ***absorbed*** (soaked up) through the walls of your small intestine, leaving only the waste materials and water. These pass into your large intestine, which is wider than your small intestine but only about seven feet long. There most of the water is absorbed back into your body, and what is left passes out of your body through a hole called the anus.

EXERCISE 9: DIGESTION

Directions: Match the words to their definitions.

______ 1. mouth

______ 2. saliva

______ 3. salivary glands

______ 4. esophagus

______ 5. stomach

______ 6. small intestine

______ 7. liver, pancreas, and gallbladder

______ 8. large intestine

______ 9. anus

a. organ that absorbs water from waste
b. tube that runs from mouth to stomach
c. organ that absorbs nutrients from food
d. glands that produce saliva
e. organs that dump enzymes into the small intestine
f. liquid that moistens food in the mouth
g. place where solid wastes leave the body
h. place where food enters the body
i. organ that mixes food with acid

Directions: Circle the best answer to each question below.

10. Your digestive tract is

(1) a system of many organs
(2) used only when you're an adult
(3) an organ that produces enzymes
(4) a very hot place
(5) used only on certain types of foods

11. The correct order in which food moves through your digestive system is

(1) stomach, esophagus, small intestine, large intestine
(2) large intestine, small intestine, stomach, esophagus
(3) stomach, large intestine, esophagus, small intestine
(4) esophagus, stomach, small intestine, large intestine
(5) esophagus, small intestine, stomach, large intestine

Answers and explanations start on page 212.

THE NERVOUS SYSTEM: Seeing, Thinking, and Acting

Your ***nervous system*** is the communication network of your body. Your ***brain*** is the center of the system. It is like a computer that runs your body, only your brain is much more amazing than any computer. It can teach itself without anyone to program it. It can handle problems that are much more complicated than those handled by any computer.

Your ***spinal cord*** is the main link between your brain and the rest of your body. Most of the nerves in your body connect into it. Only some nerves in your head connect directly to your brain. Your spinal cord runs down the middle of the vertebrae in your backbone. Your brain and your spinal cord together are called your ***central nervous system***.

Two kinds of nerves run throughout the rest of your body. ***Motor nerves*** carry messages *from* the brain and spinal cord *to* other parts of your body. These messages tell your body to do things, like move an arm or wink one eye. ***Sensory nerves*** carry messages *to* your brain and spinal cord *from* your body. These nerves tell your brain what is going on around you. They send messages of sights, sounds, tastes, smells, pain, heat, and pressure. There are many sensory nerves in your head, coming from your eyes, nose, mouth, and ears. There are sensory nerves all over your skin, like those in your fingertips, and even some inside your body.

EXERCISE 10: THE NERVOUS SYSTEM

Directions: Trace the path of these messages through your nervous system by filling in the blanks.

1. You are lying in bed on a cold winter night. The nerve endings in your ________ (a) feel the air getting colder. This message travels up a ________ (b) nerve to your ________ ________ (c) and then up to your ________ (d). Your ________ (e) decides to do something about the cold. It sends a message down a ________ (f) nerve, through your spinal cord, down your arm to your ________ (g), telling it to pull up the blankets. All this happens more quickly than you can realize it, because these messages, called ***nerve impulses***, travel at about one hundred feet per second.

Directions: Circle the best answer.

2. What would happen to a man if the sensory nerves leading from his foot were cut but the motor nerves were still all right?
   (1) He wouldn't be able to feel or move his foot.
   (2) He would still be able to feel and move his foot.
   (3) He would be able to feel and move his foot a little.
   (4) He would be able to feel, but not move, his foot.
   (5) He would be able to move, but not feel, his foot.

Answers and explanations start on page 212.

STRESS AND WELLNESS:
The Body-Brain Link

It's 2008. You feel sick, so you go to the doctor. She checks your fever, looks at your throat, and asks what you've been thinking about lately. When you leave, she gives you some medicine, but also a list of thought techniques that you are supposed to practice daily. She says that the way you think is causing some of your illness.

Sound like science fiction? Maybe so, but doctors and other scientists who study the mind, called ***psychologists***, are starting to believe it. You know that your brain is connected to every part of your body through your nervous system. Now there is scientific proof that how you think and feel can affect the health of your body.

Stress is caused whenever there is a problem or a change in your life. Of course, everybody has a certain amount of stress; nobody's life is perfect. In fact, stress is necessary. Without stress, we would never learn anything or grow or change. We would probably be bored to death. But too much stress can hurt you. It can cause ulcers, heart attacks, and migraine headaches. It can weaken your body's defenses so that you are more likely to catch diseases. It can even make you more likely to have an accident.

When you feel stress, your brain sends a message to your body to release a chemical called ***adrenaline***. Adrenaline speeds up your breathing and your heartbeat. It also makes your muscles tense up. Long ago, your ancestors needed this extra boost of energy to fight or run for their lives in stressful situations. Today you have a different kind of stress. Problems like unpaid bills or troubles with your kids are the kind of things you can't fight or run away from, so you don't use up all that adrenaline. It just stays bottled up inside you, and that's what can do some damage.

What can you do about stress? First, you can try to find ways of changing things so you aren't under so much stress. You can set up a plan to pay those bills or go to a counselor to try to work things out with your kids. But sometimes you can't change a stressful situation. Sometimes you don't even want to. A big change might be a good change, but it will still be stressful.

The body-brain link works in two ways. Your body can help your mind deal with stress. If you are under stress, you need to take especially good care of your body. It's important to get enough sleep and eat nutritious meals. Some people take a vitamin-mineral pill every day. Another thing that can help you handle stress is daily exercise. If you go jogging or do aerobic dancing or work out at the YMCA, you give your body a chance to burn up some of that adrenaline. Of course, a person who isn't used to much physical activity should start slowly. Anyone with a continuing physical problem should check with a doctor before starting any exercise program.

EXERCISE 11: STRESS

How do you know when you are under too much stress? One way you can tell is when you begin to feel run-down. Maybe you get a lot of headaches or stomachaches. Another clue can be found by looking at the sources of stress in your life.

The chart that follows outlines some events that cause stress. All of the events are stressful, but some of them are harder to handle than others. The events are listed in order, from the hardest to the easiest to cope with.

Directions: Look at this chart and answer the questions that follow.

Events That Often Cause Stress	
1. Death of husband or wife	**11.** Small children in home
2. Divorce	**12.** Tension at work
3. Trouble with the law	**13.** Change in working hours
4. Major personal injury	**14.** Changing to a new school
5. Getting married	**15.** Change in social life
6. Losing a job	**16.** Change in church
7. Retirement	**17.** Taking out a mortgage
8. Pregnancy	**18.** Change in sleeping habits
9. New family member	**19.** Change in eating habits
10. Loss of close friend	**20.** Vacation

1. Some of the events in the list are positive. Why do you think that they cause stress?

2. What do *all* the events in the list have in common?

3. List four ways you can reduce or handle some of the stresses in your life.

Directions: Circle the one best answer.

4. According to the chart, which of these life events is *least* likely to cause stress?
   (1) having a baby
   (2) getting a ticket for speeding
   (3) getting fired
   (4) going on a diet
   (5) breaking your leg

Answers and explanations start on page 213.

PREGNANCY PRECAUTIONS

People used to believe that an unborn baby (called a ***fetus***) was protected from most things that happened to its mother. Now doctors are discovering that the fetus is affected by many things.

If a pregnant woman catches German measles or certain other diseases, her baby might have a ***birth defect***; that is, the baby might be born with something wrong with his or her mind or body. Some medicines taken by the mother can also cause birth defects. Even some of the most common drugs, like aspirin and sleeping pills, can cause trouble for the fetus. Almost all illegal drugs can cause birth defects. If a pregnant woman drinks too much alcohol, even just beer or wine, it may hurt her baby and may cause it to be mentally handicapped. No one is sure how much alcohol is "too much." For some babies, it might be only a glass or two a day.

Regular smoking can cause a woman's baby to be born too small or too early. If a mother doesn't get enough of the right kind of foods, especially protein, her baby might also be born weak or underweight. Government programs, such as the WIC program, were set up to make sure pregnant women and small children get enough of the right foods.

Because doctors are discovering new things all the time, a pregnant woman should ask her doctor what is good for her to eat and drink. It is safest if she doesn't drink alcohol or smoke at all. If she gets sick, she should check with her doctor before taking any kind of medicine.

Some problems with fetuses happen for reasons that no one could know or prevent, but if a pregnant woman follows her doctor's advice and takes good care of herself, she is giving her baby the best possible chance to be born healthy.

EXERCISE 12: PREGNANCY PRECAUTIONS

Directions: List five things mentioned in the article that could hurt a fetus.

1. ______________________________

2. ______________________________

3. ______________________________

4. ______________________________

5. ______________________________

Answers start on page 213.

SCIENTIST IN THE SPOTLIGHT: Dr. Elizabeth Blackwell

"Unfeminine," "bold," "vulgar," "disgusting," and "positively indecent"—these were some of the things Elizabeth Blackwell was called. What horrible thing had this small, polite young woman done? She had gone to a school of medicine and graduated as the first woman doctor in the United States. What was worse, she intended to practice her profession! How unladylike!

Elizabeth Blackwell was born in England in 1821 into a family that was very unusual for its time. Her father gave his daughters as good an education as his sons. He encouraged them to learn Latin and Greek, read great literature, learn arithmetic, and study science. This was a very strange thing to do at a time when few women had any education at all. Women who were educated learned subjects like painting, music, and sewing. Because of her father, Elizabeth grew up to be much more independent than most women of her time.

When she was eleven, Elizabeth and her family moved to the United States. Her father started several businesses, but he was never able to do very well. When Elizabeth Blackwell was seventeen, her father died, leaving no money for his family. For several years Blackwell taught school to help support the family. She became more and more interested in antislavery work and in campaigns for women's rights.

In the early 1800s, women could not vote. They could not own property. In fact, they had no legal rights. They belonged to their fathers and brothers before marriage and their husbands afterward. If a woman did not marry, the only respectable thing for her to do was to live with her parents or one of her relatives, doing housework and helping with the children in return for her food and shelter. Women were not expected to work outside the home or to support themselves.

Blackwell was very shy with men, and she did not marry. She hated the idea of becoming dependent on one of her brothers. She thought and thought about how she could support herself and do something worth doing. Then one day she visited an old friend who was dying of cancer. The old friend said that one of the worst parts of her disease was that she had to be treated by a male doctor. She wished there were women doctors who could treat her. The idea of becoming a doctor grew stronger and stronger in Blackwell. She had found something worthwhile to do.

Most people she talked to were very discouraging. There were no women doctors; women could not become doctors. Finally she found one doctor who would let her study with him privately. This was a common way for people to study medicine in those days. After she worked with him for three years, she applied to twenty-nine different medical schools and was finally accepted by Geneva College, a small school in Geneva, New York.

Medical school was not easy for Elizabeth Blackwell. Many people were against her. Some of the lectures embarrassed her, especially the ones on male and female bodies. Even so, she graduated from Geneva College and received her license to practice as a doctor. Then she went to Paris and London to study and learn more about medicine.

When she returned to the U.S., she had more training than most doctors, but she had a very hard time starting out. No male doctors wanted to work with her. Few patients wanted a woman doctor. Finally, she opened her own office.

She became very upset by the horrible living conditions of many poor people in New York. Whole families lived in a single dirty room with no running water or heat. Over half the babies died in their first year. Since she didn't have many patients, Blackwell began to write articles and give lectures about these problems. She said that disease could be stopped if people lived in decent, clean places. Because of her lectures and articles, she slowly became better known and respected. More and more women came to be her patients. Her younger sister Emily also became a doctor, and together they opened their own hospital, the New York Infirmary for Women and Children.

By the end of her life, Blackwell was famous. She had done a lot to teach people healthier ways to live. She also taught doctors many ways to cut down on pain and danger of infection during medical treatment, especially during childbirth. She had written books and given hundreds of lectures on many topics, including medicine, slavery, women's rights, and even sex education. Her ideas were far ahead of her time.

In 1949, thirty years after her death, the American Medical Women's Association established the Elizabeth Blackwell Gold Medal. It is given each year to the woman who has done the most to advance the cause of women in medicine. It is given in honor of the first woman doctor in the United States, Dr. Elizabeth Blackwell.

EXERCISE 13: DR. ELIZABETH BLACKWELL

Directions: Below are listed some opinions that Elizabeth Blackwell held. Write whether you agree or disagree with each statement and why. There are no right or wrong answers to these questions, but be sure you back up your ideas with some reasons.

1. Female doctors are just as good as male doctors.
2. A person can do anything if he or she is willing to work hard.
3. You should not pay attention to the opinions of other people if you are doing what you believe is right.
4. It is more important to do something worthwhile than to be happy.

Answers start on page 213.

EXERCISE 14: CHAPTER 3 REVIEW

Directions: Read each passage carefully. Then circle the number of the best answer to each question.

Questions 1–3 are based on the following passage and diagram.

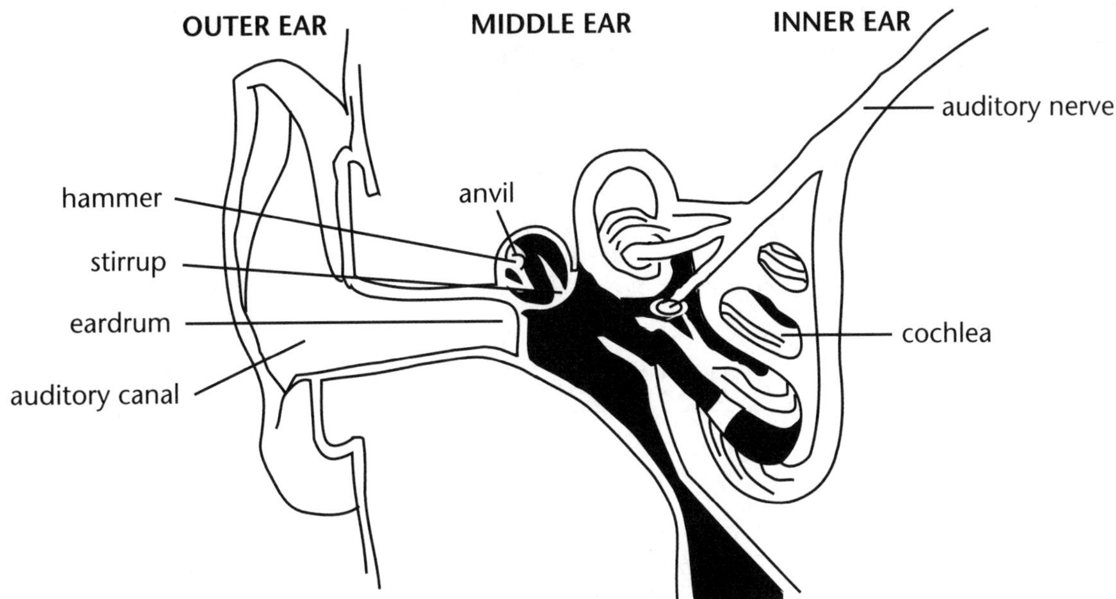

Look at this diagram of the ear. Sound enters the outer ear and travels down the auditory canal to the eardrum. The sound causes the eardrum to vibrate, just as a regular drum vibrates when you hit it. The vibration of the eardrum moves three little bones called the hammer, the anvil, and the stirrup. These three bones transfer the vibration to the inner ear, which contains the cochlea. The cochlea is a coiled tube filled with liquid. The vibrations in this liquid are changed to nerve impulses, or messages, that travel along the auditory nerve to the brain.

1. The cochlea is
   (1) a tube filled with air
   (2) three little bones
   (3) a nerve
   (4) a tube filled with liquid
   (5) a vibration

2. According to the diagram, the part of the ear that contains the hammer, anvil, and stirrup bones is called the
   (1) outer ear
   (2) auditory canal
   (3) middle ear
   (4) inner ear
   (5) auditory nerve

3. When a person gets an ear infection, the middle ear gets full of fluid. Which hypothesis best explains why someone with an ear infection can't hear as well as usual?

(1) The fluid prevents the eardrum from vibrating easily.
(2) The pain makes it hard to hear.
(3) The fluid makes the inner ear too cold for nerve impulses to travel.
(4) The fluid helps the sound travel better.
(5) The pain keeps the person from paying attention.

Questions 4–6 are based on the following chart.

Recommended Energy Intake for Average-Sized People

Category	Age (years)	Energy Needs (calories)
Children	1–3	(900–1,800)
	4–6	(1,300–2,300)
	7–10	(1,650–3,300)
Males	11–14	(2,000–3,700)
	15–18	(2,100–3,900)
	19–22	(2,500–3,300)
	23–50	(2,300–3,100)
	51–75	(2,000–2,800)
	76+	(1,650–2,450)
Females	11–14	(1,500–3,000)
	15–18	(1,200–3,000)
	19–22	(1,700–2,500)
	23–50	(1,600–2,400)
	51–75	(1,400–2,200)
	76+	(1,200–2,000)

4. According to the chart, about how many calories does a 45-year-old man need?

(1) 2,000–3,700
(2) 2,000–2,800
(3) 1,600–2,400
(4) 2,300–3,100
(5) 1,400–2,200

5. Which of these statements is true, according to the information in the chart?
   (1) The older you get, the more calories you need.
   (2) All men need more calories than all women.
   (3) Men need more calories than women of the same age.
   (4) Girls need more calories than boys.
   (5) Children need more calories than teenagers.

6. From the trend of the chart, how many calories would you predict that women over ninety years old would need?
   (1) the same as or fewer than women aged seventy-six
   (2) more than men aged ninety
   (3) more than women aged seventy-six
   (4) more than teenaged girls
   (5) fewer than 500 calories

Questions 7–9 are based on the following passage.

A sexually transmitted disease (STD) is a disease that is passed from one person to another primarily by sexual contact. Chlamydia, genital herpes, gonorrhea, and syphilis are some of the most common STDs being reported today. Chlamydia, gonorrhea, and syphilis can be cured by antibiotics if treated in the early stages. If left untreated, they can do very serious harm. Chlamydia and gonorrhea, for instance, can cause a severe infection that makes a woman unable to have children.

Because STDs can be so dangerous if not treated, a person who might have an STD should see a doctor. Signs of infection include burning, itching, or sores on the sexual organs. One way to avoid catching an STD is by using latex condoms.

Many people are embarrassed to talk to a doctor about STDs, but doctors are used to talking about private matters. Good doctors treat their patients with respect. Doctors are also required to keep medical information private. Being a little embarrassed is better than having to worry about STDs.

7. An STD is any disease that
   (1) creates an infection
   (2) leads to sterility
   (3) causes burning or itching
   (4) is mostly passed by sexual contact
   (5) can be cured by antibiotics

8. The main idea of the passage is that
   (1) people shouldn't get STDs
   (2) doctors are used to talking privately
   (3) people with an STD should see a doctor
   (4) many people are embarrassed by STDs
   (5) STDs cannot be cured

9. Many sexually transmitted diseases can be cured by
   (1) taking vitamins
   (2) waiting for them to go away
   (3) taking over-the-counter drugs
   (4) drinking plenty of fluids
   (5) taking antibiotics

Questions 10–12 are based on the following graph.

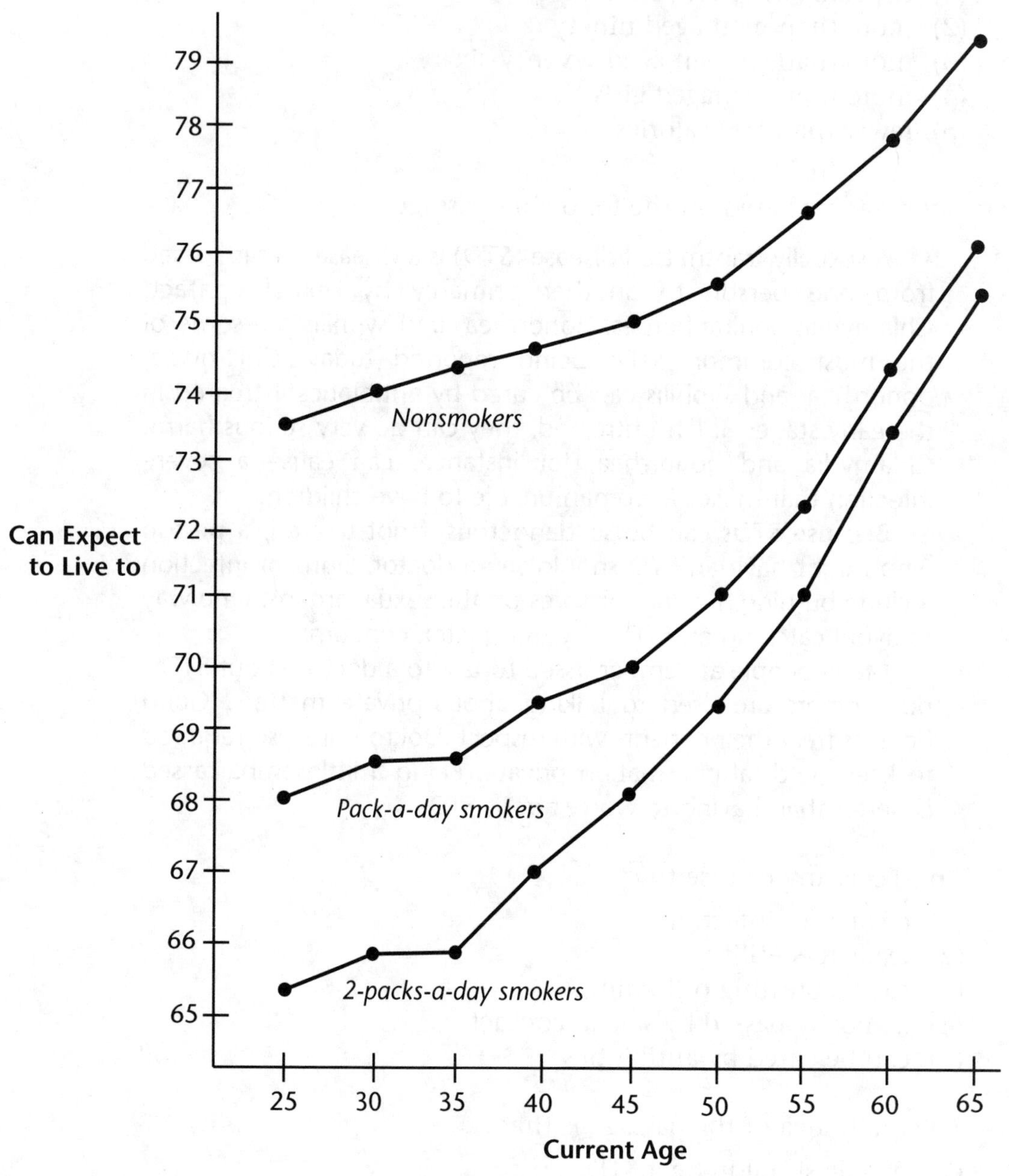

10. An average 25-year-old who smokes a pack a day can expect to live about how many more years?

(1) 25 years
(2) 32 years
(3) 37 years
(4) 43 years
(5) 68 years

11. An average 45-year-old nonsmoker can expect to live about how many years longer than an average 45-year-old who smokes two packs a day?

(1) 2 years
(2) 5 years
(3) 7 years
(4) 68 years
(5) 75 years

12. What is one reasonable hypothesis you could form from the information in this graph?

(1) It doesn't really matter whether you smoke one pack or two each day.
(2) On the average, the less you smoke, the longer you can expect to live.
(3) Women tend to smoke less than men do, which is why they live longer.
(4) Young people smoke less than older people do.
(5) Not smoking is the most important thing you can do for your health.

Answers and explanations start on page 213.

CHAPTER 4

READING SKILL
ANALYZING IDEAS

One main purpose of education is to make your life easier. This may be hard to believe at times, but it is true. The more you know about the world you live in, the better you can handle the decisions and problems that are always coming up. That's why some of the science topics in this book cover knowledge you can use in daily life. It's also true that the more you know about reading, the easier it will be to do many ordinary things, like filling out job applications, reading instructions, and understanding articles in the newspaper. The reading skills covered here will help you pass tests, but they will also be useful at many other times in your life.

SEQUENCE:
When Did It Happen?

In science it is important to know when something happened. The veterinarian (animal doctor) wants to know when your dog got sick—before or after eating the new food? The lab director wants to know when the explosion happened—before or after you mixed the chemicals together?

Many questions on tests ask when something happened. Words like *first, then, next, later, before,* and *after* can give you clues about the ***sequence*** (time order) of events. Groups of words, like *in the meantime* and *during that week,* can also give you clues about time.

Look at these examples:

> **Before** he did the experiment, he got all his equipment together.
> Children learn to crawl **first; following that** they learn to talk.
> The doctor will see you **next, after** Mrs. Jones.

Notice that the thing that happens first is not always written first in the sentence. You must use the "time" words to determine the sequence.

Sequence Tip

Here is a list of some words that show time order.

first	before	then	afterward
second	after	finally	in the meantime
third	next	later	today

▶ Now read these examples. Underline the time words in the sentences and answer the questions.

1. Louis Pasteur developed a rabies vaccine after he did his famous work on bacteria.
   Which did he work on first, the bacteria or the rabies vaccine?

   ____

In this sentence, *after* is the time word clue. It tells you that the bacteria work came first, and the vaccine came after that.

2. Before Pasteur's vaccine, a person bitten by a rabid animal was almost sure to die.
   Did more people die of rabies before or after Pasteur's vaccine was developed?

   ____

Before is the time clue here. It tells you that many people died before the vaccine was invented.

3. A boy to whom Pasteur gave the vaccine was saved; then Pasteur announced his new discovery to the world.
   Did Pasteur announce his discovery before or after he treated the boy?

   ____

The word *then* shows the announcement came after he treated the boy.

Now try your sequence skills on this paragraph. As you read this passage, underline the time words and answer the questions that follow.

> A monarch butterfly, like most insects, goes through four different stages during its life. First, it is only an egg laid on a milkweed plant. Then the egg hatches into a caterpillar, also called a ***larva***. After it grows to its full size, the caterpillar hangs from a twig and splits open its skin. The third stage, called a ***pupa***, emerges. Next, a hard skin forms to cover and protect the pupa. Inside this hard skin, the insect's body parts are slowly changing. Finally, the pupa splits. Out comes an adult butterfly with beautiful orange and black wings. About an hour later, the wings are dry. Then the butterfly flies away.

1. Which stage comes before the caterpillar? ______________________

2. What are the two names for the second stage?

   ______________________ and ______________________

3. What does the caterpillar do before it splits its skin?

   ____

4. What happens to the insect after it forms a pupa? ______________

5. What is the last stage? ______________________________

6. How long must the butterfly wait before it can fly away? __________

Now check your answers. You should have underlined these time words in the paragraph: *during, First, Then, After, third, Next, slowly, Finally, About an hour later, Then*. Here are the answers to the six questions above:

1. the egg
2. caterpillar and larva
3. It hangs from a twig.
4. A hard skin develops, and its body parts change.
5. the adult butterfly
6. about an hour

If you had trouble with this example, reread the section or talk with your teacher before trying the following exercise.

EXERCISE 1: SEQUENCING

Directions: Read the following passage. Then order the list of events from earliest to latest by numbering them from 1 to 5. If you want to, underline the time word clues as you read.

Sir Isaac Newton is known today as the Father of Modern Physics. He is best known for his theory of gravitation.

When Newton was a small boy, no one would have guessed that he was going to be a famous scientist. He was more interested in building mechanical things than in studying. He was considered a poor student. At fourteen, he had to leave school to help his mother manage the farm. But later, he went back to school. He graduated from Cambridge University in 1665.

The same year, Newton was sitting in his backyard drinking tea. He saw an apple fall from a tree. He said that this gave him the idea of ***gravity***, the idea that all objects in the universe pull toward each other. Objects that are close together pull harder than objects that are far apart. Objects that are heavier pull harder than light objects. Gravity is the force that pulls us down to the Earth. Gravity keeps the moon orbiting around the Earth, and it also keeps the Earth in its place, orbiting the sun.

Newton did most of his work on gravitation in 1665 and 1666, but he was not satisfied with it and put it away. Over twenty years later, after he was already a professor and a well-known scientist, a friend persuaded him to publish his theory. After it was published, he received many honors. He was knighted by the queen of England in 1705.

_____ **a.** Newton published his theory of gravitation.

_____ **b.** Newton was knighted by the queen of England.

_____ **c.** Newton dropped out of school.

_____ **d.** Newton started work on his theory of gravitation.

_____ **e.** Newton became a professor.

Answers start on page 213.

Using Your Head

Sometimes there are no word clues to tell you the sequence of events. But your own common sense can often tell you which event probably came first. Look at these two statements.

a. The moons of Jupiter were discovered.
b. The telescope was invented.

Logic tells you that **b** happened before **a** because a telescope is necessary to see the moons of Jupiter.

▶ Which of these two happened first?

a. Many children were paralyzed or killed by polio.
b. Jonas Salk discovered a vaccine against polio.

If you said **a** came before **b**, you used good logic. Before the polio vaccine was discovered, many children caught the disease.

▶ Now see if you can put these three statements in logical order.

a. Mr. Jones's flowers are growing well.
b. Mr. Jones sees that his flowers are wilting.
c. Mr. Jones waters his garden.

The logical order is **b, c, a.** First Mr. Jones notices that his flowers are wilting, then he waters them, and then they grow well.

EXERCISE 2: LOGICAL SEQUENCE

Directions: List these groups of events in logical order.

1. **a.** Steam locomotives pulled the first trains.
   b. The steam engine was invented.

   Logical order: ________, ________

2. **a.** The seeds are planted.
   b. The beans are picked.
   c. The plants come up out of the ground.

   Logical order: ________, ________, ________

3. **a.** Benjamin Franklin discovered that lightning is a form of electricity.
   b. People believed that lightning was a weapon of the gods.
   c. Franklin invented lightning rods to keep buildings safe.

   Logical order: ________, ________, ________

4. a. Stir the raisins into the mixture.
   b. Mix the oatmeal, flour, sugar, and butter in a bowl.
   c. Measure all the ingredients.
   d. Bake at 350°F for 10 minutes.

   Logical order: ________, ________, ________, ________

Answers and explanations start on page 213.

CAUSE AND EFFECT:
Why Did It Happen?

What causes heart attacks? Why does gold conduct electricity so well? What happens if a person is exposed to radioactive fallout? Science is concerned with many questions like these, questions about cause and effect.

A ***cause*** is whatever makes something happen. An ***effect*** is the thing that happens because of the cause. For example, if you do well on a test because you have studied hard, your studying is the cause, and your good score is the effect.

Many questions on tests will ask you about cause and effect. Sometimes there will be words like *because, since,* or *therefore* to give you a clue. Other times you must use your own logic to discover the cause and effect.

▶ Look at these two statements. Which one is the cause and which the effect?

a. John forgot to fill up his car.
b. The car ran out of gas.

Statement **a** is the cause; **b** is the effect. That is, *because John forgot to fill up his car, it ran out of gas.*

▶ For practice, write a possible effect for the given cause.

Cause: A person is exposed to a cancer-causing chemical.

Effect: ______________________________

There are many possible effects from any cause. For example, you could have said that *the person became afraid of getting cancer* or that *the person got cancer.*

▶ Now try writing a possible cause for the given effect.

Cause: ______________________________
Effect: Many drivers buy radar detectors.

There can also be more than one possible cause for an event. You could have said that *police started to use radar to catch speeders* or that *radar detectors were advertised in many magazines.*

▶ Now try these two:

Cause: Birth control methods were invented.
Effect: ______________________________

Cause: ______________________________
Effect: May Chen's garden grew its best crop of lettuce ever.

There are many possible answers for these causes and effects. Discuss your answers with a teacher or someone else you know.

Often a single cause will have more than one effect. For instance, say that Lester Hollis got up late one morning. Since he got up late, he missed the bus, forgot to pack his lunch, and had a headache all morning. Getting up late caused three separate effects.

A single effect can also have several causes. A great scientific discovery may be the result of one scientist's curiosity, another scientist's lucky accident, and a government program that brought the two of them together.

Cause and Effect Tip

As you read, look for cause-and-effect clue words like *because, since, therefore,* and *as a result of.*

EXERCISE 3: CAUSES AND EFFECTS

Directions: Read each paragraph. Identify the causes and effects by filling them in when called for.

> In nature, uranium is found mixed with many other minerals. Because of this, uranium ore must be refined and purified before it can be used in atomic power plants.

1. **Cause:** Uranium comes mixed with other minerals.

   Effect: ______________________________

The pure uranium is shipped to fuel fabrication plants. There it is put into fuel rods that fit into the cores of atomic power reactors. In the power plant, a chain reaction, which is a series of tiny atomic explosions, is kept under careful control. If the chain reaction goes very fast, the whole plant could blow up. If the reaction is slowed down too much, it won't make enough heat.

2. **Cause:** ______________________

   Effect: The power plant would blow up.

3. **Cause:** ______________________

   Effect: Not enough heat is formed.

The heat from the chain reaction is used to boil water. The steam that is formed is used to turn giant generators, which make electricity.

4. **Cause:** The chain reaction makes heat.

   Effect: ______________________

5. **Cause:** ______________________

   Effect: Electricity is made.

Because a nuclear explosion is so dangerous, atomic power plants have many safety devices to prevent the chain reaction from going too fast. Companies that run atomic power plants say that an explosion is almost impossible.

6. **Cause:** Nuclear explosions are very dangerous.

   Effect: ______________________

Answers start on page 213.

Science or Superstition?

A common mistake is to think a time order relationship is also a cause-effect relationship. They seem very similar. A cause happens before its effect. But be careful not to confuse these two relationships. Even if one event happens before another, the first event does not necessarily *cause* the second.

This kind of confusion is what causes superstitions, like these:

I saw a black cat just before I had a bad accident. The black cat must have caused my accident.

I wore my new green dress to the job interview, and I got the job. My green dress must be lucky.

My best cow died after I had an argument with that old woman. She must have put a hex on it.

▶ For practice, read these sentences. Circle those that probably show a true cause-effect relationship.

1. It was minus 25°F last night; now my car won't start.
2. It was minus 25°F last night; now I can't find my mittens.
3. John forgot his vitamins yesterday; now he has a cold.
4. John's sister had a cold last week; now John has a cold.
5. Helen walked under a ladder yesterday; today she slipped and fell on the ice.
6. Helen didn't wear her rubber boots; then she slipped and fell on the ice.

Did you circle numbers 1, 4, and 6? These are probably true cause-effect relationships. Numbers 2, 3, and 5 are simply in time order: cold weather can't make you lose your mittens; John had to catch his cold from someone else, not just from forgetting his vitamins one day; and Helen's slipping on the ice was really caused by her not wearing her boots, not by walking under a ladder.

EXERCISE 4: FINDING CAUSES AND EFFECTS

Directions: Read the passage and circle the best answer to each question.

Niels Bohr was a Danish scientist who originated the first practical theory about the structure of the atom. His father had been a professor, so when he was a child, many people had come to the house to discuss the latest scientific discoveries. When he was older, Bohr went to the University of Copenhagen and earned a doctoral degree in physics.

After he developed his theory of atomic structure, Bohr became very famous. When the Nazis invaded Denmark during World War II, they wanted Bohr to work for them in atomic research. Bohr refused, so they tried to arrest him. He escaped to Sweden and returned to his home only after the war was over.

1. One reason Bohr became interested in science was that
   (1) he was born in Denmark
   (2) he wanted to become famous
   (3) his father was a professor
   (4) he studied physics at a university
   (5) he hated the Germans

2. One effect of his scientific fame was that
   (1) the Nazis invaded Denmark
   (2) the Nazis wanted him to work for them
   (3) he refused to work for the Nazis
   (4) he hated the Nazis
   (5) he went home after the war

Answers and explanations start on page 213.

MAKING INFERENCES: Reading Between the Lines

Sometimes a writer doesn't directly tell you everything he means. Instead, he ***implies*** (hints at) some things by the way he writes. Here is an example:

> As the sun got higher, Juan wished he had brought a bigger canteen.

Consider all that is implied by this one sentence. Juan is hot and thirsty. He is in a place where water is not easy to get. Also, either he has run out of water or he is worried about running out. None of these things is said directly, but you can tell that they are true.

When a writer implies things without saying them right out, you have to ***infer*** (figure out) what he or she is trying to say. The skill of figuring out what a writer is implying is called ***making inferences***. Let's look at another example.

> The study showed that the medicine was perfectly safe. Of course, the study was done by the company that sells the medicine.

▶ What do you think this writer is implying? ______________________

____

He or she is implying that the company *might have rigged the results of the study* so that it could keep selling its medicine.

Try one more:

> The recent rise in oil prices has caused many people to change over to natural gas heat.

▶ What is this writer implying about the cost of natural gas?

____

He or she is implying that *natural gas costs less than oil*. Notice that the writer never says that it costs less; this idea is just implied.

EXERCISE 5: MAKING INFERENCES

Directions: Read the following statements. Then write your inferences on the lines provided. Notice that some statements imply more than one thing.

1. Use Saf-T mouthwash and dare to be close.

   What does the writer imply about people who don't use Saf-T?

   ____

2. Cancer of the mouth is increasing among young males, the group most likely to use smokeless tobacco.

   What does the writer imply about smokeless tobacco?

   ____

3. The new easy-care fabrics that followed the invention of polyester fiber have really changed the clothing industry.

   a. What does the writer imply that the new fabrics are made of?

   ____

   b. What does the writer imply about the fabrics before polyester?

   ____

4. The typical American still eats a diet high in fat and sugar, even though heart disease is the number one killer in America.

   a. What does the writer imply about fat and sugar?

   ____

   b. What does the writer imply that a person should do to avoid heart attacks?

   ____

5. Orange growers have been hard hit by the unusually cold weather in southern Florida.

   a. Where does the writer imply that many oranges are grown?

   ____

   b. What weather does the writer imply is needed to grow oranges?

   ____

Answers start on page 214.

SCIENCE TOPIC
EVERYDAY PHYSICS

The universe is made up of matter and energy. ***Matter*** is anything that takes up space. A brick, a person, water, the sun, and even air are all matter, because they all take up space. (If you don't understand how air takes up space, think about blowing up a balloon.)

Energy is anything that can do work. Common forms of energy are electricity, gravity, heat, and light. ***Physics*** is the branch of science that studies matter and energy and the relationship between them.

SIMPLE MACHINES: Doing Work with Less Effort

Uggle the cavewoman was in a real fix! During the night a tree had fallen across the front of her cave. Now she couldn't get out. She pushed and pulled at the tree, but it was too heavy for her. Then a large branch broke off in her hand. She wedged the tip of the branch under the tree trunk and pushed down hard. The tree rolled away from her door! Uggle ran right out to find some berries for breakfast. Uggle was too busy to know it, but she had just invented the first machine.

When you think of machines, you probably think of things like lawn mowers, electric drills, and bulldozers. These machines get power from gasoline and electricity. But some machines, like crowbars and wheelbarrows, use human muscle power. These are called ***simple machines***.

Work

A ***machine*** is anything that helps you do work. Scientists say that ***work*** is using force to move something. (***Force*** is the amount of push needed to move something.) To figure how much work is done, you multiply the force applied by the distance moved. For example, if you lift a 20-pound box 5 feet, you have just done 100 ***foot-pounds*** of work. You multiply the force needed to move the box (20 pounds) by the distance it is moved upward (5 feet).

Now figure the amount of work done in each of these cases. Your answers will be in foot-pounds.

1. A 10-pound fish is lifted 3 feet into a boat. ________________
   The force is 10 pounds; the distance is 3 feet. 10 × 3 = 30 foot-pounds of work done.

2. A 200-pound man climbs an 8-foot ladder. ________________
   The force is 200 pounds; the distance is 8 feet. 200 × 8 = 1,600 foot-pounds of work done.

Many times a person wants to do something that requires more force than his or her muscles can give. For example, Uggle wanted to move a tree that was too heavy for her. So she used a simple machine, a lever, to move the tree. Like most simple machines, the lever trades force for distance. If you use less force, you must move the end of the lever over a longer distance. Uggle didn't need as much force to move the tree, but she had to move the end of her stick a long way just to move the tree a little bit.

Inclined Planes

An ***inclined plane*** (a slope) is another type of simple machine. As with all simple machines, **the work you put into it must equal the work that is done**. Both the work you put in and the work done are figured by multiplying the force times the distance, as shown in this equation:

WORK PUT IN		WORK DONE
F × D	=	F × D

For example, imagine that you want to load your 300-pound motorcycle onto the tailgate of your pickup, which is two feet off the ground. You can't just lift 300 pounds, so you use a ramp, a type of inclined plane.

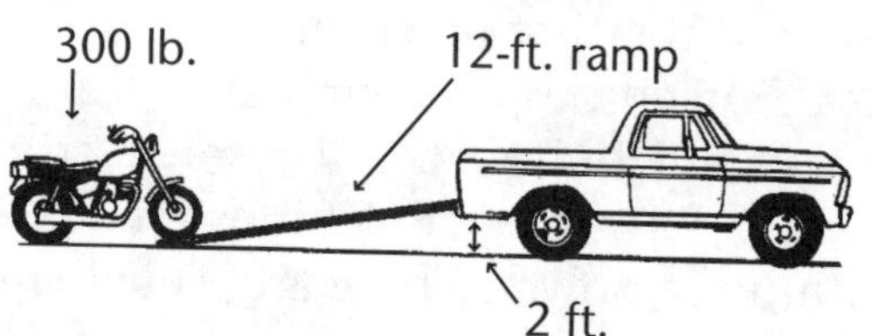

The force is 300 lb., the weight of the motorcycle. The distance is 2 ft., the vertical distance (distance straight upward) that the motorcycle must be moved. Therefore, the ***work that must be done*** is 300 lb. × 2 ft., which equals 600 foot-pounds.

Since the work put in must equal the work done, you know that the ***work put in*** will also equal 600 foot-pounds. You would use an equation like this:

WORK PUT IN		WORK DONE
force × 12 ft.	=	600 foot-pounds

Your ramp is 12 feet long, so 12 feet is the distance. Since you *multiplied*, to find the work done you *divide* the amount of force needed. You will only need to use a force of 600 ÷ 12, which is 50 pounds, to push the motorcycle up the ramp.

Now suppose that you had a motorcycle that weighed 450 pounds. How much force would you need to push it up the same ramp? The equation would look like this:

WORK PUT IN		WORK DONE
force × 12 ft.	=	450 lb. × 2 ft.

The work to be done is 450 lb. × 2 ft. = 900 foot-pounds. You get this equation:

WORK PUT IN		WORK DONE
force × 12 ft.	=	900 foot-pounds

Dividing 12 into 900, you discover that you will have to use 75 pounds of force.

EXERCISE 6: SIMPLE MACHINES

Directions: Fill in the blanks with the appropriate words.

1. Crowbars, wheelbarrows, and inclined planes are all types of __________ __________ (a). With each of these, the work you put in must equal the __________ __________ (b). Work is using __________ (c) to move something. Force is the __________ __________ __________ (d) needed to move something. When you figure how much work is done, your answers are in units of measurement called __________ (e).

Directions: A hill is also a type of inclined plane. Look at this diagram to answer questions 2 and 3.

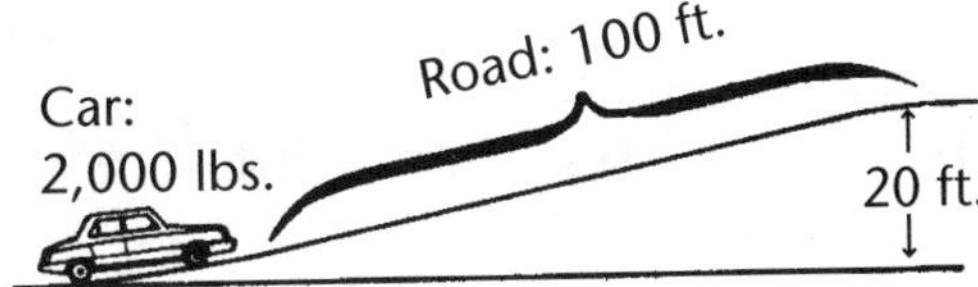

2. You drive your 2,000-pound car up a road to the top of a 20-foot hill. How much work is done?
   (1) 20 foot-pounds
   (2) 2,000 foot-pounds
   (3) 4,000 foot-pounds
   (4) 40,000 foot-pounds
   (5) 200,000 foot-pounds

3. If the road up the hill is 100 feet long, how much force will your engine have to use?
   (1) 100 pounds
   (2) 400 pounds
   (3) 1,000 pounds
   (4) 2,000 pounds
   (5) 40,000 pounds

Answers and explanations start on page 214.

WHAT IS A COMPUTER?

Input and Output

Science fiction movies and newspaper articles sometimes make us think that computers are mysterious, powerful things. The truth is that computers are only machines.

Because a computer is only a machine, it can do only what a person tells it to do. No computer can do as much as the "computer" you have in your head, your brain. But computers can do arithmetic and other things much faster than people can, and they can store a great deal of information and recall it perfectly. Computers have thousands of uses in our society.

You have probably used a computer without even knowing it. Computers control the hookups in the phone system. They do all the accounting for banks and many businesses. Many schools use computers for teaching. Writers and secretaries use word processors, computers that work like typewriters. Even the games in video arcades are run by small computers.

Parts of a Computer

When you add 13 and 41, you need to take in the problem with your eyes, do the arithmetic in your head, and then write out the answer with your hands. A computer works the same way: it must have parts for input, processing, and output.

Input is how information is given to a computer. Many computers have a keyboard, like a typewriter keyboard, for inputting information. Computers also get information from disks and tapes. Some computers read paper cards or tapes with specially coded holes punched in them. Computers in grocery stores use a light device to read a coded group of lines on each can or box of food. Computers that are hooked up to ***modems*** can get information over telephone lines, using a code of very fast beeps. These are only some of the many different ways that computers input information.

Output, as you may have guessed, is how the computer gives out information. It would do no good to have a computer figure something out if it couldn't tell you the answer. Many computers have a screen that shows the output in words or graphics (pictures). Computers are often connected to ***printers***, which type out information just like a typewriter, only much faster. Computers can also output information onto disks, tapes, and cards and over telephone lines.

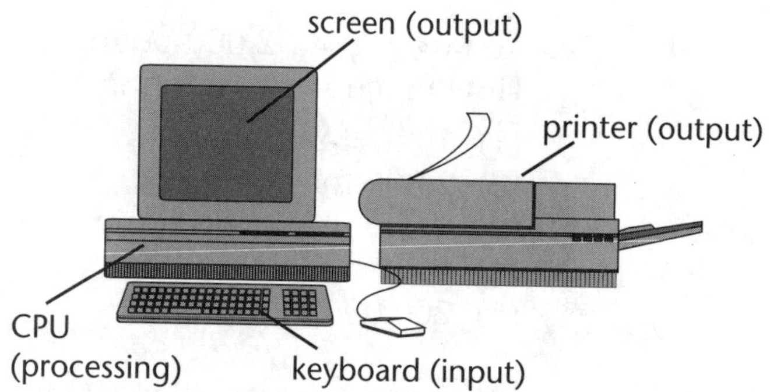

Processing Information

The main work of the computer is done in the ***central processing unit*** (CPU). The CPU is like the computer's brain. It is the part of the computer that makes decisions, does the figuring, and controls the input and output parts. Attached to the CPU are the arithmetic unit, which does the mathematical calculations, and the computer ***memory***. The memory holds the ***program*** (set of instructions) and information needed to do a particular task. When the task is done and the computer is shut off, the memory is wiped clean. If you want to hold on to some of the information in the memory, you must store it by outputting it onto cards, tapes, or disks.

Many people now own small personal computers, which cost between $100 and $2,500. These computers are not very difficult to use. Personal computers can help you keep track of your budget, write letters, or run a small business. They can help your kids do their homework and learn new things. The whole family can enjoy the many games available for personal computers. Computers are tools that can make your life easier and fuller.

EXERCISE 7: COMPUTERS

Directions: List the information required.

1. List four ways that computers are used in our society.

2. List five input devices for computers.

3. List five output devices for computers.

4. List some ways that you would like to use a computer.

Directions: Circle the number of the best answer.

5. A computer needs parts for three main jobs. What are these jobs?
   (1) input, memory, and processing
   (2) arithmetic, memory, and output
   (3) input, processing, and output
   (4) processing, memory, and output
   (5) input, arithmetic, and output

6. Which of these would probably *not* be something computers can do better than people?
   (1) correct multiple-choice tests
   (2) write music
   (3) count pills
   (4) record stock market prices
   (5) figure interest payments

Answers and explanations start on page 214.

ATOMS AND MOLECULES:
Building Blocks of Matter

All matter is made up of billions of tiny particles called ***atoms***. You often hear about atoms in the news, but no one has ever seen one. They are too small to be seen, even with the most powerful microscope. Even so, scientists have learned a lot about atoms by doing experiments.

Each atom is like a tiny sun surrounded by planets. In the center of the atom is the ***nucleus***. The nucleus is made up of ***protons***, which carry a positive electrical charge, and ***neutrons***, which are electrically neutral. ***Electrons*** orbit around the nucleus. They carry a negative electrical charge and move in levels called ***shells***. The drawing of an aluminum atom below shows these parts of an atom.

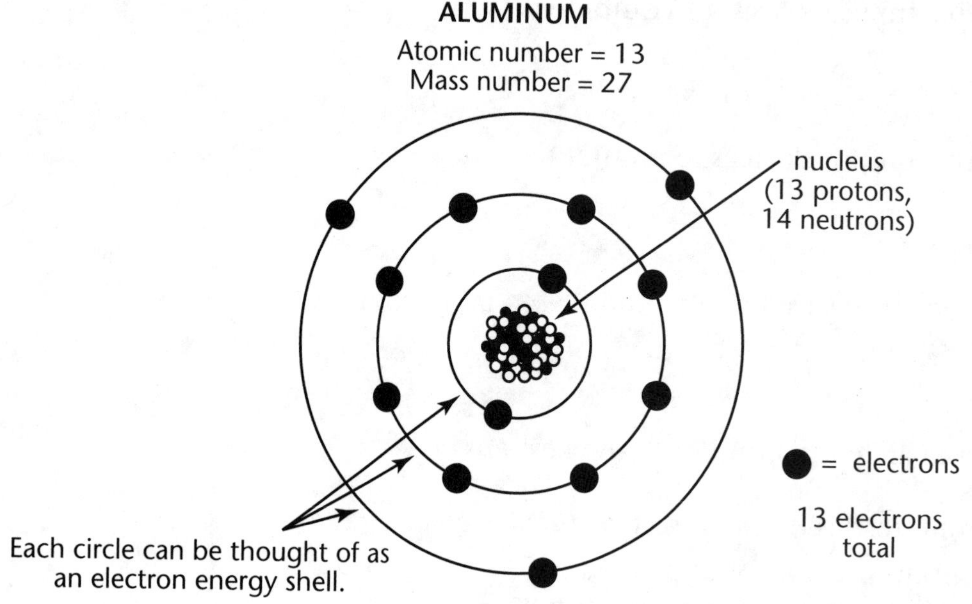

Scientists have found only 108 different kinds of atoms. A material containing only one kind of atom is called an ***element***. Most things are made of more than one kind of atom. When two or more atoms combine, they form a group called a ***molecule***. For example, a molecule of water is made up of two hydrogen atoms and one oxygen atom. There are millions of different ways that the 108 elements can combine, so there are millions of different substances in the universe.

Atomic Energy

The most powerful kind of energy in the universe is the energy that holds the nucleus of every atom together. This energy is called ***atomic energy***. Another name for it is ***nuclear energy***. When the nucleus of an atom is blown apart, an enormous amount of energy is released.

Some elements with many protons in the nucleus, like radium and uranium, lose particles from the nucleus all the time, not just when there is an atomic explosion. We call these elements ***radioactive***. Other elements may become radioactive if they have lots of extra neutrons. Radioactive substances are dangerous to us because the extra neutrons and protons they give off can enter our bodies and cause cancer and other illnesses.

EXERCISE 8: ATOMS AND MOLECULES

Directions: Match the words with their definitions.

______ **1.** atoms

______ **2.** electron

______ **3.** element

______ **4.** molecule

______ **5.** neutron

______ **6.** nucleus

______ **7.** proton

______ **8.** radioactive

______ **9.** shell

a. the center of an atom
b. positively charged particle in the nucleus
c. tiny things that all matter is made up of
d. material made up of just one kind of atom
e. a level in which electrons orbit
f. giving off particles from the nucleus
g. a group of combined atoms
h. negatively charged particle orbiting nucleus
i. neutral particle in the nucleus of an atom

Directions: Circle the number of the best answer.

10. According to this article, which of the following is true?
    (1) All molecules contain just two atoms.
    (2) There are 108 kinds of molecules in the universe.
    (3) There are three kinds of atoms.
    (4) There are 108 known elements.
    (5) There are 108 atoms in the universe.

11. Which type of worker might need special clothing to protect against radiation?
    (1) a truck driver
    (2) a nuclear power plant worker
    (3) a person who fixes home radiators
    (4) a police officer
    (5) an automobile mechanic

Answers and explanations start on page 214.

ELECTRICITY:
A Charged Subject

Imagine a world with no telephones, no refrigerators, no TVs, and no washing machines. Just over a hundred years ago, this was the world that everyone lived in. Then, in 1884, Thomas Edison built the first electric power station in New York City. Now power companies supply electricity to almost every part of the country.

Electricity is the movement of electrons. The atoms of some substances do not hold on to their electrons very tightly. Friction, magnetism, heat, or an outside source can start the electrons flowing from one atom to another. This flow is called an electric ***current***.

Substances that electricity flows through easily are called ***conductors***. Gold, copper, steel, and silver are examples of good conductors. Materials that electricity does not flow through well are called ***insulators***. Rubber, glass, plastic, and most fabrics are insulators. The wires that carry electricity in your home are made of copper or aluminum. They are surrounded by insulation made of plastic, rubber, or fabric.

TYPICAL HOUSEHOLD CIRCUIT

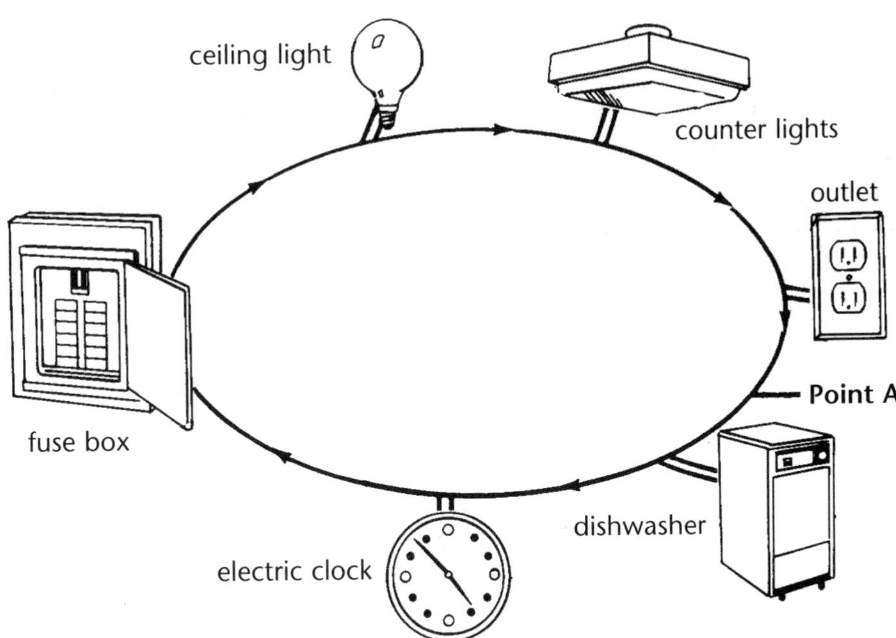

Electricity always flows in a ***circuit***. A circuit must be a complete circle. If there is not a complete circle, then electricity will not flow. For example, there is electric wiring to each side of the wall sockets in your house. When you plug in a toaster, the metal prongs of the plug complete the circuit. Electricity flows through the toaster. A light switch works the same way. When you turn it on, you complete the circuit and allow electricity to flow through the light.

A ***short circuit*** happens when the insulation on a wire wears through or when there is a loose connection or break somewhere. The wire touches some other conductor, and the electricity flows along a path different from the one it was supposed to take. An electric current in the wrong place can cause something to get very hot and may even start a fire. An electric current flowing through you can kill you or burn you badly.

Every circuit in a house has a ***fuse***. A fuse is a small strip of metal designed to burn out if too much electricity flows through it. If you have a short circuit, or you try to use too many appliances on one circuit, the fuse will blow, and the circuit will be broken. No more electricity will flow in that circuit until you find the problem and replace the fuse. More modern electrical systems have ***circuit breakers*** instead of fuses. A circuit breaker is a switch that turns off whenever too much electricity goes through it.

Electricity is useful, but it can also be dangerous. Electrical cords should be checked regularly for breaks or worn spots. Worn cords or bad plugs on appliances should be replaced. A blown fuse must never be replaced with a penny or another piece of metal. The next time, instead of a blown fuse, there could be a fire. No electrical appliance, even a radio, should be used near water. If it touches the water at the same time you do, you could get a deadly shock, because water is a very good conductor. Children must not be allowed to play with appliances or electric plugs. If there is a young child in the house, all unused outlets should be covered with plastic outlet blanks, available at many hardware and department stores.

EXERCISE 9: ELECTRICITY

Directions: Look at the sample circuit diagram on page 115. Beginning at the fuse box and following the arrows, number these in order according to the electrical flow. Then, in the spaces below, write down the order in which the electricity flows from object to object. Use the items from the list at right.

1. ______________________
2. ______________________
3. ______________________
4. ______________________
5. ______________________

outlet
counter lights
ceiling light
dishwasher
electric clock

Directions: Circle the number of the best answer.

6. In the diagram on page 115, what would happen if there was a break in the wire at Point A?
   (1) The ceiling light, counter lights, and outlet would still work, but the dishwasher and clock wouldn't.
   (2) The lights would still work because they draw so little electricity.
   (3) The dishwasher and the electric clock would work, but nothing else would.
   (4) Everything would still work.
   (5) Nothing would work.

7. What causes a fuse to blow?
   (1) very hot weather
   (2) electricity flowing the wrong way
   (3) too much electricity flowing
   (4) a penny
   (5) a fire

Answers and explanations start on page 214.

NUCLEAR POWER: Friend or Foe?

Like every new discovery, nuclear power has advantages and disadvantages. Here are two selections discussing some of the pros and cons of nuclear power.

Speaker A

America needs nuclear power. Fossil fuels such as coal, natural gas, and oil are becoming more expensive and harder to find. Air pollution laws have also made fossil fuels expensive to burn, due to the multimillion-dollar antipollution devices now required. In addition, depending on fossil fuels means depending on foreign countries for much of our energy needs. This limits our political options and ruins our balance of trade.

Radical environmental groups say that nuclear energy is too dangerous to use. They are ignoring the excellent safety record of nuclear power in the United States. American nuclear power plants are now built with so many safeguards that it is virtually impossible for a serious accident to occur.

In the long run, nuclear power will save the consumer money. The small amount of fuel needed to run a nuclear power plant is much less expensive than the barrels of oil or tons of coal needed to fuel regular power plants. The environment will benefit, too, since nuclear power plants release no acid smoke or filthy discharge.

Speaker B

Nuclear power is just not worth the risks involved. These risks are in three main areas.

First, there is the direct risk of accident. Every year, accidents happen at nuclear power plants, and "small" amounts of radiation leak out. The accident at Chernobyl showed how damaging a major accident can be. Chances are that sooner or later there will be an accident in the United States that cannot be stopped.

Second, there is the constant risk of pollution. Nuclear power plants release large amounts of heated water from their cooling devices. This water increases the growth of algae, killing off some types of fish. This water also carries slight amounts of radiation. The authorities assure us that these amounts are too small to be dangerous, but how can they be sure? The solid nuclear waste produced by nuclear power plants is especially polluting. If just small amounts of it got into our water system, many people would die. No one has yet solved the problem of what to do with these wastes.

Third, there is the danger of terrorist attacks and sabotage. When uranium is being shipped all over the country for power plants, it would be fairly easy for a small group of terrorists to steal enough for a bomb. Nuclear power plants can't have tight enough security to stop a terrorist from getting in and maybe causing a major "accident."

EXERCISE 10: NUCLEAR POWER

Directions: Read the following statements. Put an *A* in front of the ones that you think Speaker A would agree with. Put a *B* in front of the statements that Speaker B would agree with.

_____ 1. Security checks at nuclear power plants should be tougher.

_____ 2. People worry too much about radiation leaks.

_____ 3. Scientists don't know enough about the effects of small doses of radiation.

_____ 4. Some people exaggerate the dangers of pollution.

_____ 5. The United States should not be dependent on foreign countries.

Directions: Circle the number of the best answer.

6. Which of these is a fact from selection B?
   (1) Other nations are going full speed ahead to develop nuclear power.
   (2) It would be fairly easy for a small group of terrorists to steal enough uranium for a bomb.
   (3) America needs nuclear power.
   (4) The United States would be better off developing solar and wind power and forgetting about nuclear power.
   (5) Every year accidents happen at nuclear power plants.

7. Which of these is most likely to be Speaker A?
   (1) a doctor studying the effects of radiation
   (2) a public relations person for a utility company
   (3) a member of an environmental protection group
   (4) a scientist doing research on solar energy
   (5) a engineer working for an oil company

Answers and explanations start on page 214.

LIGHT AND SOUND: If You Like It Bright and Loud . . .

Light

Light is the energy that allows us to see. Scientists say that light travels in waves, but they aren't really sure what this means. They do know it travels very fast, about 186,000 miles per second. That means light can travel to the moon and back in less than three seconds. Nothing else in the universe is that fast.

The sun is our main source of light. Only a little of the sun's light reaches Earth. The white light we get from the sun is really a mixture of all different colors of light. Light that goes through a specially shaped piece of glass called a ***prism*** will split into all its different colors. The same thing happens when drops of water in the air split sunlight to make a rainbow.

When light strikes an object, three different things can happen. Light either goes through the object, or it is absorbed or reflected. If the light goes easily through it, we say the object is ***transparent***. You can see through transparent objects. Glass, water, and air are mostly transparent. Light rays bend a little when they go through a transparent object. This is how eyeglasses work. The lenses bend the light rays to focus them correctly for your eyes.

Light that doesn't pass through an object is either ***reflected*** (bounced back) or ***absorbed***. Most things reflect some colors of light while absorbing others. The reflected colors are what we see. For example, a blue sofa reflects blue light but absorbs all the other colors. The darker something is, the more light it is absorbing. If something absorbs all light, it looks black.

Sound

Sound is caused by the vibration of molecules. This is how it happens: Someone plucks a guitar string, making it ***vibrate*** (move quickly back and forth). The vibrating string hits the molecules of air around it, making them vibrate. These molecules hit other molecules, until eventually the vibration comes to your ear. The vibrating air moves against your eardrum, making it vibrate too. A nerve carries a message about the vibration from your eardrum to your brain, and you say, "Wow! Isn't that great music?"

Sound also moves as a wave, but it moves much more slowly than light. Sound only travels about a fifth of a mile per second in ordinary air. If there is a thunderstorm a distance away from you, you will see the lightning before you hear the thunder because the light travels faster than the sound. The farther apart the light and sound seem, the farther away the storm is. Sound waves are of different lengths, too. Shorter sound waves make higher tones, while longer waves make lower tones. Mixed-up combinations of waves just sound like noise.

Unlike light, sound can travel best through solid objects. This is because the molecules are closer together in solid things. Try this sometime: put your ear against a water pipe. Have someone tap lightly on the other end of the pipe. You'll be amazed at how loud the tapping sounds.

EXERCISE 11: LIGHT AND SOUND

Directions: Circle *T* if the sentence is true; *F* if it is false.

T F **1.** Light and sound both travel as waves.

T F **2.** Sound travels faster than light.

T F **3.** White light has no colors in it.

T F **4.** A lens is used to bend light.

T F **5.** A red dress absorbs red light.

T F **6.** You hear sound when your eardrum vibrates.

T F **7.** Sound waves of different lengths make different tones.

T F **8.** Sound travels best through air.

Directions: Choose the best endings for these sentences.

9. According to the article, scientists do not know
(1) what a light wave is
(2) the speed of light
(3) how to break light into colors
(4) what causes sound
(5) how we hear sounds

10. Transparent objects
(1) absorb all sound
(2) let sound pass easily through them
(3) let light pass easily through them
(4) are always made of glass
(5) reflect all light

Answers and explanations start on page 214.

SCIENTISTS IN THE SPOTLIGHT:
Marie and Pierre Curie

On November 7, 1867, Manya Sklodowska was born in Warsaw, Poland. Looking at the tiny infant, no one would have guessed that someday she would become a famous scientist, the first person ever to receive two Nobel prizes. Women did not become scientists in those days.

Manya learned to read by herself at the age of four. Later, she did very well all the way through high school. She was fascinated by science, especially physics and chemistry. Unfortunately, the University of Warsaw did not admit women. It seemed that Manya would not be able to continue her education.

For a while, she and her older sister, Bronya, attended classes in private homes. A famous scientist, scholar, or artist would give a lecture. At that time, Russia ruled part of Poland. All education was under the control of the Russian government. The lecture meetings were illegal, and they were eventually stopped.

Next Manya got a job as a governess (a private teacher) and started saving her money. She had a dream. She wanted to go to France, to a famous university called the Sorbonne. There, women were allowed to study science.

After six years, at the age of twenty-four, Manya made her dream come true. She took her money, went to Paris, and enrolled at the Sorbonne. She also changed her name to Marie, the French version of her given name Manya.

Marie did well at the university and soon was studying for her master's degree. Then she met Pierre Curie, who worked at the School of Physics and Chemistry. Pierre was already gaining a reputation as a brilliant scientist, while Marie was still an unknown student. Marie and Pierre were attracted to one another right away, but Marie did not want to get married. She thought it would interfere with her work in science. Finally she agreed, and the two were married in 1895.

Pierre Curie was an unusual man, and he realized that he had married an unusual woman. He never expected Marie to cook and keep house as almost all women did in those days. He encouraged her to continue her scientific work. In turn, Marie helped him in his research. They made a very good team.

In 1896, a scientist named Henri Becquerel discoverd that uranium gave out strange rays. For her doctorate degree, Marie decided to investigate these "Becquerel" rays. She got lots of ore with uranium in it, called ***pitchblende***, and started measuring the strange energy rays, which she named ***radioactivity***. She made a surprising discovery. The pitchblende ore had much more radioactivity than could be caused by the uranium alone.

In 1898, Marie wrote an article suggesting that there was a new, undiscovered element in the ore. Now she had to find it. Pierre realized how important this discovery could be, and he gave up his own research to work with his wife. That year, the Curies hypothesized that there were two new elements in pitchblende, which they named ***polonium*** and ***radium***.

For the next four years, the Curies worked to prove their hypothesis. They had very little money, and most of their money went for equipment and materials for their experiments. They had to get a pure sample of radium so that other scientists could examine it. The work was very hard. First Marie boiled down many tons of pitchblende. What was left had to be treated chemically and separated again and again. This was Pierre's work. Radium is a very rare element, and there was only a tiny trace of it in each pile of pitchblende. Finally, on March 28, 1902, the Curies had about a teaspoonful of pure radium. They had proved their discovery to the world.

In 1903, the Curies were awarded the Nobel Prize in physics for their discovery of radium. In 1906, Pierre Curie was killed in an accident. Marie took his job at the Sorbonne. She was the first woman professor there. Then, in 1911, she was awarded the Nobel Prize in chemistry, becoming the first person ever to win two Nobel Prizes.

Through all of this time, her health was not good. She and Pierre had been exposed to enormous amounts of radiation while working in their lab, long before anyone knew how dangerous it was. In 1934, Marie Curie died of leukemia, a blood cancer caused by her years of radiation poisoning. Scientists from around the world honored her at her death. The discoveries she and Pierre made were the beginnings of modern nuclear physics.

EXERCISE 12: MARIE AND PIERRE CURIE

Directions: Put these steps in the discovery of radium in the correct order by numbering them from 1 to 7.

______ **a.** The Curies win the Nobel Prize in physics.

______ **b.** Pierre joins Marie in looking for the new element.

______ **c.** Becquerel discovers uranium ore gives off strange rays.

______ **d.** The Curies come up with about a teaspoonful of pure radium.

______ **e.** The Curies hypothesize that there are two new elements in pitchblende ore.

______ **f.** Marie discovers that the pitchblende ore shows more radioactivity than she had expected.

______ **g.** The Curies boil down, separate, and analyze tons of ore.

Answers start on page 214.

EXERCISE 13: CHAPTER 4 REVIEW

Directions: Read each passage and study each diagram carefully. Then circle the number of the one best answer to each question.

As you know, a lever is one type of simple machine. A basic lever is just a straight object, like a board, balanced on top of a pivot point. Each side of the board can be thought of as an "arm." The pivot point is called the fulcrum. A seesaw is a good example of this type of lever.

To check whether or not a lever is balanced, we can use the following equation:

LEFT ARM		RIGHT ARM
Force × Distance	=	Force × Distance

When this equation is used with levers, the *force* is equal to the weight on each arm. We measure the *distance* from each weight to the fulcrum. Look at this example:

In this diagram, the force exerted on the left arm is 50 pounds, and there are 8 feet between the weight and the fulcrum. The force on the right arm is 100 pounds, with 4 feet from the weight to the fulcrum. If you plug these numbers into the equation, it looks like this:

LEFT ARM		RIGHT ARM
50 lb. × 8 ft.	=	100 lb. × 4 ft.

OR

$$400 = 400$$

Since both sides of the lever are the same, we know that this lever would balance.

Question 1 is based on the following diagrams.

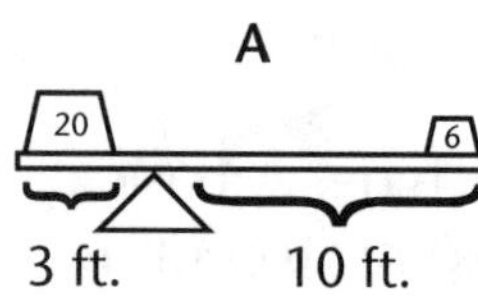

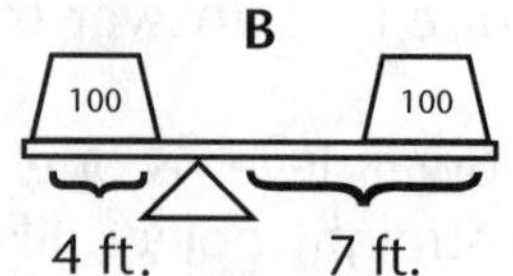

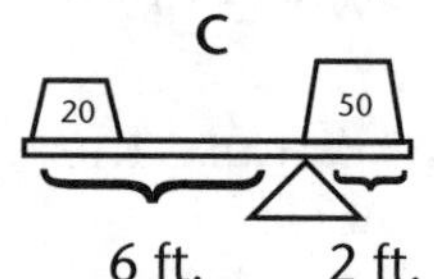

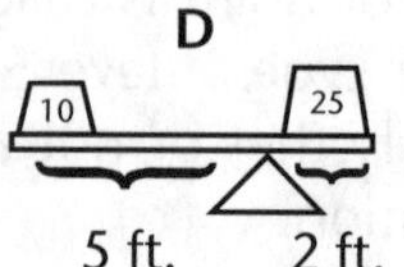

1. Which of the levers above are balanced?
   (1) Lever A only
   (2) Lever B only
   (3) Levers B and C only
   (4) Levers A and D only
   (5) Levers B and D only

2. How much force is needed to balance this lever?
   (1) 30 pounds
   (2) 45 pounds
   (3) 60 pounds
   (4) 75 pounds
   (5) 90 pounds

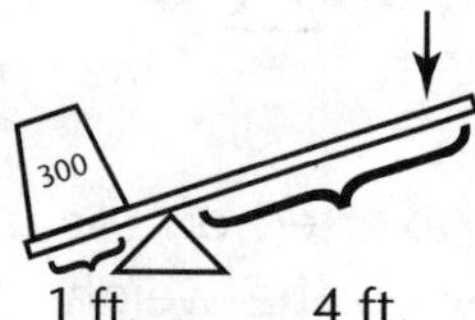

3. Look at this drawing of a balanced lever. What will happen if a one-pound weight is added to side A?
   (1) The lever will stay balanced because there are two weights on each side.
   (2) Side B will go down because the weight on top is heavier.
   (3) Side A will go up because it is heavier.
   (4) Neither end will go up or down because one pound isn't enough to make any difference.
   (5) Side A will go down because it is heavier.

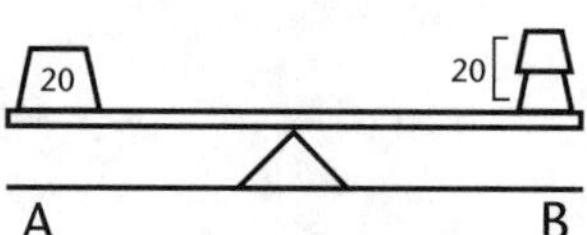

Questions 4–6 are based on the following passage.

One common cause of bad starting in cars is corrosion between the battery terminals and the ends of the battery cables. Corrosion can interfere with the circuit between your engine and the battery. This means that sometimes your car can't draw on the battery for starting power, and other times the battery can't recharge correctly.

If you have trouble starting your car, look under the hood at the place where the heavy wire cables connect to your battery. Often you will see whitish crystals on the connections. With your car turned off, take the cables off the terminals. Scrape all the crystals and the dark corrosion off the terminals and the ends of the cables. Make sure there is bright metal on both sides of the connection. This will allow for the best flow of electricity. Replace the cables and try your car again; it may surprise you by starting easily.

4. What does corrosion on battery terminals often look like?

(1) bright metal
(2) whitish crystals
(3) red plastic
(4) heavy wire cables
(5) sticky liquid

5. When should you check your battery terminals for corrosion?

(1) every five years
(2) when your car is using too much gas
(3) whenever you buy a new battery
(4) in the winter
(5) when your car isn't starting well

6. With which of these statements would the author of this passage be most likely to agree?

(1) Only professional mechanics should work on cars.
(2) Most people don't understand written directions.
(3) Most car problems are very difficult to fix.
(4) Most people can learn to do simple car repairs.
(5) Men are better at fixing cars than women.

Questions 7–9 are based on the following passage.

Most people heat their homes by burning oil, wood, or gas to give off heat, but some people are getting some of their heat directly from the sun, in a process called solar heating.

When sunlight hits an object, some of the light rays are absorbed and changed into heat. This is why the sun feels so good on your back on a chilly day. Some of the sun's rays are being absorbed by your body and warming you up.

The darker the object, the more light it will absorb and change to heat. The simplest kind of solar heating uses this principle. Large windows are placed on the south side of the house (where the most sunlight comes in). The floors under those windows are covered in dark carpeting, which absorbs the sunlight and releases heat into the room. This type of solar heating, using no special machines or instruments, is called passive solar heating.

Active solar heating systems use special heat collectors lined with black material. Light is often concentrated in these collectors by reflecting metal foil or mirrors. Small electric motors are used to pass air or liquid over the heated metal. This air or liquid is then pumped into the heating system of the house.

7. Solar heat collectors use black material because

(1) black is cheaper than colors
(2) black material reflects light best
(3) black material absorbs light best
(4) it is traditional to use black
(5) black cannot be stained by the liquid used

8. What is probably the main cause of recent interest in solar heating?

(1) The cost of fuel is rising.
(2) Solar heating is modern and fashionable.
(3) Most houses have large windows facing south.
(4) People want to try new scientific discoveries.
(5) Solar heat is more comfortable.

9. What is one big problem with solar heat?

(1) Solar heat collectors are hard to find.
(2) Solar heat can be collected only when the sun shines.
(3) Most people don't like dark carpeting.
(4) Solar heat is less polluting than other heat sources.
(5) Large windows are expensive to install.

Questions 10–12 are based on the following passage and chart.

Sound travels as waves. The stronger the wave, the more pressure it puts on our eardrums and the louder the sound seems to us.

The strength of a sound wave is measured in decibels (dB). On the decibel scale, each increase of 10 units means a sound 10 *times* louder. Therefore, a noise rated at 80 decibels is 10 times louder than one at 70 dB. A noise at 90 dB is 100 times louder than one at 70 dB. Repeated exposure to levels of 90 to 115 dB can cause permanent hearing loss. Lower levels of continuous noise may not damage hearing, but they add to stress and may contribute to stress-related diseases like ulcers and migraines.

Here is a chart showing the decibel ratings for some common noises. Use the chart to answer the following questions.

Sound	Rating
Ordinary conversation	60 dB
Busy street traffic	75 dB
Office adding machines	80 dB
20 feet from a subway train	90 dB
Can manufacturing plant	100 dB
Newspaper printing press	102 to 108 dB
Caterpillar tractor, idling	104 dB
Circular saw	105 to 116 dB
Drills, shovels, trucks operating	108 dB

10. The sound of office adding machines is how many times the sound of ordinary conversation?

(1) 2
(2) 10
(3) 20
(4) 100
(5) 200

11. Loud sounds can damage hearing because

(1) they are very confusing
(2) they make it hard to hear other things
(3) they could cause accidents
(4) they give people headaches
(5) they put pressure on the eardrum

12. Which of these workers is *most likely* to have job-related hearing loss?

(1) a heavy-equipment operator
(2) a worker in a can factory
(3) a teacher
(4) a traffic cop
(5) a secretary

Answers and explanations start on page 215.

CHAPTER 5

READING SKILL
BUILDING VOCABULARY

"I hate reading science stuff! It's got so many big words!" If you've ever felt like this, you're not alone. Scientists do use a lot of big words, but most of them are made up of smaller pieces. If you understand the pieces, you can often figure out the bigger words. Other times you can guess the meaning of a word from the way it is used in a sentence.

COMPOUND WORDS:
Sum of the Parts

The easiest words to figure out are ***compound*** words. These are words made by putting two other words together. *Mailman*, *lighthouse*, and *bookstore* are all common examples of compound words. What do you think a *breakwater* is? It's a line of concrete or rocks that breaks the force of the waves in front of a harbor. Where does *buttermilk* come from? It's the milk left after butter is made.

EXERCISE 1: COMPOUND WORDS

Directions: Write each word in the blank after its definition.

sunspot	horsepower	earthquake	rattlesnake
lifetime	spaceship	catfish	wavelength

1. Power equal to one horse pulling: ____________________
2. A ship that travels in outer space: ____________________
3. A spot on the surface of the sun: ____________________
4. A fish with whiskers like a cat's: ____________________
5. The length of time a person lives: ____________________
6. A time when the earth quivers and shakes: ____________________
7. A snake with rattles on its tail: ____________________
8. How long a wave of light or sound is: ____________________

Answers start on page 215.

BEFORE AND AFTER:
Roots, Prefixes, and Suffixes

Many long words are made up of several word parts put together. The main part of the word is called the ***root*** of the word. For example, the root of *careful* is the word *care*, and the root of *unpleasant* is the word *please*. As you can see, beginnings and endings can be added to root words to change the meaning. An addition to the beginning of a word is called a ***prefix***. Something added to the end is called a ***suffix***. Two root words can also be put together to form another word.

Scientific words are often made from roots, prefixes, and suffixes that come from Latin or Greek words. This is because when modern science first began, hundreds of years ago, most scientists could understand these two languages. On the next page is a chart of some common word parts used in science and their meanings. Read the chart carefully.

Prefixes	Roots	Suffixes
mono- (one, single) di-, bi- (two, double) tri- (three) multi- (many) anti- (against) re- (to do again) un- (not) micro- (very tiny)	meter (instrument for measuring) bio (life, living) cardio (heart) hydro (water) nuclear (central, atomic) neur (nerves) derm (skin) therm (heat)	-graph, -gram (writing, record) -logy (the study of) -ist (person who does something) -itis (disease or inflammation of) -al (having to do with)

You can form words by putting these parts together and by using them with other words you know. For example, *biology* is the study of living things, a *biography* is a piece of writing about someone's life, and *biochemistry* is the chemistry of living things. Every time you see the root *bio* in a word, you know it has something to do with life or living things. Likewise, *redo* means to do over again, *return* means to go back again, and an instant *replay* shows a sports play over again. The prefix *re-* always means back or over again.

Knowing the meanings of common word parts can help you figure out many new words. Let's say you read an article about antinuclear protestors. The chart above shows that *anti-* means "against" and *nuclear* can mean "atomic," so you could tell that antinuclear protestors are probably people protesting against atomic weapons. How would you use the chart to figure out what neuritis is? Since the root *neur* means "nerves," and the suffix *-itis* means "disease," neuritis is a disease of the nerves.

EXERCISE 2: WORD PARTS

Directions: In each group of sentences, choose the correct word for each blank. Do this exercise without a dictionary. Use the chart above and some words you already know. The first one is done for you.

-logy (study of)—dermatology, ~~hydrology~~, neurology

1. ___Hydrology___ is the study of water on the Earth.

2. The study of the skin is called ________________.

3. ________________ is the study of the nervous system.

therm (heat)—thermometer, thermonuclear, biothermal

4. ________________ energy is heat that comes from living things.
5. A ________________ is an instrument that measures heat.
6. Heat from nuclear reactions creates ________________ power.

tri- (three)—trimonthly, tricycle, trifocals

7. A ________________ magazine is published every three months.
8. Glasses that focus at three different distances are ________________.
9. A ________________ is a cycle with three wheels.

cardio (heart)—cardiologist, cardiogram, cardiac

10. Hospital patients in ________________ care have heart problems.
11. A written record of your heartbeat is a ________________.
12. A doctor specializing in heart disease is a ________________.

micro- (tiny)—micrometer, microbiology, microfilm

13. The study of very tiny living things is called ________________.
14. Pictures reduced to a very small size are put on ________________.
15. A ________________ is used to measure very small distances.

Answers start on page 215.

CONTEXT CLUES:
The Company It Keeps

There's an old saying that "You can tell a person by the company he keeps." This saying may not really be true about people, but it certainly is true about words. Many times you can figure out a new word by looking at the sentence it is in. This is called getting the meaning from the ***context*** of the word.

Using the context is easiest when the meaning of a new word is given clearly in the sentence. You have already been using this skill throughout this book. Here are some sentences that give clear definitions of new words:

> Ichthyologists, scientists who study fish, may find the next solution to the world's hunger problem.
>
> One of the worst childhood diseases, scarlet fever, can now be controlled by antibiotics.

From these sentences you can tell that *ichthyologists* are scientists who study fish and that *scarlet fever* is a disease that children used to get. Notice that the explanations of the new words are separated from the rest of the sentence by commas. Commas are often used this way, so look for them when you are trying to figure out a new word.

▶ Unfortunately, the sentence where you first see a new word does not always give a complete definition. Even so, there may be ***context clues*** that will tell you at least part of the meaning. Look at this sentence:

> She poured the mixture into the crucible and put it on the burner.

From this sentence you can tell that a crucible must be *some kind of pot that things are heated in*. Now try this one.

> Pregnant women should avoid catching rubella.

▶ What do you think rubella is? ______________________________

If you said it was *some kind of disease*, you used the context well.

EXERCISE 3: USING THE CONTEXT

Directions: Read each sentence. Then write what you think each boldfaced word means. Don't worry if you cannot guess them all exactly. Just for this exercise, do not look the words up in the dictionary. Instead, use the context clues in the sentence to help you.

1. The astronomer used her **astrolabe** to measure the distance between the two stars.

   An astrolabe might be ______________________________.

2. Use only **pasteurized** milk to avoid bacterial disease.

   Pasteurizing milk probably gets rid of ______________________.

3. Information sent into **cyberspace** can be viewed by computer operators across the nation.

   Cyberspace might be ______________________________.

4. The mountain climber drove his **piton** into the rock, then tested it to make sure it could hold his weight.

   A piton is probably ______________________________.

5. Most plastics are only one color, but this one was **polychromatic**.

   Polychromatic probably means ______________________.

6. Cats, wolves, and dogs are all **carnivores**, but mice, rabbits, and horses are not.

   Carnivores are probably animals that eat ____________________.

7. **Hydroponic** farming makes it possible to grow vegetables in areas with no fertile soil.

   Hydroponic farming is probably farming without ______________.

8. The **paleontologist** was delighted to find the dinosaur bones.

   A paleontologist might be ______________________________.

Answers start on page 215.

SCIENTIFIC LANGUAGE:
Translating from Science to English

Many textbooks are not written in the kind of English that we speak every day. In fact, sometimes the reading is so difficult, it almost seems like a foreign language. In a way, it is—the language of science. You should not expect to be able to read a difficult science passage the same way you read a romance or spy story; that is, you should not expect to read it easily and all at once. Instead, you may have to read it several times through, figuring out the meaning of difficult words, going back over tough sentences, and finally putting the whole thing together. Do not be discouraged if the whole passage doesn't make sense to you at first. You need to pick it apart patiently until you can understand it.

These are the steps to follow when you are reading something difficult:

1. Start to read normally until you run into a sentence that doesn't make sense to you.
2. When a sentence doesn't make sense, go back and read it again more slowly. Sometimes it helps to read it out loud quietly.
3. Look for any words you don't know in the sentence. Try to figure out their meanings using word parts and context clues. If you have to, look them up in the dictionary.
4. Look at the next few sentences to see if they explain more about the sentence you are working on. Do not read very much farther ahead until you understand what is being said.
5. Finally, read the sentence again. Try to put it into simpler words. This helps you be sure that you have understood it.
6. Read through the passage once this way. Figure out all the hard parts as well as you can. Then read the whole passage once more at a regular speed. This helps you to put all the ideas together.

This process sounds a lot harder than it is. It is really just the normal way good readers figure out anything that is difficult to read. After you have done the best you can this way, you should always feel free to ask for help from your teacher, if you have one available.

Remember, you may not be a perfect reader, but no one is a perfect writer either. Sometimes writers don't write very clearly, even when they try to. Also, some things are very hard to explain in writing. For instance, imagine trying to write directions telling someone how to tie her shoe. It is a simple thing to show somebody but very hard to put into writing.

Restating Ideas

One of the key steps in understanding difficult writing is being able to put complicated sentences into simpler words. Here is an example:

> In considering the experimental results, it would not be wise to take too optimistic a view of the eventual usefulness of the new drug in the treatment of cardiac diseases.

This is not an easy sentence to understand. There are three words that may be new to you: *optimistic, eventual,* and *cardiac*. The first two you may need to look up. You discover that being optimistic means "always expecting the best thing to happen." *Eventual* means "at the end" or "in the long run." Your knowledge of scientific root words tells you that *cardiac* means "something to do with the heart."

Now let's translate the sentence piece by piece. The original writing will be on the left-hand side, and the simpler translation will be on the right-hand side.

Original	Simpler Version
In considering the experimental results,	When you look at the results of the experiments,
it would not be wise to	you shouldn't
take too optimistic a view of the eventual usefulness of	expect too much good, in the long run, from using
the new drug in the treatment of cardiac diseases.	the new drug to help people with heart disease.

Putting the simpler version all together, we get

> When you look at the results of the experiments, you shouldn't expect too much good, in the long run, from using the new drug to help people with heart disease.

or even more simply:

> The experiments don't show for sure that the new drug will help people with heart disease.

Now that is a lot easier to understand.

▶ Of course, normally you wouldn't try to write down your simpler translation. You would just do it in your head. For practice, though, try writing an everyday translation of this sentence.

> A person acquiring a high school diploma has demonstrated industriousness and perseverance, as well as mastery of a certain large body of knowledge generally regarded as likely to be of use in adult life.

____

____

Your translation should go something like this: *Someone who gets a high school diploma shows that he can stick to a job and has learned a lot of useful things*. Obviously, there are many different ways to say this, but whatever you wrote should be fairly short and clear. If you aren't sure about how to do this, check with your teacher before doing the following exercise.

EXERCISE 4: TRANSLATING SCIENCE TO ENGLISH

Directions: Rewrite the following sentences in simpler words. Use your knowledge of context clues and word parts and look words up in a dictionary if you need to.

1. The effects of atmospheric pollution are among the most seriously adverse.

   ____

2. Experimental medications are frequently ineffective and may result in unfortunate consequences for the uninformed user.

   ____

3. The generation of hydroelectric power was the primary development necessary to provide inexpensive residential electricity.

   ____

4. Playthings for young individuals should be constructed to provide intellectual as well as recreational experiences.

   ____

Answers start on page 215.

SCIENCE TOPIC
CHEMISTRY

Early ***chemists***, scientists who studied chemistry, used their test tubes and burners to try to find out about chemicals they saw in the world around them. Many of today's chemists are more concerned with discovering new combinations of chemicals that do not occur naturally. They use these chemicals to make new types of fabrics, plastics, and many other things. Other chemists are investigating the chemistry that goes on in living things. They are responsible for many new medicines and medical treatments. Without the discoveries of chemistry, our world would be very different.

HOW CHEMICALS COMBINE: Getting Together

Chemicals are similar to people. Some people are friends with everybody, while others don't seem to get along with anyone at all. In just the same way, some chemicals seem to combine easily with other chemicals, other chemicals will combine only with certain special partners, and a few chemicals are complete loners; they won't combine with anything.

No one knows exactly what makes a person friendly or unfriendly, but we do know something about how chemicals get together. Chemicals can combine in simple mixtures, in solutions, and in chemical compounds.

Simple Mixtures

The simplest way that chemicals get together is in a ***mixture***. A mixture is formed when two or more things are simply mixed together. The materials in a simple mixture are not changed at all. The mixture itself may be uneven, with more of one material at the bottom, for example, and more of another at the top.

A good example is a mixture of sugar and sand. In a sugar-sand mixture, the sugar is still white and the sand is still brownish. If you tasted it, the mixture would taste like both sugar and sand. Nothing is changed. Another good example is a salad, which is a mixture of vegetables. All the vegetables are in the same salad bowl, but the tomatoes are still red, the lettuce is still green, the peppers still taste sharp, and the onion still smells. None of the vegetables have changed; they have just been put together.

Solutions

A ***solution*** is a special type of mixture. It has two parts. The material that is dissolved is called a ***solute***. The material it dissolves in is called a ***solvent***. For example, when salt dissolves in water, the salt is the solute and the water is the solvent. The most familiar solutions are formed when solids dissolve in liquids, but you can have a solution using any two types of materials, such as a liquid and a liquid or even a gas and a liquid.

A certain amount of solvent can only hold so much of any one solute. For instance, if you try to dissolve more and more salt in a glass of the water, it finally can hold no more. We say that the solution is ***saturated***. Any more salt that is added will just sink to the bottom of the glass; it will not go into solution.

A solution is different from a simple mixture in several ways. For one thing, you can't see any separation between the solute and the solvent. Another difference is that a solution is ***homogenous***, which means it is the same all the way through. Finally, a solution cannot be separated by ***filtration***. This means that both parts of the solution will stay together if you try to separate them by using a screen or pouring them through filter paper.

	Sugar & Sand —SIMPLE MIXTURE	Salt & Water —SOLUTION	Water (hydrogen & oxygen)—COMPOUND
Can you see the separate parts?	**YES.** You can easily see the separate bits of sugar and sand.	**NO.** You can't see the particles of salt at all.	**NO.** Water does not look at all like hydrogen and oxygen.
Is it homogenous?	**NO.** You can see that in some parts of this mixture there is more sand, while in others there is more sugar.	**YES.** The solution is the same all the way through.	**YES.** The water is the same all the way through.
Can you separate it by sifting or filtering?	**YES.** A small sifter would let the sugar through, while holding the coarser sand particles back.	**NO.** The salt particles in solution would slip through even the finest filter paper along with the water.	**NO.** You cannot separate water into hydrogen and oxygen by sifting or filtering it.
Is the result a totally new substance?	**NO.** The sugar and sand still look, taste, and feel like sugar and sand.	**NO.** The water still looks the same, and even though you can't see the salt, you know it is still there because you can taste it.	**YES.** Water is completely different from hydrogen and oxygen. You can see it, you can drink it, but you can't breathe it.

Compounds

A chemical ***compound*** is very different from a solution or an ordinary mixture. Obviously, the materials in a simple mixture like sugar and sand stay the same. In the saltwater solution, even though you couldn't see the salt, the solution's salty taste told you the salt was still there, basically unchanged. But when two or more materials combine chemically, they form something that can be totally different from the original materials.

For example, hydrogen and oxygen are both invisible gases in the air you breathe. When they combine chemically, they make water, a liquid you can easily see but certainly not breathe. Carbon is a black solid like coal in its pure form. It combines with hydrogen and oxygen to make sugar, something much better to eat than coal!

Compounds are formed when atoms of two or more elements are bonded together into a single molecule. As you may remember from Chapter 4, elements are pure substances. An atom is the smallest particle of an element. Two or more atoms can become bonded together by sharing electrons. A group of atoms bonded together is called a ***molecule***. If the atoms are from different elements, the result is a chemical compound. (You may want to go back and review the article on atoms and molecules in Chapter 4.)

To review the information in this article, look at the chart on page 139 comparing a simple mixture, a solution, and a compound.

EXERCISE 5: MIXTURES, SOLUTIONS, AND COMPOUNDS

Directions: Tell whether each of the following forms a compound, a solution, or a simple mixture by writing *C*, *S*, or *M* in the blank.

______ 1. popcorn and caramel making popcorn balls

______ 2. carbon and oxygen making carbon dioxide gas

______ 3. sugar stirred into hot coffee

______ 4. different types of candies in a dish

______ 5. oxygen and nitrogen gas making nitrate fertilizer

______ 6. pancake mix and water making pancake batter

______ 7. chocolate powder and hot milk making hot cocoa

______ 8. scraps of different-colored paper making confetti

Directions: Circle the best answer for each question.

9. A student is told to find out whether a colored liquid is an ordinary mixture or a solution. One thing she could do to find out is to
   (1) boil it
   (2) filter it
   (3) freeze it
   (4) microwave it
   (5) mix it with salt

10. Chlorine is a poisonous gas. When chlorine gets together with sodium, it forms a white solid called *salt,* which people eat every day. From this information, you can tell that salt is a
   (1) simple mixture
   (2) poison
   (3) compound
   (4) solution
   (5) solvent

Answers and explanations start on page 215.

CHEMICAL FORMULAS:
The Chemical Code

It is a dark and stormy night. Agent 770 waits in the shadows. A man appears out of the fog. He stops to light a cigarette and whispers out of the side of his mouth, "I've got it! It's hydrogen sulfate, nitrous oxide, and calcium chloride." Then he hands Agent 770 a piece of paper. The camera zooms in, and we see:

H_2SO_4, N_2O, $CaCl_2$

It's the secret invisibility formula! But it seems to be in some kind of special code. Can Agent 770 figure it out in time?!

Certainly he can, if he remembers his high school chemistry. Actually, the formula isn't in any kind of secret spy code. It is written in the ordinary abbreviations used by chemists all over the world. It isn't too hard to learn how this "code" works.

Chemical Names

Some chemicals have common names that we use every day: things like water, bleach, alcohol, and cleaning fluid. All chemicals also have a scientific name, using the names of the elements as root words plus some prefixes and suffixes.

The chemical name tells you just what is in a compound. For example, calcium chloride is a compound of calcium and chlorine. Iron oxide is made of iron and oxygen. Sodium hydroxide is a combination of sodium, hydrogen, and oxygen. Notice that the suffix *-ide* is often added to the name of the last element in a compound. This suffix indicates a compound; nothing else has been added to it.

Two other common suffixes do indicate a change, though. The suffixes *-ite* and *-ate* both mean that oxygen has been added to the compound. For instance, hydrogen sulfate is a compound of hydrogen, sulfur, and oxygen. Calcium nitrite contains calcium, nitrogen, and oxygen.

Chemical Symbols and Formulas

Chemical names can get quite long, especially if there are many elements in a compound. Chemists, just like the rest of us, want to save time and energy. Instead of writing out the whole name of every chemical they use, chemists usually use symbols for chemicals.

Each of the 108 elements has its own chemical symbol. These symbols are one or two letters taken from the name of the element in either English or some other language. If there are two letters, the first letter is the only one capitalized.

You certainly do not need to memorize the symbols for all 108 elements, but there are a few very common ones that you should know. Some of these are listed below.

Name	Symbol
Hydrogen	H
Carbon	C
Nitrogen	N
Oxygen	O
Sodium	Na
Sulfur	S
Chlorine	Cl
Calcium	Ca
Iron	Fe

The chemical formula for every compound is written using the symbols of the elements in it. For instance, hydrogen chloride is written HCl, while sodium chloride is NaCl.

You probably already know the chemical symbol for water; it's H_2O. The H and the O tell you that water is made of hydrogen and oxygen, but why is there a small 2 after the H? That small 2 shows that it takes two atoms of hydrogen to combine with one atom of oxygen to make a molecule of water. Whenever there is more than one atom of an element in a molecule, chemists show how many are needed by putting that small number after the symbol for the element. For example, $C_6H_{12}O_6$ is the chemical formula for a simple kind of sugar. This formula shows that it takes 6 carbon atoms, 12 hydrogen atoms, and 6 oxygen atoms to make one molecule of this sugar.

While the number of *atoms* is shown with a small number after the symbol for an element, the number of *molecules* is shown with a large-size number in front of all the elements. For example, two molecules of the simple sugar would be described this way: $2C_6H_{12}O_6$.

EXERCISE 6: CHEMICAL NAMES AND SYMBOLS

Directions: From the list below, write the correct symbol after each chemical name. Look back at the chart on page 142 if you need to.

CaO $CaCl_2$ CO Fe_2O_3 $NaSO_4$

HNO_2 H_2S NO_2 NaH

1. calcium chloride __________
2. calcium oxide __________
3. hydrogen sulfide __________
4. sodium sulfate __________
5. carbon monoxide __________
6. sodium hydride __________
7. hydrogen nitrite __________
8. iron oxide __________

Directions: Circle the best answer for this question.

9. Carbon tetrachloride is the chemical name for a common cleaning fluid. (*Tetra-* is a prefix meaning "four.") Which of these equations correctly describes one molecule of carbon tetrachloride?
   (1) CCl
   (2) $CaCl_2$
   (3) $4CO_2$
   (4) C_4Cl
   (5) CCl_4

Answers and explanations start on page 216.

ACIDS AND BASES: Household Chemicals

You are probably wondering why you should bother with all this chemistry, anyway. What does it have to do with real life?

The rest of the articles in this unit are about different applications of chemistry in daily life. Some of the most common uses of chemistry are in cooking and cleaning.

One common group of chemicals is called ***acids***. Many foods contain ingredients that are acids. Vinegar, used in pickling, is mainly acetic acid ($HC_2H_3O_2$). Citric acid ($HC_6H_7O_7$) is found in oranges, lemons, and grapefruits and is used as a preservative in many canned foods. Sour milk contains lactic acid ($HC_3H_5O_3$), and baking powder also contains a type of acid.

Acids are also used for cleaning. Vinegar and lemon juice are old standbys for cleaning glass or china. Boric acid (H_3BO_3) is used in eyewash, and sulfuric acid (H_2SO_4) is used to clean corroded metals.

From the examples above, you might guess that most acids have a sour taste. The chemical formula for an acid usually shows an H for hydrogen at the beginning. Chemists test for acids using ***litmus paper***, a special kind of paper that turns red in acid.

Another group of chemicals is known as ***bases***. Many common household chemicals are bases. Most drain cleaners contain sodium hydroxide (NaOH), a very strong base that is commonly known as lye. Washing soda ($NaCO_3$) and baking soda ($NaHCO_3$) are both bases. Ammonia (NH_3) is a base that is used in many kinds of household cleaners. Milk of magnesia ($Mg(OH)_2$) and aluminum hydroxide ($Al(OH)_2$) are both bases used in common antacid medicines.

Most bases are bitter-tasting and have a slippery feel to them. The chemical formulas for many bases show an (OH) group on the end. Litmus paper can be used to test for bases, too, because it turns blue when it touches a base.

Both acids and bases are very ***reactive***; that is, they react easily with other chemicals. This is part of what makes them such good cleaners; they react with the dirt and grease. But this also makes them very dangerous. A strong acid or base can burn a person very badly, because it reacts with the water and other things in the skin. Acids and bases react very easily with each other. If an acid and a base are combined, they will react together to form water and some kind of salt. When this happens, the acid and the base have ***neutralized*** each other.

EXERCISE 7: ACIDS AND BASES

Directions: Complete this review by filling in the blanks.

1. ______________ (a) and ______________ (b) are two common groups of chemicals that are very reactive. ______________ (c), ______________ (d), and ______________ (e) are examples of foods containing acids. Three cleaners that are bases include ______________ (f), ______________ (g), and ______________ (h).

   There are many ways to tell an acid from a base. Acids taste ______________ (i), while bases taste ______________ (j). ______________ (k) also feel slippery to the touch, but ______________ (l) don't. Scientists test acids and bases using ______________ (m) paper. This special paper turns ______________ (n) when it touches an acid and ______________ (o) when it touches a base.

Directions: Circle the best answer for the question.

2. This passage tells how the chemical formula for an acid should look. According to the information in the passage, which of these compounds is likely to be an acid?

   (1) HCl
   (2) $NaCl$
   (3) Li_2CO_3
   (4) $Ca(OH)_2$
   (5) FeO

3. What would be a good way to test a chemical to see if it was a base?

   (1) Taste it to see if it's bitter.
   (2) Touch it to see if it reacts with your skin.
   (3) Pour it into an acid to see if it reacts.
   (4) Feel it to see if it feels slippery.
   (5) Touch it with litmus paper; see if the paper turns blue.

Answers and explanations start on page 216.

POISON!
Safety Is No Accident

Each year hundreds of people die from being poisoned by common household items. Thousands more are badly injured, sometimes crippled for life. Knowledge and some simple precautions can prevent most of these poisonings from happening.

Children under five are the most common victims of poison. Young children do not know what is food and what isn't. They taste everything they find, and many poisons are so strong that even a taste can be very dangerous.

People are often surprised at how many common household items have dangerous chemicals in them. Bleach, drain cleaner, floor polish, and most cleaning supplies can all be deadly. Children have been poisoned by relatively small amounts of ordinary medicines like cough syrups, laxatives, and Tylenol. Cosmetics like eye shadow, face cream, and even lipstick can be ***toxic*** (poisonous) when eaten. Vitamins may seem like candy, but an ***overdose*** (too much) can be toxic.

Adults, too, can be poison victims, but the chemicals that get adults in serious trouble are often not the same chemicals that cause poisoning in children. The most common cause of adult poisoning is drug overdose. Most drug overdoses are accidental. A half-asleep person may accidentally take extra doses of sleeping pills. Someone else may take extra prescription medicine, thinking that if a little is good, a lot will be even better (not true!).

Adults can also be poisoned while working around the house. They may breathe toxic fumes (gases) from insecticides, paints, and solvents. Dangerous chlorine gas can be created just by mixing ammonia with bleach or other chlorine-based cleaners. Siphoning gasoline by mouth is not safe; just a few drops of gasoline in the lungs can kill a person.

Safety Precautions

An accident with poison can be a real tragedy. People can help prevent poisonings in their own homes by taking these basic safety precautions:

1. Keep all chemicals, cleaners, cosmetics, and medicines in high cupboards with childproof hooks or locks on them. Return things to these cupboards immediately after use; never leave them out on a countertop or table.
2. Put warning stickers on all poisons. These stickers are available free from your local hospital or poison control center.
3. Don't get children to take medicine by telling them that it is "candy." Never encourage a child to take "just a sip" of your drink. Don't leave tobacco, ashes, or alcoholic drinks in rooms where little children may be alone.

4. Read the information on containers of all household products and pay attention to the warnings.
5. Use materials that put out strong fumes only in well-ventilated areas. If you start to feel sick, go out into the fresh air. If you still feel funny, call a doctor or a hospital emergency room.
6. Never put a nonfood substance, like oil or cleaning fluid, in a food container, like a Coke bottle or milk carton. Check the label every time you take or give medicine and use only the amount prescribed.
7. On the wall by your telephone, keep a list of the phone numbers of the hospital emergency room and the nearest poison control center. If someone does take poison, call one or the other immediately.
8. Get a bottle of syrup of ipecac from your drugstore and keep it handy with your other medicines. Syrup of ipecac can be used to make a person vomit (throw up) if he has swallowed poison. Sometimes vomiting will help; sometimes it will just make things worse, so *do not use the ipecac until told to by a health professional.*

EXERCISE 8: POISONS

Directions: Go through your home, checking everything on the list of safety precautions in this article. In the space below, list three ways you could make your home safer from accidental poisonings.

1. ____________________

2. ____________________

3. ____________________

Directions: Circle the best answer for the question.

4. Which of these is *not* recommended in this article?
   (1) Put all poisons out of the reach of children.
   (2) Tell children that medicine is like candy.
   (3) Put warning stickers on all poisons.
   (4) Read and follow the label directions on all chemicals and medicines.
   (5) Keep emergency phone numbers on the wall by the phone.

Answers and explanations start on page 216.

CHEMICALS THAT CAUSE DISEASE: The Cost of Progress

Modern chemistry has made our lives longer, fuller, and more comfortable. Without chemistry, there would be no plastic for dishes, toys, building materials, or medical supplies. There would be no nylon, rayon, or polyester for clothes, fabrics, and carpeting. There would be no detergents or photographs or contact lenses. Every day of our lives we use the products of modern chemistry.

But chemicals can harm as well as help. Terrible chemical weapons, like nerve gas and napalm, have been used in wars since World War I. Even now they are being made by many countries, including our own, for use in future wars. Often, however, the damage done by chemicals is not done on purpose. Many times a chemical that people thought was harmless has turned out to have unknown side effects.

Medicines are the most important chemicals to many people. Before 1940, people used to die from infected wounds and from diseases like strep throat and pneumonia. Now we don't even worry about these things. We just get a prescription for an antibiotic from the doctor, and we feel fine in a few days. People with heart disease, high blood pressure, and many other illnesses depend on modern medicines to help them lead normal lives.

But scientists don't know everything about new medicines, and big mistakes have been made. For example, in just the last few years, doctors have discovered that giving children aspirin when they have the flu or certain other viruses may cause a deadly reaction called ***Reye's syndrome***.

Another area in which chemistry has been important is the construction business. Modern chemical-based materials are lighter, stronger, cheaper, and easier to work with than old-fashioned materials. Unfortunately, they are not always healthier.

Asbestos is one of the most useful chemicals in construction. It is fireproof; it makes good insulation; it helps strengthen other materials like concrete and plastic. Millions of tons of asbestos were used in our schools, homes, and stores. Now scientists have discovered that asbestos can cause cancer. There are plans to remove all the open asbestos in public buildings, but for the many people who got cancer the damage is already done.

Chemicals in Food

Another problem involves ***food additives***, chemicals that are added to foods. Preservatives help keep foods from spoiling or going stale. Artificial flavors and flavor enhancers are added to foods to make them taste better. Artificial colors make foods more attractive and appealing. Almost all prepared foods, and many other canned and frozen foods, contain food additives. Food additives have made a great variety of foods available to us in easy-to-fix forms. But scientists are discovering that some additives can be dangerous to our health.

Artificial sweeteners have been a big problem for manufacturers. According to some tests, cyclamates and saccharin, two popular sweeteners, may cause cancer. Another sweetener called *aspartame* (NutraSweet and Equal) was carefully tested before it was used, but some people still say that it gives them headaches and other problems.

Sodium nitrite is a preservative that keeps meat from spoiling. It is used in meats like hot dogs, salami, and bacon. Before sodium nitrite was used, people sometimes got food poisoning from these foods. Now some people say that sodium nitrite should be banned because experiments show that it can cause cancer in animals.

As you can see, decisions about using chemicals are not easy to make. We need chemicals to fight disease, to build houses, and to produce and preserve food. Yet chemicals can be very dangerous, too. No one is saying that we should stop using all chemicals; that would be impossible. However, many people are saying we must be more careful about the chemicals we use. This can be accomplished through the cooperation of manufacturers, concerned individuals, and government agencies such as the FDA (Food and Drug Administration) and the EPA (Environmental Protection Agency).

EXERCISE 9: DECISIONS ABOUT CHEMICALS

Directions: There are no right or wrong answers to these questions. Write your opinions. Give reasons for your ideas.

1. Who do you think should have to pay for taking out all the asbestos used in buildings? Should it be the taxpayers, the building owners, the original builders, the asbestos manufacturers, or someone else?

2. Do you think people should be allowed to buy artificial sweeteners, even if they may cause cancer?

3. In the mid-1980s, the budgets of agencies like the EPA and FDA were cut. At the same time, more and more money was spent on the military. Do you believe that this was a wise way to spend money?

Directions: Circle the best answer for each question.

4. Which of the following is an opinion, not a fact?
   (1) Some tests show that saccharin may cause cancer.
   (2) Manufacturers should work to make sure that chemicals are safe.
   (3) Artificial colors are intended to make food more appealing.
   (4) Chemistry has been important in the construction business.
   (5) Sodium nitrite can cause cancer in animals.

5. The rate of cancer has increased a lot in recent years. Which of these possible causes is indicated by the information in this article?
   (1) Doctors are getting better at finding cancer.
   (2) People don't take care of their health.
   (3) People are smoking more than they used to.
   (4) Nuclear weapons testing has released radiation.
   (5) More artificial chemicals are being used.

Answers and explanations start on page 216.

DRUG ABUSE:
A Dangerous Habit

Drugs and medicines can be divided into two groups. Most drugs mainly affect the body. These drugs are rarely ***abused*** (taken when they should not be) because they are not fun to take. But there are many drugs that affect the mind. They can make a person feel very happy or relaxed or full of energy. Because these drugs can make someone feel good in a bad situation, they are often abused.

Drugs may make a person feel good, but they can have some bad effects. Drugs can change a person's picture of reality. He may believe he is driving well when he is really all over the road. He may jump from a window, believing that he can fly. Some drugs can cause ***hallucinations***; that is, they can make a person see or hear things that aren't real.

If a person uses a drug regularly, he may come to need that drug. He is ***addicted***. That drug becomes the most important thing in his life. Usually he needs the drug just to handle everyday stress. Without it, he feels like he would fall apart. This is called a ***psychological dependence***. Some drugs also cause chemical changes in the body. The body comes to need the drug. If a person stops taking the drug, he becomes very sick. This is called a ***physical dependence***.

Both kinds of dependence can ruin a person's life. When people abuse drugs, they do not learn well. They cannot pay attention to the real business of life, because much of their time goes into getting and using the drugs. Much of their money has to go for drugs, too. Sometimes there is not enough left for food or rent. Sometimes people become criminals to get enough money for the drugs they need. Often they neglect or abuse their families and lose their jobs because of needing and using drugs.

Commonly Abused Drugs

Marijuana (grass, pot) is a dried plant that is usually smoked or eaten. It makes a person feel relaxed, lazy, and a little silly. Once in a while it will make a person feel frightened or depressed. It can cause psychological dependence. Marijuana smoke causes lung damage, just as cigarette smoke does. Heavy use may affect the sex hormones and the ability to have healthy children. THC, the main chemical in marijuana, is used by doctors to treat an eye disease and to help cancer patients tolerate chemotherapy. Hashish is a concentrated form of marijuana.

Hallucinogens are a group of drugs that cause hallucinations. Included in this group are LSD (acid), STP, PCP, mescaline, psilocybin, and others. These are very powerful, unpredictable drugs. A person taking these drugs may see beautiful visions or have nightmarish delusions. Some people have gone crazy while using these drugs. Some hallucinogens can become active in the body again, long after they have been used, causing "flashbacks." There is some evidence that hallucinogens may cause brain damage and birth defects.

Amphetamines (uppers, speed) are drugs that make a person feel very energetic, awake, and alive. People using speed often don't eat or sleep for days. It is very easy to damage the body, especially the nervous system, using speed. Amphetamines are sometimes prescribed by doctors to treat obesity and depression, but they are not used very much anymore because they are so addictive, psychologically and physically.

Barbiturates (downers) are drugs that depress and slow down the whole body. They can make a person feel very relaxed and peaceful. Doctors use them to treat sleeplessness, epilepsy, and many mental illnesses. Barbiturates are very physically addictive, and if a person suddenly stops taking them, he or she may die. Taking an overdose of barbiturates, or combining even a small amount with alcohol, can make a person stop breathing.

Cocaine (coke) is a drug made from the leaves of a South American plant. It is a strong stimulant, and it makes people feel very confident and well. It causes a very strong physical and psychological addiction; once a person starts using cocaine often, it is very hard to stop. One form of cocaine, called "crack," can be deadly even on the first use.

Heroin is the drug many people think of when they think of addicts. Heroin is strongly addictive, both physically and psychologically. Heroin users waste away physically. Because this drug is usually injected, users can get diseases like hepatitis and AIDS from using unclean needles.

Alcohol is not considered a drug by many people, yet it can be a dangerous one. People addicted to alcohol are called alcoholics, who number in the millions in this country alone. Researchers say that one in four families is affected by alcoholism. Frequent abuse of alcohol can cause permanent damage to the kidneys, liver, and brain.

Nicotine is the main drug in cigarettes. It is probably the most commonly abused drug in this country. It is a stimulant that speeds up the heartbeat and breathing and raises the blood pressure. Over a period of years, nicotine and other chemicals in tobacco smoke damage the lungs, heart, and blood vessels.

Treatment of Drug Addiction

Drug addiction can affect anyone: male or female, young or old, rich or poor. People who are psychologically or physically dependent on drugs are caught in a trap. Even if they do not want to use the drugs anymore, often they cannot stop. Sometimes they need medical treatment to be able to stop safely. They almost always need help from a counselor or special group, like Alcoholics Anonymous or Narcotics Anonymous. The telephone book lists programs that help people free themselves from a chemical dependency.

EXERCISE 10: DRUG ABUSE

Directions: Match the drugs in the column on the left with the phrases in the column on the right by writing the correct letters in the blanks.

_____ 1. marijuana

_____ 2. hallucinogens

_____ 3. amphetamines

_____ 4. barbiturates

_____ 5. cocaine

_____ 6. heroin

_____ 7. alcohol

_____ 8. nicotine

a. one deadly kind is called "crack"
b. can damage lungs, heart, and blood vessels
c. usually smoked or eaten
d. can damage kidneys, liver, and brain
e. may cause "flashbacks"
f. should never be combined with alcohol
g. users may not feel the need to eat or sleep
h. usually injected, very addictive

Directions: Circle the best answer for each question.

9. According to this article, what is one common reason that people abuse drugs?
   (1) They want to get well faster.
   (2) They are natural troublemakers.
   (3) They have nothing to do.
   (4) They want to feel good in bad situations.
   (5) They don't know that drugs can be dangerous.

10. Which of these drugs is physically addicting?
   (1) marijuana
   (2) hallucinogens
   (3) barbiturates
   (4) hashish
   (5) aspirin

Answers and explanations start on page 216.

SCIENTISTS IN THE SPOTLIGHT:
Early Scientists and Alchemy

From the beginning of civilization, people have tried to discover why things in nature happen and how to control them. The first scientist was probably the cave dweller who discovered fire. But for a long time, science was confused with magic and religion. The first true scientists were Greeks living three to four hundred years before Christ.

Hippocrates is known as the Father of Medicine. He was the first doctor that we know of who believed that diseases were caused by natural things, not by demons or evil spirits. Because he believed this, he kept careful records of the various illnesses he treated and how he cured them. Two thousand years later, people were still studying his notes and using his treatments. Even today, graduating doctors still take the Hippocratic Oath. They promise to treat the sick honestly, to the best of their ability, and confidentially, just as Hippocrates's students swore to do over twenty-four hundred years ago.

Archimedes was a famous Greek mathematician. He was also what today would be called a ***mechanical engineer***. He designed ships and invented war machines that were effective enough to hold off the Roman army for ten years. He was the first person to apply scientific ideas to the tools of everyday life, inventing a water pump, the block-and-tackle, and many other things. He also discovered many principles of modern geometry and mathematics. Legend has it that he died like a true scientist. When his city was captured by Roman soldiers, he refused to surrender until he finished a problem he was working on, so he was killed by an impatient soldier.

Aristotle was the most famous of ancient scientists. He was one of the first scientists to do organized research. He wrote in his *History of Animals* about the bodies and habits of over 540 kinds of animals. He also was the first to try to classify animals into related groups. During the Middle Ages (about A.D. 500–1500), he was considered the absolute authority in all matters of science. Unfortunately, people believed his wrong ideas just as strongly as his right ones. Aristotle was one of a group of Greek scientists who believed that everything was made out of four basic elements: fire, air, water, and earth. This idea, combined with religious ideas about spirits and devils, led to the development of alchemy.

Alchemy was a strange combination of science and magic that grew up during the Middle Ages. Alchemists were looking for a way to turn common metals like lead and iron into gold. This would make them very rich, but they also believed this knowledge would reveal to them all the secrets of the construction of matter. Some alchemists believed in the existence of the Philosopher's Stone. This magic stone would not only turn lead to gold, but would also heal all disease and give eternal life.

Alchemists did hundreds, probably thousands, of experiments, trying to discover the Philosopher's Stone. Often they spoke magical words over their incredible mixtures. Of course, they never discovered the Philosopher's Stone, but the many experiments of the alchemists were the beginning of modern chemistry.

EXERCISE 11: EARLY SCIENTISTS

Directions: Give brief answers to the following questions.

1. According to this article, why have people always been interested in science?

____

____

2. Why is Hippocrates considered the Father of Medicine?

____

____

3. List three inventions of Archimedes. How did he use science in a new way?

____

____

4. Describe the theory of the four elements that Aristotle and many other Greeks believed.

____

____

5. What were the alchemists searching for? What was it supposed to do?

____

____

6. If you could find a magic Philosopher's Stone, what would you like it to do?

____

____

Answers and explanations start on page 216.

EXERCISE 12: CHAPTER 5 REVIEW

Directions: Using the information given, circle the best answer for each question.

Questions 1–3 refer to the chart below.

Some Elements and Their Chemical Symbols		
Cl—Chlorine Si—Silicon	N—Nitrogen Cu—Copper	O—Oxygen Ag—Silver

1. Which of these is the correct formula for silicon dioxide?
   (1) SiCu
   (2) CuO_2
   (3) SiN_2
   (4) SiO_2
   (5) $SiCl_2$

2. How many of these compounds contain silver?

   $AgNO_3$ Cu_2O Ag_2O Ag_2S Au_2O

   (1) 1
   (2) 2
   (3) 3
   (4) 4
   (5) 5

3. What is the correct name for CuCl?
   (1) silver calcite
   (2) chlorine sulfate
   (3) copper oxide
   (4) silver chloride
   (5) copper chloride

Questions 4–6 are based on the label below.

CAUTION: KEEP OUT OF REACH OF CHILDREN
If bleach is splashed in eyes, flood with water.
Harmful if swallowed. If swallowed, feed milk.
Call a physician or Poison Control Center.
If splashed on skin, flood with water.

4. According to this label, laundry bleach can be harmful to which parts of the body?
   (1) eyes
   (2) stomach
   (3) skin
   (4) all of the above
   (5) none of the above

5. If a person swallows bleach, you should
   (1) flood the person with water
   (2) have the person drink milk
   (3) have the person drink water
   (4) rinse the person's eyes with water
   (5) rinse the person's eyes with milk

6. Why must you keep bleach out of the reach of children?
   (1) They might drink it.
   (2) They might spill it on the floor.
   (3) They might get it on their clothes.
   (4) Children are too young to do laundry.
   (5) It is too expensive to waste.

Questions 7–9 are based on the chart on page 157.

Many people are exposed to dangerous conditions on the job. On the next page is a chart of some symptoms and possible causes.

7. Betty Rundell works in a chemical factory. She has been having problems with her nervous system. According to this chart, what is one possible cause?
   (1) solvents
   (2) metal poisoning
   (3) ozone
   (4) acid fumes
   (5) radiation

8. Workers in another plant are exposed to many different kinds of dust. According to the chart, which of these problems is probably *not* caused by dust?
   (1) irritated eyes
   (2) sore throat
   (3) dry cough
   (4) sneezing
   (5) headache and dizziness

Some Work-Related Health Problems		
Area Affected	**Symptoms**	**Common Causes**
Head	headache, dizziness	excessive noise
Nose and Throat	coughing, sneezing, sore throat nasal cancer	ozone, solvents, ammonia, caustic soda, dusts hardwood dusts and resins
Chest and Lungs	dry cough, wheezing, congestion flu-like symptoms shortness of breath after mild exercise	cotton dust, detergent enzymes, beryllium, solvents, TDI metal oxides from welding long-term exposure to asbestos
Ears	ringing, temporary deafness, hearing loss	excessive noise
Eyes	irritation, redness, watering "welder's flash," grainy feeling	gases, fumes, smoke, metal dust, acids ultraviolet radiation
Skin	itching, dryness, redness ulcers, skin cancer	epoxies, solvents, oil, fiberglass, nickel, caustic soda arsenic, pitch, tar, mineral oils, radiation
Nervous System	nervousness, irritability, stress tremors, sleeplessness, speech changes	speed-up, noise metal poisoning (mercury, lead)
Reproductive System	irregularities in menstruation miscarriage damage to chromosomes or fetus sterilization	polystyrene production, xylene, solvents pesticides, radiation, lead, anesthetic gas lead, mercury, radiation, benzene radiation

9. Dave Miklasz has just found out he has cancer. He works cutting and gluing lumber. According to the chart, which of the following could be a cause of his cancer?
   (1) epoxy glues
   (2) noise
   (3) hardwood dust
   (4) solvents
   (5) fumes

Questions 10–12 are based on the following opinions.

Speaker A

There has been a lot of discussion about the "problem" of marijuana. The biggest problems are caused by the laws that make marijuana illegal. If marijuana were legalized, ordinary students would not get a criminal record just for smoking it. People who wanted marijuana would not be forced into contact with criminals who also sell other, more dangerous drugs. If marijuana sellers were licensed, users would not have to worry about poisons or other drugs being mixed with it. Finally, if marijuana were controlled the way alcohol is, people would learn to use it responsibly, just as they do with alcohol.

Speaker B

Some people are calling for the legalization of marijuana. This would be a big mistake. If marijuana were legal, more people would smoke it more often. This would cause an increase in car accidents due to driving under the influence of marijuana. It would slow production and cause more accidents in factories. If marijuana were legal for adults, it would also be easier for underage children to get. Many immature people would try to avoid their problems by getting high, instead of learning to deal with their problems. Also, there is new evidence that smoking marijuana may cause sterility, brain damage, and birth defects. Look at all the problems society has with legal alcohol; legalized marijuana would be even worse.

10. What is the main topic of these articles?
   (1) How can marijuana be used?
   (2) How is marijuana like alcohol?
   (3) Should children smoke marijuana?
   (4) Should marijuana be legalized?
   (5) Should alcohol be legal?

11. Speaker A would probably agree with which of these statements?
    (1) Governments should pass laws to protect people against drugs, even if people don't want to be protected.
    (2) People should be allowed to do what they want, as long as they don't harm others.
    (3) People who smoke marijuana are mostly delinquents and criminals.
    (4) Most people cannot be trusted to take care of themselves.
    (5) Smoking marijuana usually leads to hard drug addiction.

12. Both of these articles are mostly opinion. What is one fact mentioned by Speaker B?
    (1) Some people are now calling for the legalization of marijuana.
    (2) Legalizing marijuana would be a big mistake.
    (3) If marijuana were legal, people would smoke more of it.
    (4) Children should not smoke marijuana.
    (5) Marijuana would be a bigger problem than alcohol if it were legalized.

Answers and explanations start on page 216.

CHAPTER 6

READING SKILL
EVALUATING IDEAS

Should our country make and store nuclear weapons, or should we ban them?

Should businesses be required to protect the environment, even if that means that jobs will be lost and prices will rise?

Should new medicines that might cure diseases like AIDS be put on the market right away, or should they first go through a regular five-year testing program to make certain they are useful and safe?

Should the government spend millions to put astronauts in space, or should it spend that money on health care for the elderly?

These are just a few of the questions that our modern society faces because of scientific progress. Scientists are making discoveries every day that will allow us to do things that we have never done before. For example, we can save lives with modern medical techniques like heart transplants. We can also make weapons that can kill millions. Our factories make things so quickly and cheaply that ordinary people in the United States today live better than kings did 200 years ago. On the other hand, the same factories may ruin our air and water if we don't control their pollution. Every scientific discovery brings problems as well as benefits.

Questions about how science should be used cannot be answered by scientists alone. There is no "scientific" answer that will tell us what we should do. Science can answer only questions about facts. What should be done with those facts is a question of values and beliefs.

VALUES AND BELIEFS:
Decision Making and Value Conflicts

Each person has his or her own ***value system***, a set of beliefs about what is important and what is right and wrong. We develop this value system as we grow, from our life experiences and from what our family and other people tell us. We use our value system to help us make decisions.

Sometimes our values are in conflict; we cannot do or have everything we want. Often the conflict is between short-term and long-term values. A ***short-term value*** is something that will make us feel good right now. A ***long-term value*** is something that we think is important in the long run. For instance, a person on a diet might have to decide whether to enjoy a piece of chocolate cake now or enjoy being thinner later. Someone working toward his high school diploma might have to decide whether to go out to a party or stay home and study. Short-term values pay off right away, so they are hard to resist. As we grow up, though, we learn to balance both types of values, so we get some short-term rewards but also reach our long-term goals.

Our society has value conflicts about many things, including the uses of science. Sometimes these are conflicts between short-term and long-term values. For example, an inexpensive sewage treatment plant will save the taxpayers money now, but in ten years it may have polluted the local drinking water. Other decisions about science are difficult because of conflicts between important long-term values. For example, everyone agrees that doctors should save lives and that people should die with dignity. But issues like these raise difficult questions: Should patients be allowed to refuse special medical treatment and die in peace? Or should doctors always try to keep patients alive as long as possible?

Some conflicts come about because there is only so much money, time, and effort available to solve problems. Should we spend money on weapons to defend our country or on programs like student grants and food stamps? Should we increase Medicare benefits for older people or provide more nutritious hot lunches in schools? Different groups of people will have different ideas about what is most important. Sometimes it seems as though there is no answer that will be good for everybody; we just make the best decision we can.

Every citizen in this society helps make decisions like these. Every time we vote or buy a new product, we influence these decisions. That is one reason it is important for all of us to learn as much as possible. As people who care about our country and our world, we take time to study important issues. We think about our values and beliefs, the things we consider important. Then we try to use our influence well.

Suppose your town, like many, uses chemical herbicides (weed killers) along the sides of the roads. Some people want to stop the town from doing this, because the chemicals pollute the environment and because a few children get very sick when they are exposed to herbicides. The mayor says that if the town can't use herbicides, it will have to hire extra workers to mow the roadsides. That means higher taxes. The mayor says that the town has been using these chemicals for years, and no one has really been hurt.

▶ If you were voting on this issue, would you vote for or against the use of herbicides? Here are some questions you might consider in making this decision.

1. Which is more important to you, a cleaner environment or lower taxes?
2. Should everyone have to pay more just because a few children are sensitive to these chemicals?
3. Is the mayor probably right that no one has been hurt, or do you think that a chemical that makes some people really sick might be causing less obvious problems for many people?

Now write how you would vote and list any other reasons for voting that way.

___

Do you think your answer would be different if you had a brother or sister who was sensitive to herbicides? How about if your family had a low income, and you were afraid of losing your home because you have trouble paying the taxes even now? To make fair decisions, we have to look both at what is best for us personally and what is best for everyone in our community.

EXERCISE 1: YOU DECIDE

Directions: Below are several pairs of opposite opinions on current questions about the use of science. Put a check next to the opinion you agree with. Then write three reasons that support your opinion.

1. ________ Scientists should control the genes of unborn children so that the next generation is stronger and smarter.

   ________ Scientists should not try to control the genes of unborn children.

   Reasons that support your opinion:

   a.

   b.

   c.

2. ________ Some areas of government land should be closed to all people so that some wilderness can be preserved.

________ All government lands should be open to tourists and to careful mining, ranching, or lumbering.

Reasons that support your opinion:

a.

b.

c.

3. ________ Employers should have the right to test workers to find out if they are using drugs.

________ Employers should not have the right to do drug testing.

Reasons that support your opinion:

a.

b.

c.

4. ________ Our country should develop deadly bacteria that can be used as biological weapons.

________ Our country should not develop or use bacteria as weapons.

Reasons that support your opinion:

a.

b.

c.

Answers will vary.

CRITICAL READING: Think for Yourself!

Advertisers want you to buy their products. Politicians want you to vote for them. Even your family and friends will try to persuade you to agree with them and do things their way. With all this pressure, you still have to make your own decisions according to what you believe is important and right.

To help yourself understand and make clear decisions about important issues, ask yourself these two questions: Am I getting all the facts? If not, where can I go to get more information?

All the Facts, Please

Many times someone will try to persuade you to think or do something without giving you all the facts. For example, an advertiser will say, "Strike detergent is new and improved; buy some today!" However, the ad doesn't say how Strike was improved. Does it clean better, cost less, or just smell nicer? You need this information before you can decide if Strike is the detergent you want to buy. Or a newspaper article says, "Nuclear power plants have an excellent safety record." Exactly what does the writer consider "excellent"? How many accidents have there been per plant in the last five years? How many workers have been injured? Have any members of the public been injured by nuclear accidents? You need these facts and more before you can decide whether you support nuclear power.

▶ Look at this statement from a medicine company: "Ninety percent of people surveyed prefer Sager aspirin." List two or more pieces of information you might need before deciding whether to buy Sager aspirin.

1. ______________________________

2. ______________________________

There are many different facts you might need here. *How many people were surveyed?* If only ten people were surveyed, the results don't mean as much as if thousands were surveyed. *How was the survey done?* Did the questioners choose people at random, or did they question only people who had already bought Sager? *Who did the survey,* an independent company or the Sager company itself? Finally, *why did the people prefer Sager?* Was it cheaper? Did it work best for headaches or perhaps for arthritis? You can see that even though this advertisement sounds very scientific, it is still missing most of the facts.

EXERCISE 2: THE WHOLE STORY

Directions: Read the following persuasive statements. Write at least one question that you would need answered in order to have all the facts.

1. Move to California; we have the best weather in the nation.
2. Take vitamins to improve your health.
3. Stop your taxes from going up by voting against the new park.
4. Use Bantex insecticide on your corn crop.
5. We must build more roads; we can't stand in the way of progress.
6. Chemical X must be banned because it causes cancer in mice.
7. Space travel is the next great American challenge.

Answers start on page 217.

WHERE TO GO NEXT:
Information, Please

It is not always easy to get accurate information on a subject. Your sources of information should have some special knowledge about the subject. For example, medical information from a doctor is much more reliable than the stories of "miracle cures" in grocery-store newspapers. A lawyer is the person to ask about your legal rights, not the guy down the block, who may have his facts all mixed up.

It is also important to get information from a source that is not ***biased*** (prejudiced toward one side of a question). For example, if you wanted to know which brand of stereo needs the fewest repairs, you wouldn't just ask the salesperson. After all, she wants to sell you her brand. Instead, you could check in a magazine like *Consumer Reports* for the results of independent testing. Likewise, a missile base commander is not the person to ask about the safety of nuclear weapons. His whole career is based on the existence of nuclear missiles. Instead, you might try to get information from independent scientist and citizen groups.

One good place to start looking for information is the public library. Libraries have thousands of books and articles on all sorts of subjects. Many people are not sure just where to look for things in the library, but librarians are used to helping people find the information they want.

Another good source of information about local questions is your city, town, or county government. If you ask for help with a problem, they will often explain exactly what you can do. A letter to your congressperson or senator will often get you lots of information about new laws and government programs to help individuals. If you live in the country, your county extension agent will give you free information and even personal help with any question about farming, gardening, or housekeeping.

Finally, there are citizens' groups organized to deal with many different issues, from wildlife preservation to preventing birth defects. These groups are usually more than happy to provide information on their subjects.

EXERCISE 3: INFORMATION, PLEASE

Directions: Circle the numbers of the *two* best sources of information about each of the following questions.

1. Is the factory in my town polluting our river?
   (1) a publicity release from the factory
   (2) the town health department
   (3) Citizens for a Better Environment
   (4) a friend who fishes on the river all the time

2. If a child has a fever of 101°F, does the child need to see a doctor?
   (1) the doctor's nurse
   (2) the child's grandmother
   (3) a neighbor whose child had a similar fever last week
   (4) the hospital emergency room

3. Does the space program use our tax money efficiently?
   (1) NASA (the federal agency that runs the space program)
   (2) a manufacturer of rocket parts
   (3) articles on the space program in your local paper
   (4) a citizen's group studying the space program

4. Are "health foods" really better for you?
   (1) books on nutrition from the library
   (2) the county social services department
   (3) your brother, who is always on a diet
   (4) a clerk at your local health food store

Answers and explanations start on page 217.

EXTRA EXERCISE: As you watch TV or read the paper, practice critical reading. Watch for incomplete information and biased viewpoints. Find more information on the issues that are important to you.

SCIENCE TOPIC
EARTH SCIENCE

People have lived on Earth for hundreds of thousands of years, and we have always been curious, yet there is always something new to discover about the amazing planet we live on. Even today, we know very little about the deep places in the oceans, and there are probably hundreds of plants and animals that we have not named and classified—maybe some we have not even seen. Although we still have much to learn about our own planet, we are now taking on an even bigger challenge. We have begun to investigate the other planets and the stars, the universe itself.

THE EARTH'S INTERIOR:
Journey to the Center of the Earth!

> Here we had white mushrooms from thirty to forty feet tall. . . . There were thousands of them. . . . Now over there is an uncommonly large sea lizard. And behind it a monstrous crocodile. . . . Here I am, actually face to face with two reptiles of the primitive oceans!
>
> —from *Journey to the Center of the Earth,*
> written in 1864 by Jules Verne

This is how one famous science fiction writer pictured the center of the Earth, as an underground land full of strange plants and dangerous animals. For centuries people have wondered and guessed about the inside of our planet Earth. Now scientists have discovered some of the facts, and very strange they seem.

Inside the Earth

THE STRUCTURE OF THE EARTH

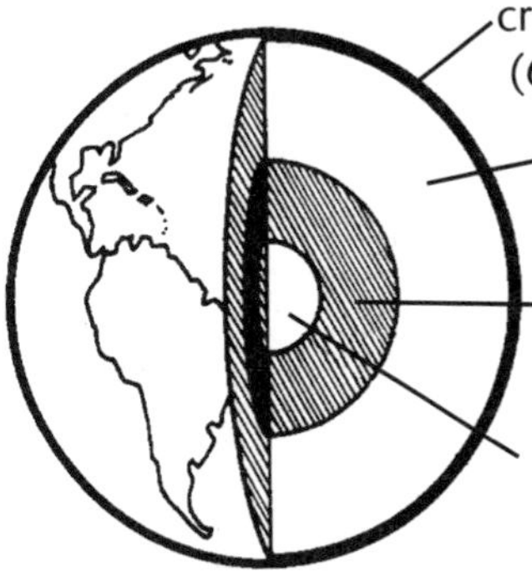

crust (6–40 miles)

mantle (1,800 miles)

outer core (1,400 miles)

inner core (800 miles)

The Earth is a little like the apple you had for lunch. It has a thin outer layer like a peel, an inner part, and a core. The thin outer part is called the ***crust***. It is very irregular, bumping up into mountains and flattening out under the oceans. The thickest part of the crust is only about 40 miles thick but it gives us everything we need for life.

Below the crust is a thick layer called the ***mantle***. No one has ever drilled down into the mantle or the layers beneath it. From studying the way vibrations pass through this layer, scientists believe the mantle is made of solid rock.

Inside the mantle are the ***outer core*** and the ***inner core***. Both cores are probably made of a mixture of iron and nickel. It is very hot inside the Earth, up to 9,000°F, so the outer core is molten (liquid). The enormous pressures at the center of the Earth have forced the material of the inner core into a solid, very dense state.

Buried Treasure

People dig mines into the Earth's crust to find all kinds of ***minerals*** (natural elements and compounds). Minerals contain materials that we need for many things.

Metals are usually found mixed with other elements in mineral compounds called ores. From different ores, we get iron to make steel for all kinds of building and machinery, copper for electric wires, aluminum for aircraft and kitchen uses, and uranium for use in atomic power plants. Gold and silver ores are especially valuable because they are used to make coins, but they are also used in industry.

Oil, coal, and natural gas, called ***fossil fuels***, are minerals that are the remains of plants that lived millions of years ago. These plants died and were buried in layers deep within the Earth, where heat and pressure gradually changed them to coal and oil. During this process, they gave off natural gas, which was trapped under the Earth. Fossil fuels took millions of years to make, but we are using them up very quickly. We burn fossil fuels to get most of the energy for our cars, homes, and industry. We also use them to make many important chemical products, from medicines to plastics. Fossil fuels are so important to us that many people are worried about what will happen if we use them all up.

The most romantic and expensive of Earth's treasures are jewels, like diamonds, emeralds, and rubies. Throughout history, people have valued jewels because of their beauty and rarity. Strangely enough, jewels are just ordinary minerals that have been changed into clear and colorful gems by exactly the right amounts of heat and pressure. For instance, rubies are made of aluminum and oxygen, while diamonds are pure carbon, the same material as in black, sooty coal. Besides being used in jewelry, gemstones are used in industry. For example, diamonds, which are the hardest natural material, are used in drills and cutting tools, and rubies are used to focus laser beams.

EXERCISE 4: TREASURE FROM THE EARTH

Directions: List two examples of things you own or use made from these earth products.

1. copper: ______________________________

2. iron: ______________________________

3. aluminum: ______________________________

4. fossil fuels: ______________________________

5. jewels: ______________________________

Directions: Choose the best answer to each question.

6. According to this article, scientists learn about the layers under the Earth's crust by
   (1) drilling down under the crust
   (2) reading science fiction
   (3) going down into the center of the Earth
   (4) measuring vibrations that pass through the Earth
   (5) studying the material that comes out of volcanoes

7. As fossil fuels become scarcer and harder to find, which of the following will probably *not* happen?
   (1) Houses will be insulated better.
   (2) More sun and wind energy will be used.
   (3) People will drive more.
   (4) Scientists will search for substitutes for fossil fuels.
   (5) Oil prices will rise.

Answers and explanations start on page 217.

SOIL CONSERVATION:
Modern Farming

When the pioneers first settled our country, a farmer mainly had to have a strong back and lots of energy. Everything had to be done by hand. First the farmer had to clear his land by chopping down the trees and pulling out the largest stumps and rocks. Then he plowed it with a single-bottom plow pulled by an ox or horse. He scattered the seed by hand and then spent hours hoeing around each plant to keep the weeds from growing. Finally, if everything went well, he gathered his crops by hand and stored them in his barn. Year after year, most farmers planted the same crops, often corn or cotton. When the land was worn out, they moved on to new, uncleared land and started again.

Today a successful farmer still needs a lot of energy, but he also needs a lot of scientific knowledge. New machines and chemicals have changed the way people farm. Almost all the good farmland is settled, so farmers can't just move on if they wear out their land. Instead, successful farmers have learned to keep the land from wearing out through soil conservation, taking care of the soil.

Soil is the loose material found on the top of the Earth's crust. Plants get most of their nutrients (the materials they need to grow) from the soil. Most of the available nutrients are found in the upper layer of the soil, called the ***topsoil***. Topsoil is a mixture of sand, clay, and humus. ***Humus*** is decaying plant and animal material. It provides many nutrients and keeps the soil spongy so it can hold air and water. Sand makes the soil loose so water and air can get in and plant roots can grow easily. Clay helps the soil hold water and provides some necessary minerals. All three materials are needed for good soil.

Beneath the topsoil is the ***subsoil***, which may be sand, clay, gravel, or a mixture of all three. Since subsoil has no humus in it, most plants cannot grow in it directly, although some plants have very deep roots that allow them to get some of their minerals from the subsoil. Both layers of soil rest on the ***bedrock*** that makes up the crust of the Earth.

Soil Damage

If ground is left bare, wind and running water can carry away the topsoil. This process is called ***erosion***. Water erosion is more likely on hilly land, while wind erosion happens most often on large fields with no hedges or windbreaks. Fall plowing adds to the problem of erosion. So do crops like corn and cotton that grow in rows, leaving the soil bare between the plants.

Every year the plants take minerals out of the soil. If these minerals aren't returned to the soil, soon the soil is worn out. Since different crops use different amounts of minerals, soil gets worn out faster when only one type of crop is grown year after year.

Keeping Soil Healthy

Farmers do many things to prevent erosion. They plant lines of trees or bushes, called ***windbreaks***, to slow down the wind as it crosses their fields. They avoid plowing in the fall and plant ***cover crops*** to hold down the soil after they take their main crop off the land. Farmers with hilly land plow sideways around the hills (called ***contour plowing***). Contour plowing leaves the soil in horizontal ridges that catch water, preventing the water from running straight downhill. Some farmers use ***conservation tillage***, a modern method of plowing that leaves plant material in the top layer of soil to protect it from erosion. All these things help keep valuable topsoil from being blown or washed away.

Farmers add ***fertilizer*** to their soil to keep it from getting worn out. ***Inorganic*** fertilizers are chemicals made in a laboratory that can be added to the soil. Some commonly added chemicals are nitrogen, phosphorus, and potassium. ***Organic*** fertilizer comes from living things, like manure from farm animals, compost, or waste material from crops. Organic fertilizer can be more expensive, and its chemical content is harder to measure exactly, but only organic fertilizer contains humus, which is necessary for healthy soil.

To preserve the minerals in the soil, farmers sometimes let a field lie ***fallow***, which means letting it rest for a year without taking any crop off it. Farmers also ***rotate*** their crops, growing different crops on the same piece of land each year. A crop like corn, which takes a lot out of the soil, may be followed by a planting of clover or alfalfa, crops that actually help replace some soil minerals.

EXERCISE 5: SOIL CONSERVATION

Directions: What follows is a list of farming practices. On the line next to each farming practice, write whether the practice *harms* or *helps* the soil. The first one is done for you.

1. Using fertilizer helps

2. Planting the same crop every year ____________

3. Fall plowing ____________

4. Letting a field lie fallow ____________

5. Planting windbreaks ____________

6. Plowing straight up and down hills ____________

7. Planting cover crops ____________

8. Conservation tillage ____________

9. Rotating crops ____________

10. Having big fields without windbreaks ____________

11. Contour plowing ____________

12. Leaving soil bare between row crops ____________

Directions: Circle the number of the best answer.

13. If you had a garden patch with sandy, worn-out soil, what would be the best thing you could do to improve it?

(1) plant only easy-to-grow things like radishes and beans
(2) dig in lots of dried manure for fertilizer
(3) plow it well before planting
(4) leave it bare all winter to soak up water
(5) spread pure nitrogen fertilizer on it

14. From the way the term *organic fertilizer* is used in this article, the word *organic* probably means

(1) from a living thing
(2) brown or black in color
(3) modern and scientific
(4) artificially made
(5) inexpensive and useful

Answers and explanations start on page 217.

ECOLOGY AND POLLUTION:
A Balancing Act

> There was an old lady who swallowed a dog; she swallowed the dog to catch the cat; she swallowed the cat to catch the bird; she swallowed the bird to catch the spider; she swallowed the spider to catch the fly; I don't know why she swallowed the fly. Perhaps she'll die.

Did you ever sing this old nonsense song when you were young? Of course, it's just meant to be silly and fun, but it is actually a pretty good description of how the natural world is set up: everything eats something else.

The study of the balance of nature is called ***ecology***. Ecologists study how living things are related to each other and to the world around them, their ***environment***. All living things depend on their environment and on each other in very complex patterns.

MEADOW FOOD WEB

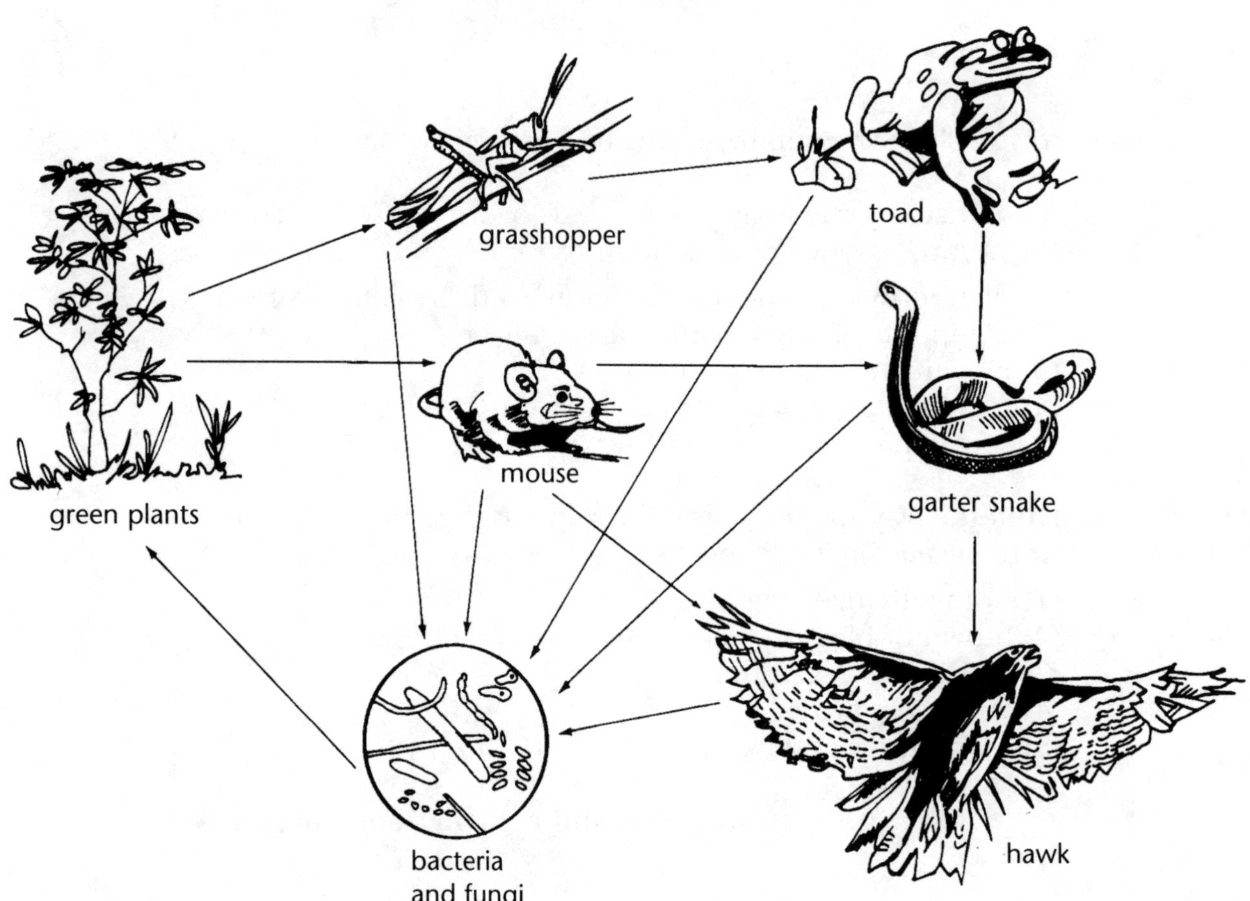

One pattern that ecologists study is called a ***food web***. The basis of any food web is green plants. Green plants are called ***producers*** because they use energy from the sun to produce food by photosynthesis. Every other living thing depends on the food made by green plants. Animals that eat plants, like grasshoppers and mice, are called ***primary consumers***. Animals that eat other animals, like the toad, the snake, and the hawk in this food web, are all ***secondary consumers***. Finally, ***decomposers*** like bacteria and fungi break down wastes and dead plants and animals, returning their nutrients to the soil for plant food.

If just one link in a food web is disturbed, all the other parts are affected. For an example, look at the food web on page 172.

- If a sudden dry spell prevented the toads from breeding, there would be fewer toads to eat grasshoppers.
- Millions more grasshoppers would survive, so farmers' crops in the area would be under attack from the hungry grasshoppers.
- Snakes would not do well either because there wouldn't be so many toads for them to eat.
- Because there were fewer snakes, there might be fewer hawks, too.

The whole thing is even more complicated than we can picture here, because there are many more animals involved in a real food web.

People and the Environment

Humans are the only animals that try to control their environment. Because of this, we often disturb the balance of nature. We cut down forests that provided food and shelter for many kinds of animals and plants. We dam rivers and water our lawns. We burn fossil fuels to heat our homes in winter and cool them in summer. We kill off whole groups of animals for sport or for food.

Our industrial society produces many chemicals that are sometimes released into the environment, causing ***pollution***. Air pollution comes from the chimneys of factories and furnaces and from automobile exhaust. Water pollution can be caused by wastes from homes and factories. Even fertilizers can pollute the water if they wash off farm fields instead of soaking into the ground where they can be used by plants.

As you can see, it is easy for people to disturb the balance of nature without meaning to. It usually takes a lot of knowledge, money, and work to protect or repair that balance. Unfortunately, not everyone is willing to spend the money and effort needed. Because we can partly control our environment, many people do not realize that we still depend on the balance of nature. Many people also do not realize how we can be affected by problems in nature that seem far away. Scientists know that all living things, including people, are woven together into one overall system. We depend on the natural environment for our food, water, and air—for our very lives—so it is up to all of us to keep the environment safe and healthy.

EXERCISE 6: A FOREST ECOSYSTEM

Directions: A group of plants and animals and the local environment they live in are called an ***ecosystem***. Use this diagram of a food web in a forest ecosystem to answer the following questions. Notice that all of the arrows in the food web point to consumers.

FOREST FOOD WEB

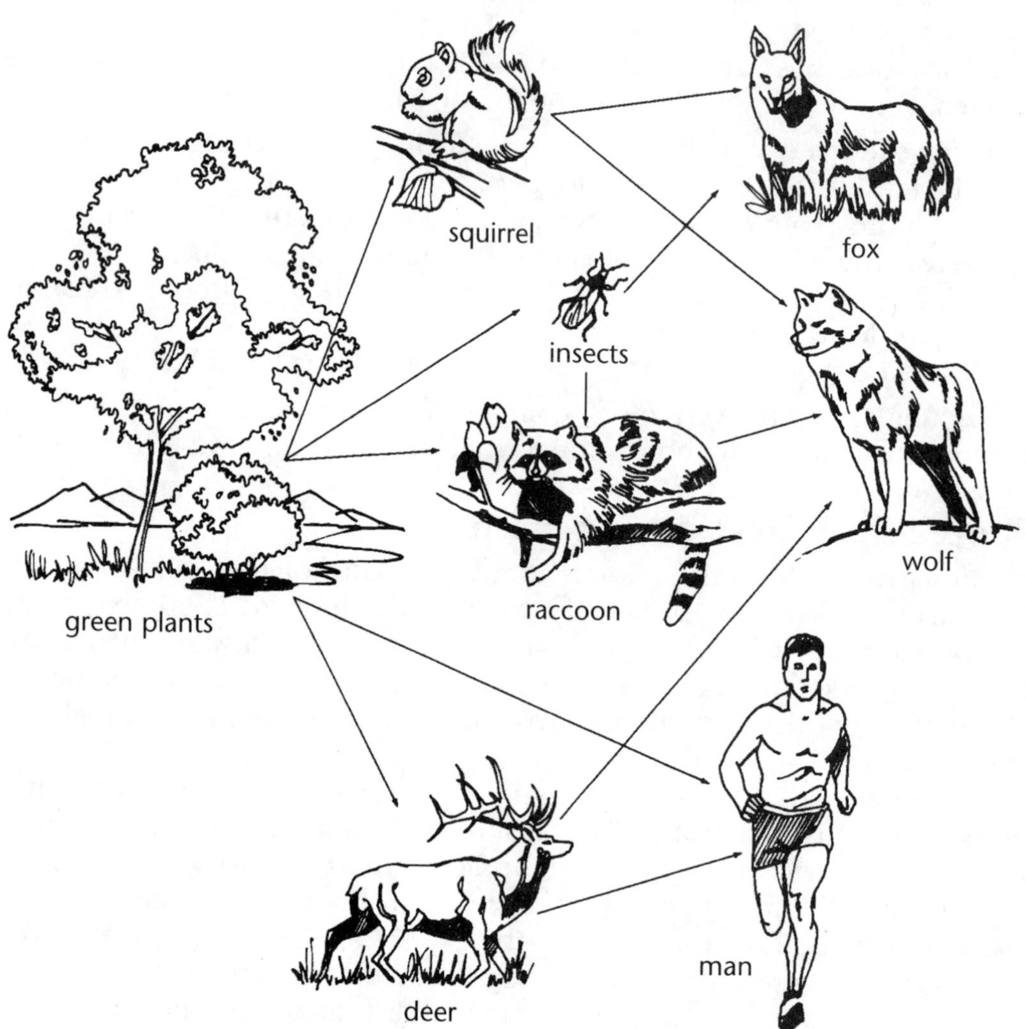

Note: All dead organisms are decomposed by bacteria and fungi, and their nutrients return to the soil to be used by plants.

1. What are the producers in this food web?
2. What are the primary consumers?
3. What are the secondary consumers?
4. What are the decomposers?

5. If all the wolves were killed off by hunters, what would probably happen to the deer population?

Directions: Circle the number of the best answer.

6. Looking at the diagram on page 174, if the trees were sprayed with a pesticide that killed most of the squirrels, what other animal population in this web would be most affected?
   (1) wolves
   (2) deer
   (3) raccoons
   (4) humans
   (5) foxes

7. The main point this author is trying to make is that
   (1) people can control their environment
   (2) living things depend on each other and the environment
   (3) some animals eat other animals
   (4) green plants are the most important things on earth
   (5) people often pollute the environment

Answers and explanations start on page 217.

WEATHER: What's It Like Outside?

One of the first things most people do in the morning is check the weather. We look out the window to see if the sun is shining or if it has rained during the night. As we dress, we listen to the weather report. The weather affects how we live every day, from the clothes we wear to the prices of the food we eat. Yet the weather is a part of the environment that we really cannot control. We don't even predict it very well, as anyone who has been rained out unexpectedly at a picnic or ball game can tell you.

The Earth is surrounded by a blanket of air many miles thick, our ***atmosphere***. Everything that affects the lower part of the atmosphere affects our weather.

Air Pressure

Because air is so light, we don't usually think of it as weighing anything. But each of us has miles of air above our head. Like everything else on Earth, this air is pulled down by gravity. It presses on us with a force of about fourteen pounds per square inch. Because we're so used to it, we don't usually feel this ***air pressure*** unless it suddenly drops. When this happens before a storm, or when we go up in an airplane, it makes our ears pop and can give some people a headache.

Warm air is lighter and cold air is heavier, so weather forecasters can use changes in air pressure as one way to predict the weather. They measure air pressure with an instrument called a ***barometer***, so air pressure is sometimes called ***barometric pressure***.

Wind

Wind is the movement of air. Large masses of air move in predictable patterns around the Earth due to the Earth's rotation (spinning). Weather patterns in the United States mostly move from west to east. Small masses of air move in different directions because of differences in temperature. When air is warm, it becomes lighter and rises. Colder, heavier air moves in close to the ground to take the place of the warm air. This movement of air causes wind. A light wind feels good on a hot day, but strong winds like tornadoes and hurricanes can be very destructive.

Clouds

Clouds are part of the natural water cycle. Water evaporates into warm air. As the air rises, it cools, and tiny droplets of water form. These droplets are so small and light that they just hang in the air, forming a cloud.

Clouds come in many sizes and shapes. ***Cirrus*** clouds are thin, feathery-looking clouds that are usually high up in the atmosphere. ***Cumulus*** clouds are the familiar soft, puffy clouds that look like pieces of cotton wool as they blow across the sky. Light, white cumulus clouds are usually a sign of good weather, but cumulus clouds with dark, heavy-looking bottoms mean rain or snow is probably on the way. ***Stratus*** clouds are low, flat clouds that often cover the whole sky. Fog is actually a stratus cloud that has formed near the ground.

Precipitation

Precipitation is the scientific word for any kind of water that falls from the sky, in the form of rain, snow, sleet, hail, or dew. Each type of precipitation is formed under different conditions. Raindrops are formed when water droplets in a cloud combine into larger and larger drops. When the drops of water get heavy enough, they fall to the ground as rain. If the air cools very quickly, the water droplets freeze before they can combine, and the precipitation falls as snow. If already-formed raindrops go through a very cold air layer on their way to the ground, they freeze into hard little pellets called ***sleet***. ***Hail*** develops when raindrops are blown up and down between layers of warm and cold air, freezing and refreezing. Strong winds can hold hailstones up in the clouds until they are the size of golf balls or even larger.

EXERCISE 7: WEATHER

Directions: Show whether these statements are true or false by putting a *T* or an *F* in front of them. If a statement is false, change the word in *italics* to make it true. The first one is done for you.

__F__ 1. The Earth is surrounded by a blanket of air called the ~~*lithosphere*~~ atmosphere.

______ 2. *Water* pressure is also called barometric pressure.

______ 3. Weather in the United States usually moves from *west* to *east*.

______ 4. *Cirrus* clouds are soft-looking, puffy clouds.

______ 5. Fog is a low-lying *stratus* cloud.

______ 6. Rain, snow, sleet, hail, and dew are all forms of *precipitation*.

______ 7. *Snow* is formed when frozen raindrops are blown up and down between layers of warm and cold air.

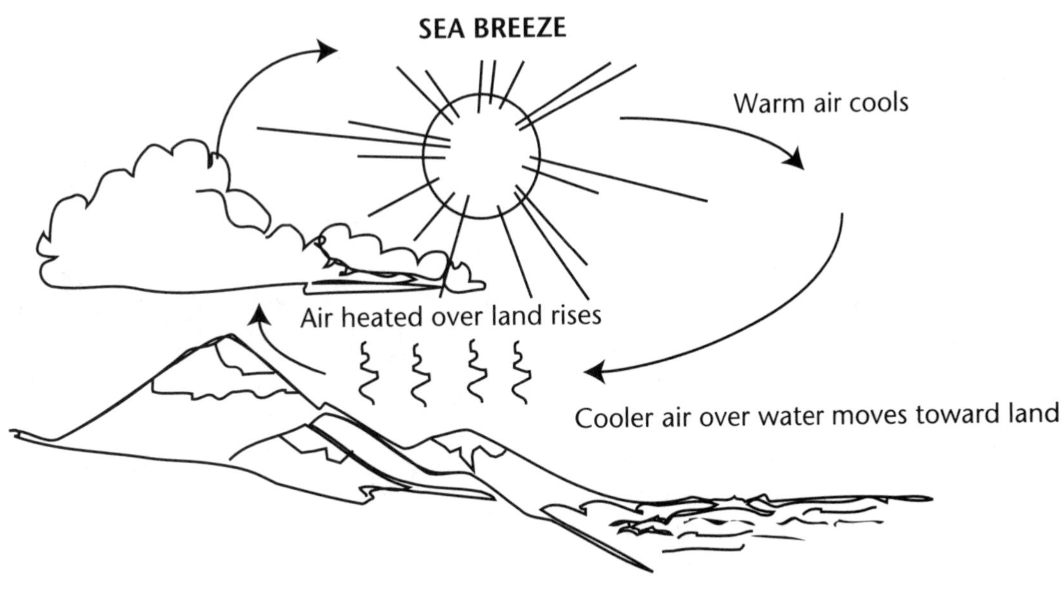

Directions: The diagram above shows why, on a warm day, you can often find a cool breeze blowing from a lake or an ocean. Use this diagram and the information about wind in this article to choose the best answer for each question.

8. Why does the air over the land rise?
   (1) The sun draws it up by gravity.
   (2) The water is warmer than the land.
   (3) The shade from the cloud makes the air cooler.
   (4) The sun heats the land and the air over it.
   (5) The strong wind causes friction.

9. At the time and place represented in this diagram, would it be safe to go out on the water in a small sailboat?

(1) Yes, because the wind is blowing toward the land.
(2) No, because the wind is too strong.
(3) Yes, because the sun is shining.
(4) No, because the water is too cold.
(5) There is not enough information to answer this question.

Answers and explanations start on page 217.

OUR SOLAR SYSTEM:
Beyond the Earth

The ***universe*** is the biggest thing we know. It is simply everything—all matter and all space. If something is not in the universe, it doesn't exist physically anywhere, because every part of space is part of the universe. No one knows where the edge of the universe is; maybe it just goes on forever.

A ***galaxy*** is a group of stars in the universe. Our galaxy is called the Milky Way. It contains millions of stars grouped in a flat spiral pattern that is about 100,000 light-years across. A ***light-year*** is a unit used to measure distance in space. One light-year is equal to about 6 trillion miles, a distance too large for anyone to really imagine.

THE MILKY WAY GALAXY

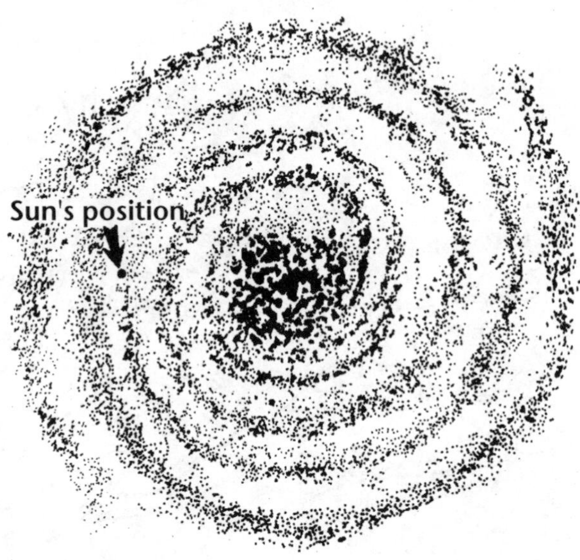

Stars are enormous balls of very hot gases in which nuclear reactions are constantly happening. These nuclear reactions produce a lot of heat and light, which are given off into space. Stars come in all different sizes, from giants to dwarfs, and in all the colors of the rainbow.

Our own ***sun*** is a yellow star about halfway out from the center of our galaxy. It is only a medium-sized star, although it looks much bigger to us because it is so much closer than any other star. There are nine known ***planets*** that orbit (go around) our sun; one of these planets is the Earth we live on. Astronomers, scientists who study the stars, think that other suns may have planets, but they don't really know.

The Solar System

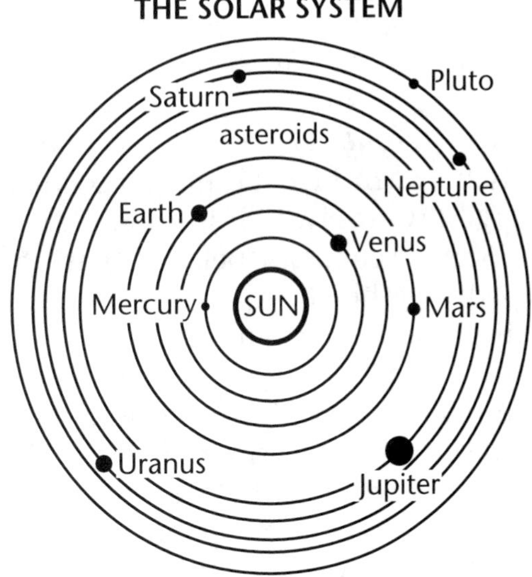

Our sun, with all its planets, their moons, and various other things, such as comets and asteroids, is called the ***solar system***. Look at the illustration at right while you read about Earth's neighbors in the solar system.

Mercury is the planet closest to the sun. Mercury rotates very slowly, taking almost 59 days to spin around once. Because of this, one side of Mercury gets very hot while the other side, away from the sun, gets very cold.

Venus is the second planet from the sun. It is about the same size as Earth, nearly eight thousand miles in ***diameter*** (distance across, going through the center). Venus is always covered with clouds, so no one has ever seen its surface.

Our Earth is the third planet. It is the only planet known to have life. This may be because it has just the right temperature range for liquid water—cool enough so it doesn't boil away, yet warm enough so that it doesn't all freeze solid.

Mars is the fourth planet, another small one, about one-half the diameter of Earth. Some scientists think there may once have been life on Mars, before the planets cooled off so much. Some even think there might still be life. Other scientists say that life is impossible because the atmosphere is very thin and cold. A space probe sent to Mars did not find any life, but no one can be sure until we do a lot more exploring.

Jupiter is the largest planet, over eleven times the diameter of Earth. The atmosphere of Jupiter is very thick and heavy, made up mostly of hydrogen, methane, and ammonia.

Saturn is the sixth planet from the sun. It is slightly smaller than Jupiter, and it is known mostly for its beautiful rings. There are at least seven rings around Saturn, probably made of ice-covered rocks that revolve around Saturn and sparkle brightly from reflecting sunlight.

Uranus and Neptune are the sixth and seventh planets. They are both very far from the sun and very cold. They are about the same size, approximately 3 1/2 times the diameter of Earth.

For most of its orbit, Pluto is the farthest planet from the sun: it is more than 3 1/2 billion miles away. Because it is so far away, and because it is only a little larger than Mercury, Pluto was not discovered until 1930.

Six of the planets have ***moons*** orbiting around them. Jupiter has at least fifteen moons, and more are likely to be discovered. Even though Earth has only one moon, it is a big one, about one-fourth the size of Earth. Most moons are smaller, with only four of Jupiter's and one of Saturn's moons being as big as ours.

The ***asteroids*** are a belt of small chunks of rock that orbit the sun mainly between Mars and the next planet, Jupiter. They range in size from the largest, Ceres, which is 480 miles across, down to tiny particles of rock dust. Some scientists believe that the asteroids are matter that never grouped together to form a planet. Others think that they might be the remains of a planet that blew up.

Other bodies in the solar system include meteors and comets. ***Meteors*** are chunks of rock like asteroids, but they do not follow a regular orbit around the sun. Sometimes meteors hit Earth, but most of them burn up in the atmosphere long before they hit the ground. When we see meteors burning up in the atmosphere, we call them "shooting stars." ***Comets*** are good-sized balls of rock and ice. They have very strange orbits; at one end they come very near the sun, while at the other end they swing way out past Pluto. When a comet comes near the sun, the ice in it begins to melt and then boil away. The gas from the boiling ice reflects the sunlight and looks like a long white "tail."

EXERCISE 8: THE HEAVENLY BODIES

Directions: Write the correct word in front of each definition.

__________________ 1. largest planet in the solar system

__________________ 2. large balls of hot gases giving off light and heat

__________________ 3. everything; all matter and space

__________________ 4. planet with visible rings

__________________ 5. chunks of rock orbiting between Mars and Jupiter

__________________ 6. smallest planet

__________________ 7. group of stars in the universe

__________________ 8. planet with thick layer of clouds

__________________ 9. the sun with all its planets, moons, etc.

__________________ 10. ball of ice and rock with a long gaseous "tail"

Directions: Circle the number of the best answer.

11. According to the article, which of the following is an opinion that some scientists have about Mars?
    (1) Mars is about one-half the diameter of Earth.
    (2) There are little men living on Mars.
    (3) Life couldn't survive on Mars due to its thin atmosphere.
    (4) A space probe did not find any life on Mars.
    (5) Mars is the fourth planet from the sun.

12. Considering how the term *solar system* is used in this article, the word *solar* probably means
    (1) very hot
    (2) having to do with the Earth
    (3) far apart
    (4) having to do with the sun
    (5) related to comets

Answers and explanations start on page 218.

A SOLAR ECLIPSE:
Now You See It; Now You Don't

> Imagine that you are living ten thousand years ago. You belong to a tribe of wandering hunters. Hunting has not been good for some time, and many people in the tribe are very hungry. At noon one day, your leader prays to the tribal gods for food. Suddenly, the sky grows dark, and slowly the sun itself seems to disappear. Everyone in the tribe shouts and prays, offering sacrifices to the gods. Gradually, the sun starts to grow and the sky gets lighter until it is normal daylight again. You are very glad to see the sun again. Without the sun, you and all your people would die.

You have just seen a solar ***eclipse***. It is not magic, though people used to believe it was. A solar eclipse happens when the moon comes between the Earth and the sun. Look at the diagram on page 182.

A SOLAR ECLIPSE

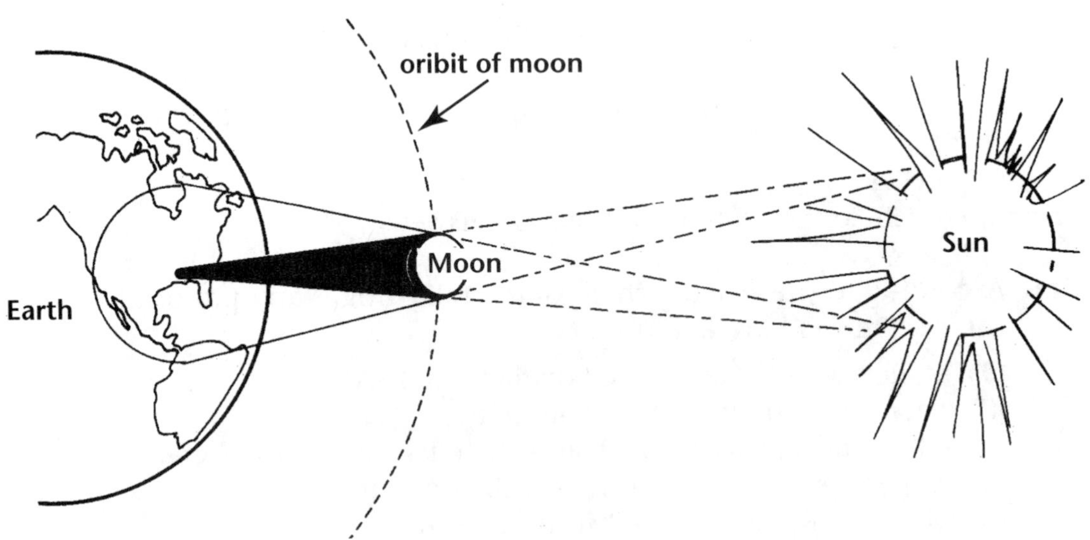

When the moon is directly between the Earth and the sun, the sun's rays cannot reach a small part of the Earth (an area 169 miles wide). If you are standing in this area where the moon's shadow falls, it will seem as if the sun has disappeared. Actually, the moon is blocking your view of the sun, just the way your hand held in front of your face can block your view of a whole tree or house. It is important, however, to avoid looking at the sun during an eclipse because doing so may cause permanent damage to your eyes.

If you are near, but not in, the shadow area, only part of the sun will be blocked. This is called a ***partial eclipse***. Total solar eclipses are rare. When there is one, scientists will travel many miles for the opportunity to do experiments and discover more facts about the sun, the moon, and our own planet Earth.

EXERCISE 9: AN ECLIPSE

Directions: Write a few sentences in answer to the following question.

1. What if you had never heard about eclipses, and you suddenly saw the sun start to disappear? Write a few sentences describing what you might think, feel, and do.

Directions: Circle the number of the best answer.

2. From the article you can tell that
   (1) people were very stupid 10,000 years ago
   (2) no one today is afraid of eclipses because we could live without the sun
   (3) solar eclipses have not always been understood scientifically
   (4) the sun stopped shining 10,000 years ago
   (5) praying can't cause solar eclipses anymore

3. Which of the following can you infer from the diagram?
   (1) During a solar eclipse, some people on Earth can't see the sun or the moon.
   (2) The Earth is almost as big as the sun.
   (3) Most of the Earth is dark during a solar eclipse.
   (4) Solar eclipses happen mostly at night.
   (5) The moon is closer to the sun than to the Earth.

Answers and explanations start on page 218.

THE FUTURE IN SPACE: "Beam me up, Scotty!"

> Christopher James was almost too excited to stay in his shuttle seat. He wasn't going far, just up to Luna to see his uncle, but it was his first time off the surface. He peered through the port to see if he could spot the station up ahead, but it was still too far away, just one bright speck against a background of stars. He slid back in his zero-weight harness, wondering how the other passengers could sit there so calmly. Why, twenty years ago, there hadn't been any regular spaceflights! The moon colony was just getting established then, so there was really nowhere to go. Now there were three commuter flights daily from the U.S. space station alone. Luna City was over 100,000 people strong and growing fast, along with that new colony on Mars. Christopher was secretly hoping to get a job in Luna City. He had a feeling his future lay in space.

Maybe someday this scene won't seem like science fiction, just an ordinary account of an ordinary trip. Even before 1969, when the first man landed on the moon, scientists and engineers all over the world have worked to find ways for people to live and travel in space.

There are many difficulties to overcome. To begin with, there is the problem of ***gravity***—first too much and then too little. Any spaceship that leaves Earth has to break free of Earth's tremendous gravity. Right now, it takes enormous amounts of fuel to do this, so launching spaceships is terribly expensive. Then, when the ship reaches space, the effects of gravity are no longer noticeable. Everything in the spaceship, including the people, becomes weightless. People need to have weight; our hearts, our lungs, and especially our stomachs are comfortable only when we can feel which way is down. All of our tools and equipment are designed to work in gravity. (Have you ever thought of how you would drink from a glass if there were no weight to hold the water down?)

Another problem is air. Space is nearly a ***vacuum***; that is, it is almost totally empty, containing practically no matter, not even air. Any ship that travels in space has to be completely airtight. For long trips, a spaceship would have to carry enough air for all the passengers to breathe, or scientists would need to find a way to break down exhaled carbon dioxide to get pure oxygen again. There would be the same problem on the moon, which has no real atmosphere. Every building would have to be airtight, and some way would be needed to supply oxygen for the people living there.

A third problem is heat. On Earth, our atmosphere controls the sun's heat for us. In the daytime, it shelters us from the direct rays of the sun, which would boil us alive. At night, it holds in heat so that we don't freeze solid. In space and on the moon, there is no atmosphere to do this. Special shielding and insulation are needed to protect us.

Space Exploration

With all these difficulties and more, why should we bother with space exploration? This is a question many people are asking now, especially when it seems that the government hasn't enough money to do everything it needs to do right here on Earth.

There are some very practical reasons for investing money and effort in space exploration. Many experiments can best be done in conditions of vacuum or weightlessness, conditions that are easy to find in space. Solving the problems of space travel and communication has already led to many inventions, like new medical monitoring techniques and the microchips used in personal computers. Many raw materials that are becoming scarce on Earth may be found in space, especially in the asteroid belt. Some nations also want to use spaceships or stations for military purposes.

However, there are other important, though less obvious, reasons for exploring space. Humanity needs a frontier, a growing edge. Two hundred years ago, that frontier was here in North America. People who didn't fit into a settled country, who wanted adventure or freedom or just a chance to make it on their own, took a long, dangerous trip across the ocean to seek a new land. Even people who didn't come here could wonder about it, could dream of unexplored mysteries. Now almost all of the land in the world has been explored; most of it is settled. Space may well be the next place we will go to learn from nature, to test our abilities and our ideals—our next, and perhaps final, frontier.

EXERCISE 10: THE FUTURE IN SPACE

Directions: Write short answers to the following questions.

1. What are the three main areas of difficulty in space exploration listed in this article?

2. From the article or from your own ideas, choose one example of a problem in space exploration and tell how scientists might try to solve it.

3. Do you agree or disagree with the author's idea that our country should spend money on space research? Give at least *three* reasons for your answer and support them.

   a.

   b.

   c.

Directions: Choose the best ending for each sentence.

4. The final paragraph in this article is mostly
   (1) fact—something that can be proven
   (2) hypothesis—a reasonable explanation based on observations
   (3) scientific principles—the laws of science
   (4) opinion—someone's personal beliefs
   (5) experimentation—testing to prove a hypothesis

5. The author of this article would probably agree that
   (1) people should stick to old, traditional ways
   (2) scientific research is too expensive
   (3) dreaming of new things is useless and impractical
   (4) humanity was never intended to travel in space
   (5) people need a challenge to bring out the best in them

Answers and explanations start on page 218.

SCIENTIST IN THE SPOTLIGHT: Galileo Galilei

Around 1580, a young Italian named Galileo went to study at the University of Pisa to become a doctor. His father, a well-born but poor musician and mathematician, hoped that his son would recover the family fortunes by becoming a doctor. Unfortunately for his family, but luckily for science, young Galileo became fascinated with mathematics and science instead. He never became a doctor, but he did become one of the most famous of the early physicists and astronomers (people who study the stars).

Galileo was one of a number of scientists then making discoveries that did not agree with traditional beliefs. Unfortunately, although a brilliant scientist and mathematician, Galileo was also a rude and sarcastic person. When he thought that traditional beliefs were wrong, he didn't hesitate to say so.

One of his best-known experiments involved the speed of falling objects. Until Galileo, scientists believed what Aristotle had written hundreds of years before—that the heavier an object was, the faster it would fall. This theory sounded so sensible that no one had ever tried it out; they just accepted it. Galileo worked out a mathematical proof that showed that this theory couldn't be true. He said that if there were no air resistance, objects of different weights would fall at exactly the same speed. When no one would listen to him, he decided to show them. He climbed to the top of the famous Leaning Tower of Pisa and dropped two iron weights, one large and one small. They both struck the ground at the same time.

He wrote a booklet about this experiment, with all kinds of nasty, sarcastic comments about the scientists who had disagreed with him. It seems like a small thing to get all excited about, but the problem was not so much what Galileo did, but rather how he did it. He made so many enemies in Pisa that he had to leave and go to Padua, a city in a different area of the country. Galileo taught at the University of Padua for nineteen years. He did much of his best scientific work there, inventing the first thermometer and a drawing machine, among other things. His lectures were so popular that the university had to build him a special lecture hall that would hold up to two thousand people.

Galileo's most famous work began in 1609, when he first heard from a passing traveler of the invention of the telescope. He had never seen one, but from the man's description he was able to figure out the main principles. The next day, he started to build his own, and soon he had built a telescope better than any other made so far. He kept on improving his telescopes and sold hundreds to wealthy Italians.

At that time, most people believed that the Earth was the center of the universe and that everything, including the sun and the other planets, went around the Earth. The Catholic Church also supported this idea (although it certainly doesn't now), declaring it to be proof that the universe had been created for the human race.

By looking through his telescope, Galileo could see that, in fact, the Earth was not the center of the universe. Some years before, a scientist named Copernicus had said that the Earth and the planets all went around the sun. Galileo saw that Copernicus's theory was right.

In his usual tactless way, Galileo began writing and speaking about what he had seen, making fun of the important people who believed the old Earth-centered theory. Some of his enemies complained to the Church authorities that Galileo's ideas went against the Bible. The Church told Galileo he had to stop teaching his new theory.

But Galileo wouldn't keep quiet. Finally, in 1632, he wrote a book called *Dialogues on the Great World Systems*. His book was an excellent explanation and defense of his sun-centered theory. It was also very insulting to those who disagreed with him, including the Church. Galileo was brought before a Church court. He was threatened with torture and forced to confess publicly that he was wrong, that the Earth did not move around the sun. But even this defeat couldn't break his spirit. As he turned to leave the court, it is said that he muttered to himself, so softly that only a few people heard him, "Yet, it does move!"

EXERCISE 11: GALILEO GALILEI

Directions: Using the information from this article, number from first to last the following seven main events of Galileo's life.

1. ________ **a.** He builds a telescope.

________ **b.** He is tried by a Church court and forced to say his book is wrong.

________ **c.** He goes to the University of Pisa.

________ **d.** He starts teaching at the University of Padua.

________ **e.** He publishes *Dialogues on the Great World Systems*.

________ **f.** He does his famous "falling objects" experiment.

________ **g.** He discovers that Copernicus's "sun-centered" theory is correct.

2. There were many value conflicts in Galileo's life. He often had to choose which of two opposing values was more important to him. Describe one of these times and say whether you think he made a good decision.

Answers and explanations start on page 218.

EXERCISE 12: CHAPTER 6 REVIEW

Directions: Read each passage carefully. Then circle the number of the one best answer to each question.

Questions 1–3 are based on the following passage.

There are over 2,000 types of minerals found in the Earth's crust, but they can all be classified in three basic groups. The first type is igneous rock. Igneous rock is formed when hot, liquid rock is pushed up from the center of the Earth and then cools and hardens. Since the whole crust of the Earth was once liquid, most of the crust is made of igneous rock.

Sedimentary rock is often formed under water. For example, some types of sedimentary rock are formed as a layer of sand, mud, small rocks, and shells drifts to the bottom of the ocean each year. As the layers pile up, more and more pressure is put on the bottom layers. As they are pressed together, they gradually turn into rock.

Metamorphic rock is rock that has been changed. If an ordinary igneous or sedimentary rock gets buried deeply under other rocks, sometimes the heat and pressure will cause the rock to change its form. For example, marble is a metamorphic rock made from ordinary limestone.

1. Most jewels are stones that have been changed under heat and pressure. What type of rocks are they?
   (1) inexpensive
   (2) igneous
   (3) sedimentary
   (4) metamorphic
   (5) any of the above

2. According to the passage, most of the Earth's crust is made of igneous rock because
   (1) there are many volcanoes in the world
   (2) metamorphic rock is changed to igneous rock
   (3) sedimentary rock is found only where oceans have been
   (4) granite is a kind of igneous rock
   (5) the crust was once all hot, liquid rock

3. Limestone contains small shells and bits of fish skeletons. What type of rock must limestone be?
   (1) metamorphic
   (2) sedimentary
   (3) igneous
   (4) useless
   (5) expensive

Questions 4–6 are based on the following passage and diagrams.

A

200 million years ago

B

present

1 North America
2 South America
3 Europe
4 Asia
5 Africa
6 Australia
7 Antarctica

One of the most interesting ideas in science is the theory of continental drift. Scientists who hold this theory believe that at one time all seven of the continents were in one giant land mass. Gradually, over millions of years, the continents broke apart and shifted to the places where they are today.

There is a good bit of evidence supporting this theory. In the above diagrams, you can see how the western edges of Europe and Africa seem to fit right into the eastern edges of North and South America. Also, similar fossil plants and animals have been found on widely separated continents, like Africa and South America. It is hard to believe that any land-living plant or animal could somehow cross a wide ocean. It is easier to explain if, at one time, Africa and South America lay right next to each other.

No one is sure what could cause such a heavy land mass to break up and move thousands of miles. Some scientists think that the drift was caused by the Earth's rotation. In fact, many scientists believe that the continents are still moving, but so slowly that we cannot measure their movement.

4. According to the diagram, which is the smallest of the continents listed below?

(1) Africa
(2) Asia
(3) Australia
(4) North America
(5) South America

5. One way to test the idea of continental drift would be to

(1) watch the continents from a spaceship
(2) try to push a continent with many large ships
(3) keep careful records of the positions of the continents over hundreds of years
(4) measure very carefully to see if the continental edges would still fit together exactly
(5) see if ancient scientists believed the idea of continental drift

6. Fossils of one certain kind of animal are found in both Africa and South America. If the continental drift theory is true, that animal probably existed
   (1) recently
   (2) only 1,000 years ago
   (3) only after the continents drifted apart
   (4) before the continents drifted apart
   (5) before Earth's crust began to cool

Questions 7–9 are based on the following passage.

Early explorers in Africa and South America wrote about the "endless jungle," the tropical rain forest, dark and tangled and teeming with life. Today, however, the jungle is disappearing; within 20 years there may not be any tropical rain forest left outside of a few parks and reserves.

People are destroying the rain forest. Every year thousands of acres of rain forest are cut down by lumber companies that take the largest trees, destroying the rest in the process. Other people clear many more acres to make farms and ranches. Towns and even cities are springing up in areas that used to be primitive forest.

Why should we care if all the rain forest is eventually gone? One reason is that unusual rain forest plants provide us with many medicines, dyes, and other chemicals. Even more importantly, the rain forest is a major part of the air renewal system of this planet. All the millions of green plants in the rain forest put out enormous amounts of oxygen every day. Without the rain forest, some scientists think there might not be enough green plants on Earth to keep the oxygen level up.

Scientists are concerned about the destruction of the rain forest and what that destruction might do to our planet. We need to listen to their concerns and take steps now to preserve and protect one of our most important natural resources, the tropical rain forest.

7. The main idea of the third paragraph of this passage is that rain forests are
   (1) beautiful
   (2) valuable to us
   (3) being destroyed
   (4) difficult to travel in
   (5) useless and unnecessary

8. How would the author of this passage probably feel about laws to protect endangered species of plants and animals?
   (1) strongly for
   (2) mildly for
   (3) neutral
   (4) mildly against
   (5) strongly against

9. Which would probably be the best source of more information about the destruction of the rain forest?
   (1) a pamphlet put out by a lumber company
   (2) your hometown daily newspaper
   (3) a high school chemistry textbook
   (4) articles in an ecology journal
   (5) advertisements for real estate in tropical countries

Questions 10–12 are based on the graph below.

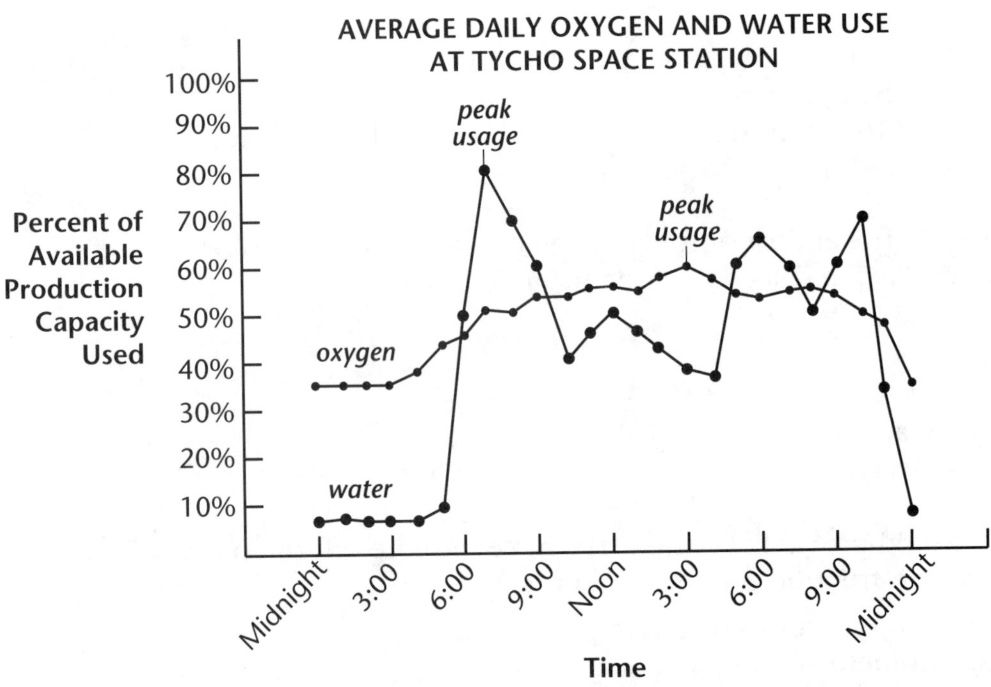

10. Which of the following can you conclude from the graph?
(1) Water and oxygen show exactly the same pattern of usage.
(2) Oxygen use changes more during the day than water use.
(3) Lowest usage of water and oxygen occur at the same time.
(4) Oxygen is more necessary than water.
(5) Water and oxygen use both peak at the same time.

11. What is the most likely reason that water use is highest from 6:00 A.M. to 9:00 A.M.?
(1) The crew members drink more in the morning.
(2) The space station is hotter when the sun rises.
(3) The water has been storing up all night.
(4) Cooking breakfast takes more water than cooking other meals.
(5) Most crew members take showers right after they wake up.

12. Which question *cannot* be answered from the information in the graph?
(1) Are more oxygen-producing plants needed?
(2) Who uses more water, male or female crew members?
(3) When is oxygen use highest?
(4) Do crew members use as much oxygen when asleep?
(5) Does the crew use all of the water that can be produced?

Answers and explanations start on page 218.

Post-Test

This is a two-part test to help you find out what you have learned from this book. Part I will test how well you remember some of the science words and ideas you have learned in this book. Part II will test your ability to understand science passages in multiple-choice format.

This test is not timed. Do the best you can without looking at the rest of the book. Then read pages 207–208 to find out how to evaluate your answers.

PART I: SCIENCE KNOWLEDGE

SECTION A: SCIENCE TERMS

Directions: These are some of the scientific words you need to know. In each group, write the letter of the correct definition in front of each word.

Group 1

1. ________ atmosphere
2. ________ chromosomes
3. ________ chlorophyll
4. ________ erosion
5. ________ fossil fuels
6. ________ galaxy
7. ________ nucleus
8. ________ litmus paper
9. ________ mammal
10. ________ work

a. the center of a cell
b. oil, coal, and natural gas
c. using force to move something
d. green chemical that plants use to make food
e. any animal that feeds its young with milk
f. threadlike groups of genes in cell nucleus
g. the layer of air around the Earth
h. a group of many stars
i. the wearing away of earth by water or wind
j. turns red in acids, blue in bases

Group 2

11. ________ conductor
12. ________ conservation
13. ________ ecology
14. ________ enzymes
15. ________ nerves
16. ________ invertebrate
17. ________ matter
18. ________ preservatives
19. ________ solution
20. ________ toxic

k. carry messages to and from brain
l. chemicals that help digest food
m. anything that takes up space
n. poisonous
o. the study of the balance of nature
p. any animal without a backbone
q. anything electricity flows through easily
r. preserving nature and the environment
s. chemicals used to keep food from spoiling
t. substance that cannot be separated by filtering

SECTION B: TRUE/FALSE

Directions: Write *T* (true) or *F* (false) in the blank before each statement. Then make all false statements into true statements by changing one or more of the words in dark type (see the example).

Example: __F__ **Proteins**, ~~**monohydrates**~~ carbohydrates, **fats**, **vitamins**, **minerals**, and **water** are the six main nutrients your body needs.

______ **21.** The **vibration** of molecules in matter is what causes **sound**.

______ **22.** Photosynthesis is how **fungus** plants use sunlight to make food from carbon dioxide, water, and minerals.

______ **23.** **Reptiles** lay their eggs in water and change as they grow up from gill-breathing tadpoles to lung-breathing land animals.

______ **24.** A **recessive** gene will always override a **dominant** gene.

______ **25.** Your lungs are the main organs in your **digestive** system.

______ **26.** **Stress** can be caused by any demand or change in your life, good or bad.

______ **27.** **Barbiturates**, often called "downers," are very addictive drugs that should never be taken with alcohol.

______ **28.** **Protons** and **neutrons** are found in the nucleus of an atom, while **zenons** orbit around the nucleus.

______ **29.** White light is really made up of **many different colors**.

______ **30.** An **atom** of a chemical compound is made up of two or more **molecules**.

______ **31.** A person who needs a drug regularly to handle everyday stress is **psychologically dependent** on the drug.

______ **32.** Cover crops, windbreaks, crop rotation, conservation tillage, and contour plowing are all ways to prevent **soil erosion**.

PART II: READING SKILLS

Directions: Read each passage carefully. Then circle the one best answer for each of the questions following. Feel free to look back in the passage to help yourself answer the questions.

Questions 1–3 are based on the following passage and graph.

John Washington is a wildlife manager in a national forest. His job is to make sure that all the animals in the forest are doing well and that there are not too many or too few of any one species of animal.

In the forest live a few wood ducks. For the past five years, John has been trying to increase the number of wood ducks by setting out artificial nesting boxes near streams and ponds. Every year he has kept records of the number of wood ducks seen in the forest, to see if his experiment is working. Here is a graph of his results.

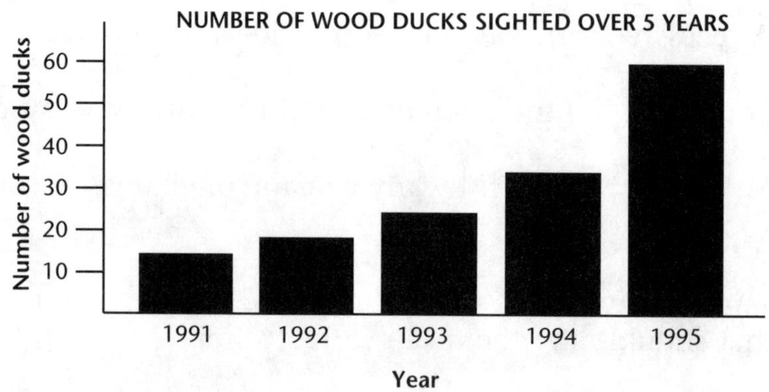

1. About how many wood ducks were sighted in the year John started his experiment?
   (1) 5
   (2) 15
   (3) 25
   (4) 40
   (5) 60

2. What is the hypothesis John is testing with his experiment?
   (1) Wildlife managers should take care of animals.
   (2) There aren't enough wood ducks in the forest.
   (3) The wood ducks need more nesting places in the forest.
   (4) People can count wood ducks accurately.
   (5) Wood ducks breed every five years.

3. What is one disadvantage with John's experiment?
   (1) There is no control area where no nesting boxes are provided.
   (2) The experiment isn't long enough.
   (3) Nobody cares very much about wood ducks.
   (4) John didn't record data every year.
   (5) John is not getting the results he hoped for.

Questions 4–6 are based on the following passage and chart.

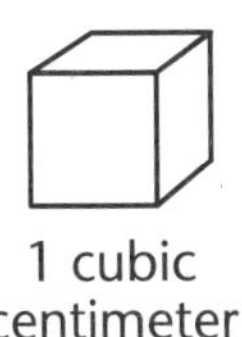

Physicists use the idea of density to describe different materials. If a material is very dense, that means that a small piece of it is very heavy. Iron and lead are dense materials. In contrast, Styrofoam is not dense at all; a very large piece of Styrofoam is still quite light.

The density of something is expressed in the number of grams that a cubic centimeter of that substance weighs. (Grams and centimeters are units in the metric system of measurement, used by all scientists and most other people outside the United States.)

For example, one cubic centimeter of pure iron weighs 7.86 grams; we say that iron has a density of 7.86 grams per cubic centimeter. The density of a pure substance is always the same. This means that pure iron will always weigh 7.86 grams per cubic centimeter. If you had two cubic centimeters of iron, they would weigh exactly twice as much, or 15.72 grams. Ten cubic centimeters of iron would weigh 78.6 grams, and so on.

The chart below shows the densities of some common substances.

Material	Density (in g/cm^3)	Material	Density (in g/cm^3)
Gold	19.3	Aluminum	2.7
Mercury	13.6	Water	1.00
Lead	11.3	Alcohol	0.79
Silver	10.5	Gasoline	0.68
Iron	7.86	Air	0.0013
Diamonds	3.5		

4. How much would a 6-cubic-centimeter diamond weigh?

(1) 3.5 grams
(2) 6 grams
(3) 9.5 grams
(4) 21 grams
(5) 35 grams

5. An archeologist dug up an old crown. There were 30 cubic centimeters of metal in the crown, and it weighed 315 grams. What was the crown made of?

(1) gold
(2) lead
(3) silver
(4) iron
(5) aluminum

6. What does the word *physicists* mean? (Use your knowledge of context, root words, and suffixes.)

(1) people who are physically strong
(2) experiments about physics
(3) scientists who study plants
(4) people who study chemistry
(5) people who study physics

Questions 7–9 are based on the following passage.

Spaceships of the future will probably be very different from our present-day rockets and shuttles. First, they will be designed to remain in space all the time, using small shuttles to carry passengers and freight up and down to planets. Because of this, they won't have any wings or the traditional pointed nose necessary to move through air. Maybe they will be completely round or shaped like a dumbbell or a doughnut.

These spaceships will also probably be much bigger. The spaceships we have today must be fairly small because it takes a great deal of fuel for even a small ship to escape the Earth's gravity. In the future, spaceships traveling between the stars may be large enough to carry thousands of people, plus enough plants for oxygen and fresh food and perhaps even some animals for meat. A really large ship could be a complete, well-balanced ecosystem, able to survive on its own for years.

7. Why are present-day rockets pointed at the nose?
   (1) They look more military that way.
   (2) They aren't big enough to be round.
   (3) They have to move through air.
   (4) The instruments have to point forward.
   (5) They have no wings.

8. Which of the following would probably be the most accurate source of more information on this subject?
   (1) a science fiction book
   (2) a college professor who teaches English
   (3) a children's encyclopedia
   (4) a congressman campaigning against the space program
   (5) a member of the astronaut training program

9. Why would you infer that a spaceship traveling to other stars might need to be a complete ecosystem?
   (1) It costs less that way.
   (2) It will take a long time to travel between stars.
   (3) It takes less fuel to travel in a large ship.
   (4) People like to have plants and animals around.
   (5) Fresh food is better than canned or frozen food.

Questions 10–12 are based on the following passage.

About one out of every twenty young children has a common behavioral problem called attention deficit disorder (ADD). Children with this problem are also called hyperactive children. All children have times when they are very active. This is not hyperactivity, even though it can drive parents crazy. A child with ADD is almost always moving, even when sleeping or watching TV. He usually has trouble paying attention to anything for more than a minute or two, so he often doesn't get very much done, even though he is so active. He often gets distracted or frustrated very easily and may have trouble waiting for anything.

Parents who suspect their child may have ADD should have the child examined by a team of experts. This team may include a child psychologist, a neurologist, and a developmental pediatrician. Children with ADD can often be helped by special behavior management techniques, special diets, or medicines, but each child is different. Treatment may have to change as the child grows and changes. No treatment should be started or medicines given on the advice of an ordinary family doctor or pediatrician alone. With the right help, children with ADD can grow up to be happy, healthy, and capable people.

10. The first paragraph mainly tells

(1) how children usually behave
(2) how to help a child with ADD
(3) how active children of different ages should be
(4) how an ADD child acts differently from other children
(5) how to keep a child from being distracted or frustrated

11. From the passage you can infer that

(1) some foods may make ADD worse in some children
(2) only boys get ADD
(3) children with ADD will probably not get better
(4) all children with ADD must take special medication
(5) children with ADD like to watch TV

12. According to the passage, who would be able to tell whether a child is hyperactive?

(1) the family's doctor
(2) a group of medical specialists
(3) the child's teacher
(4) another parent with a hyperactive child
(5) the child's grandparents, who have experience with how children act

Questions 13–15 are based on the following passage and graph.

Below is a solubility graph showing how a new vitamin powder called Vitamix dissolves in milk at different temperatures. Use this graph to answer the next three questions. (Note: Liters and milligrams are measurements from the metric system, which is different from the everyday measurement system used in the United States. Don't worry about this; you can still read the graph without knowing exactly how much a milligram or a liter is.)

SOLUBILITY OF VITAMIX IN MILK

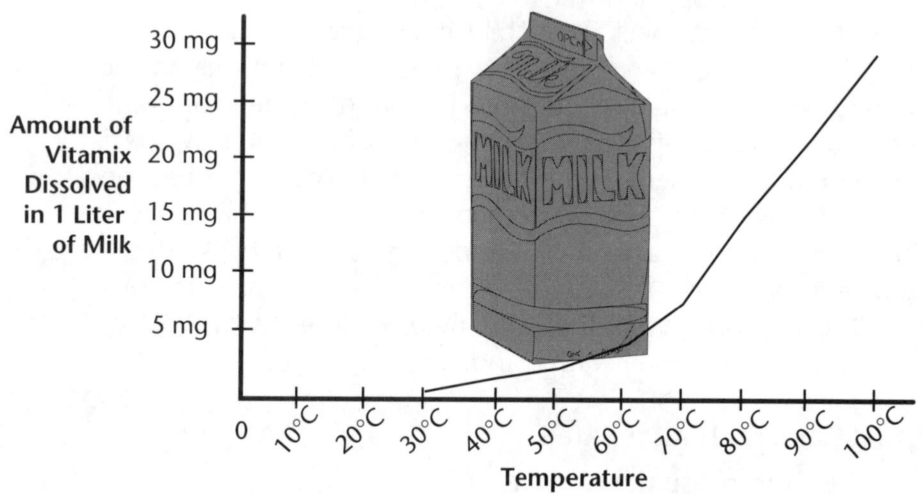

13. Approximately how hot does the milk have to be before 5 mg of Vitamix will start to dissolve?

(1) 0°C
(2) 30°C
(3) 60°C
(4) 80°C
(5) 100°C

14. The general trend of the graph line shows that

(1) hot liquids dissolve powders better than cool liquids
(2) the higher the temperature, the less Vitamix will dissolve
(3) the more liquid used, the more Vitamix will dissolve
(4) the more Vitamix was dissolved, the lower the temperature got
(5) the higher the temperature, the more Vitamix will dissolve

15. How was the information for this graph probably obtained?

(1) Many people happened to notice how much Vitamix would dissolve in milk at different temperatures.
(2) Someone did an experiment on dissolving Vitamix in water.
(3) A survey was taken.
(4) Several people did experiments on dissolving Vitamix in milk.
(5) A famous scientist predicted how Vitamix would dissolve in milk.

Questions 16–18 are based on the following passage.

> Artificial selection has been used for centuries by people who wanted to develop new, more useful types of animals. In artificial selection, a breeder chooses animals closest to the type he or she wants and then breeds them together. Then the most desirable of their offspring are bred together again.
>
> This process of breeding can continue for many generations. For example, to develop a type of dog to go down holes after badgers, some German dog owners bred together dogs with short legs and long bodies. From the offspring, they chose the puppies with the shortest legs and longest bodies and bred them together. Then they did the same with their offspring. After many years, they developed a dog with a low, long body and very short legs, called the *dachshund*, or "sausage dog."

16. According to the passage, artificial selection is used by

(1) people who want an improved breed of animal
(2) only Germans
(3) mostly dog breeders
(4) only people long ago
(5) mainly people who like to hunt and fish

17. In German the word *dachs* means "badger." Considering the meaning of *dachshund*, the German word *hund* probably comes from the same root word as which English word?

(1) dog
(2) high
(3) hound
(4) gunned
(5) hung

18. From the information in the passage, you could infer that dachshunds are nicknamed "sausage dogs" because they

(1) eat a lot of sausage
(2) used to cost the same as a sausage
(3) are the same color as sausage
(4) are shaped somewhat like a sausage
(5) were perfected by a person named Sausage

Questions 19–21 are based on the following passage.

The first "record player" was a very strange machine. It was patented by Thomas A. Edison in 1877. It didn't play actual records but instead played cylinders covered with tinfoil or wax. A recording could be made on the cylinder by speaking or singing at a large diaphragm, a flexible disk sort of like the top of a drum. This diaphragm was connected to a needle. Sound waves from the voice caused the diaphragm to vibrate, which made the needle move up and down, pressing grooves into the wax or foil.

To play the "record," the process was simply reversed. The cylinder was turned, making the needle move up and down in the groove. The needle, in turn, made a small diaphragm vibrate, causing it to reproduce the original sounds. These sounds came out through a big horn, like a megaphone, which amplified them (made them louder). As you may imagine, the sounds were not very clear. Also, the foil or wax "records" wore out very quickly. Record players have come a long way since 1877.

19. According to the passage, which of the following is *not* true?

(1) There were recording machines before 1900.
(2) Thomas Edison invented an early type of "record player."
(3) As they do today, early "record players" had a needle.
(4) Early amplifiers were not electronic.
(5) Wax or foil records could be played over a period of many years.

20. Which of these quotes from the first paragraph is an opinion?

(1) "The first 'record player' was a very strange machine."
(2) "It was patented by Thomas Edison. . . ."
(3) "It didn't play actual records. . . ."
(4) "A recording could be made on the cylinder. . . ."
(5) "The diaphragm was connected to a needle."

21. From the information in the passage, you can tell that sound waves can cause solid objects to

(1) wear out
(2) vibrate
(3) disappear
(4) get old
(5) break

Questions 22 and 23 are based on the following diagram.

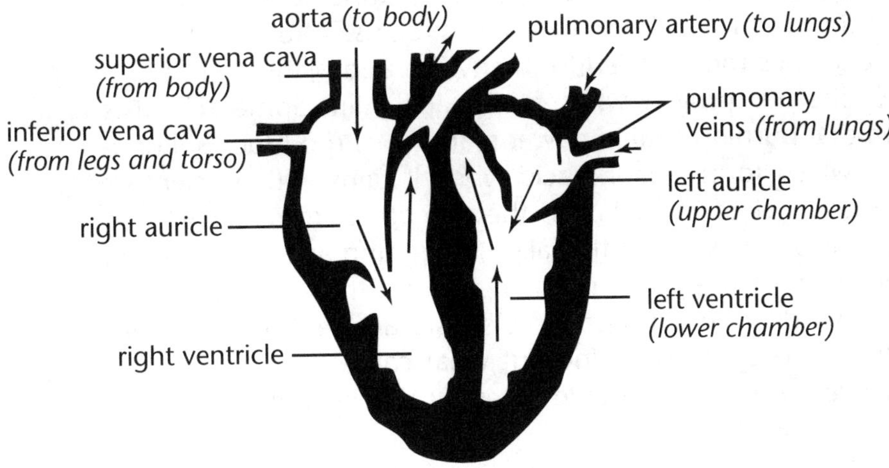

22. According to the diagram, which of these statements is true?
    (1) There are three main chambers (sections) in the heart.
    (2) Some veins lead directly into the ventricles.
    (3) Blood flows from the auricles into the ventricles.
    (4) No arteries or veins lead directly to the body.
    (5) Blood flows from one ventricle directly into the other.

23. From the diagram you can tell that the word *pulmonary* means something to do with the
    (1) heart
    (2) brain
    (3) lungs
    (4) body
    (5) blood

Questions 24 and 25 are based on the following passage.

Many ecologists today are concerned about the problem of acid rain. Acid rain is rain that picks up sulfuric acid pollution in the air and then falls into lakes and streams. After a while the water becomes too acidified for many fish and plants to live in.

No one has proven what causes acid rain. Some scientists believe that burning coal in power plants puts too much sulfur in the air, which forms sulfuric acid when it rains. Other scientists think that most of the sulfur in the air comes from car exhaust fumes. Still others say that the lakes are getting acid from the soil around them or the plants in them and not from the rain at all. Right now, different groups of scientists are testing their own hypotheses. They need to find out what causes acid rain so our grandchildren will still be able to enjoy the beautiful lakes and streams that we have.

24. Something is *acidified* when it
   (1) dies
   (2) falls like rain
   (3) becomes less acidic
   (4) is beautiful
   (5) becomes more acidic

25. The author of this passage would probably agree that
   (1) the problem of acid rain will be easy to solve
   (2) acid rain is not really very important
   (3) there should be more research on the acid rain problem
   (4) most people know the cause of acid rain
   (5) acid rain is a problem only for fishermen and boaters

Answers and explanations start on page 205.

POST-TEST ANSWER KEY

Part I: Science Knowledge
Section A: Science Terms

Group 1

1. g	**6.** h
2. f	**7.** a
3. d	**8.** j
4. i	**9.** e
5. b	**10.** c

Group 2

11. q	**16.** p
12. r	**17.** m
13. o	**18.** s
14. l	**19.** t
15. k	**20.** n

Section B: True/False

21. T

22. F Photosynthesis is how **green** plants use sunlight to make food from carbon dioxide, water, and minerals.

23. F **Amphibians** lay their eggs in water and change as they grow up from gill-breathing tadpoles to lung-breathing land animals.

24. F A **dominant** gene will always override a **recessive** gene.

25. F Your lungs are the main organs in your **respiratory** system.

26. T

27. T

28. F Protons and neutrons are found in the nucleus of an atom, while **electrons** orbit around the nucleus.

29. T

30. F A **molecule** of a chemical compound is made up of two or more **atoms**.

31. T

32. T

Part II: Reading Skills

1. (2) The bar for 1991 is halfway between 10 and 20. This can be estimated at 15.

2. (3) John is hoping that providing more nesting places will increase the number of ducks.

3. (1) John does not have a control area in which he provides no nesting boxes, to check on whether the duck population would increase anyway. It would be very hard for him to have a control group in this sort of experiment.

4. (4) According to the chart, 1 cm^3 (cubic centimeter) of diamonds weighs 3.5 grams, so 6 cm^3 would weigh 6 cm^3 times 3.5 g, which equals 21 grams.

5. (3) If you divide 315 g by 30 cm^3, you get 10.5 g per cubic centimeter, which is the density given in the chart for silver.

6. (5) The context tells you that physicists are people. You have learned that the *-ist* suffix means a person who does something.

7. (3) The passage talks about "the traditional pointed nose necessary to move through air."

8. (5) This person is likely to have the most specific, up-to-date information. Choices (1), (2), and (3) are not expert enough in the subject, and choice (4) would be very biased.

9. (2) This answer is implied by the final sentence in the passage and by your knowledge of the enormous distances between stars.

10. (4) The first paragraph describes an ADD child's behavior. Choice (1) does not cover all that is in the first paragraph. Choices (2), (3), and (5) are not covered in the first paragraph at all.

11. (1) You can tell that some foods may make ADD worse because the passage says that some children can be helped by a special diet.

12. (2) The passage says a team of doctors is needed. It specifically says that a regular family doctor or pediatrician should not handle this problem alone. A teacher, family member, or other parent would be even less expert.

13. (3) Find 5 mg on the vertical axis. Look straight across to your right until you reach the graph line. This point is directly above 60°C on the horizontal axis.

14. (5) The graph line shows that more Vitamix dissolved as the temperature of the mixture got higher, so choices (2) and (4) cannot be correct. Choice (3) is not right because nothing was on the graph about using different amounts of liquid. Choice (1) is not correct because this graph gives information only about Vitamix dissolving in milk, not about all powders in all liquids.

15. (4) The graph shows data from experiments. Choices (3) and (5) are incorrect because this graph is based on observed facts, not just opinions. Choice (1) is wrong because it is unlikely that people would just "happen" to notice exact temperatures and amounts of Vitamix dissolved. Choice (2) is wrong because the experiment is about Vitamix and milk, not water.

16. (1) See the first sentence.

17. (3) You would infer this from the information that the dachshund was a dog bred to hunt badgers and from the similarity in sound between *hund* and *hound.*

18. (4) The passage describes dachshunds as being long and low, with very short legs; thus, somewhat sausage-shaped. Choices (1), (2), (3), and (5) are not mentioned in the passage at all.

19. (5) The passage says that the "foil or wax 'records' wore out very quickly."

20. (1) "Strange" is a matter of opinion. All the other statements are provable facts.

21. (2) The passage says that "sound waves from the voice caused the diaphragm to vibrate," and the diaphragm is a solid object.

22. (3) On each side, the arrows come down from the auricles into the ventricles.

23. (3) The pulmonary artery leads to the lungs, and the pulmonary veins come back from the lungs.

24. (5) The passage says that water becomes *acidified* when acid falls into it.

25. (3) In the last sentence, the author says that scientists need to find out what causes acid rain. Choices (2) and (5) are not correct because the author says that this is a problem that many people are worried about.

POST-TEST EVALUATION CHARTS

Since the post-test is divided into two parts, you should use the following two-step method to evaluate your answers.

First, use the answer key on page 205 to check your answers to Part I: Science Knowledge. Then look at the chart below. Find the number of each question you missed on this chart and circle it in the second column. Then you will know which science topics you might need to review.

Next, use the answer key to check your answers to Part II: Reading Skills. Then go to the chart on page 208. Circle the number of each question that you missed. By looking at the row labeled "Number Correct," you will be able to decide which reading skills you need to review.

Part I: Science Knowledge

Science Topic	Question Number	Number Correct
Plant and Animal Biology pages 37–50	2, 3, 7, 9, 16, 22, 23, 24	______ / 8
Human Biology pages 72–88	14, 15, 25, 26	______ / 4
Physics pages 107–20	10, 11, 17, 21, 28, 29	______ / 6
Chemistry pages 137–52	8, 18, 19, 20, 27, 30, 31	______ / 7
Earth Science pages 166–85	1, 4, 5, 6, 12, 13, 32	______ / 7

______ /32 TOTAL

Part II: Reading Skills

	The Scientific Method pages 14–27	Understanding What You Read pages 28–36	Understanding Illustrations pages 57–72	Analyzing Ideas pages 96–106	Building Vocabulary pages 129–37	Evaluating Ideas pages 160–66
Plant and Animal Biology	2, 3	16	**1**	18	17	
Human Biology		10	**22**	11	**23**	12
Physics	20	19	**4**	**5**, 21	6	
Chemistry	15		**13, 14**			
Earth Science		7		9	24	8, 25

NUMBER CORRECT:	_____ / 4	_____ / 4	_____ / 5	_____ / 5	_____ / 4	_____ / 3

The numbers in **boldface print** are questions based on illustrations.

_____ / 25 TOTAL

ANSWER KEY

CHAPTER 1

Exercise 1: Fact and Opinion
pages 17–18

1. F You could prove this by measuring Robert.
2. O There is no way to measure beauty. What is beautiful is a matter of opinion.
3. O That Denver is nicer is a matter of opinion.
4. F You can measure 92 miles.
5. O Statements about what people should do can never be proven; they are always opinions.
6. F You could prove this by a survey.
7. F You could prove this by measuring the hearing of people who listen to a lot of very loud music.
8. O What is good is a matter of opinion.
9. O Statements about what should be done are always opinions.
10. F You could prove this by looking at the records.
11. Answers will vary for the three opinions.

Exercise 2: Everyday Hypotheses
page 19

Your answers should be a lot like these answers, but you may use different words. If you are not sure whether your answer is correct, check with your teacher.

1. There will be spaghetti for dinner.
2. The storm has caused a power outage.
3. Bill isn't really sick; he's out hunting.
4. Your family is making you a Christmas present.
5. You are going to be promoted.

Exercise 3: Choosing Hypotheses
pages 20–21

1. (3) The plants without light died, and the plants with little light did not grow well. Therefore, you can hypothesize that green plants need light to grow and live.
2. (4) The bacteria in the jars were killed by the boiling temperatures. Choice (2) is wrong because bacteria grew in a sealed jar with no air.
3. (2) The amount of oil burned is related directly to the average temperature. Choices (1), (4), and (5) are not correct because the most oil was burned in January, when it was sunny, not snowy, and not the holiday season. Less oil was burned in December than in November, so (3) is not right.

Exercise 4: Making Hypotheses
page 22

Your answers should be a lot like these answers, but you may use different words. If you are not sure whether your answer is correct, check with your teacher.

1. The detergent is coming from the town. Upstream from the town there was no detergent in the river.
2. The dog has swallowed the toy mouse and is choking on it. The dog was playing and eating just that morning, so it is probably not sick. It probably does not have food poisoning because the other dog ate the same food and is fine.
3. Carl's magnet, like all magnets, picks up only things made of iron or steel. It makes no difference how big the object is or whether or not it is wet.

Exercise 5: Errors in Experiments
page 25

Your answers should be a lot like these answers, but you may use different words.

1. **subjects were not similar OR conditions of experiment not kept the same**
   The gardener used pepper plants for one group and beans for the other, so his subjects were not all similar. He couldn't tell if the beans didn't grow because of the fertilizer, because the seeds were bad, because it was a bad year for beans, or for some other reason.
2. **conditions of experiment not kept the same**
   Alice did her test-driving on a long-distance trip, so the conditions weren't the same as in her normal driving. Perhaps she got better mileage because of the premium gas, but perhaps it was because she was doing highway driving instead of stop-and-go driving around town.
3. **not enough subjects OR the experiment was not reproduced**
   The mechanic tried only one squirt gun, so she didn't have enough subjects in her test group. Since the machine was having trouble only a third of the time, maybe the next gun or the one after that would have been flawed. The mechanic needs to reproduce the experiment.

Exercise 6: Review of the Scientific Method
pages 26–27

Your answers should be a lot like these answers, but you may use different words.

1. Why didn't milkmaids catch smallpox?
2. Getting cowpox makes you unable to catch smallpox.
3. He tested it by giving people cowpox and seeing if it protected them against smallpox.

CHAPTER 2

Exercise 1: Restating Facts
pages 29–30

Your answers should be a lot like these answers, but you may use different words.

1. Smoking increases your chances of getting lung cancer.

2. Many people who pass the GED go on to do well in business.
3. Nuclear energy is very powerful and useful, but it can also do horrible damage.
4. An older person with more experience often learns more easily than a child in school.
5. Babies who are less than a year old can get botulism from eating honey.

Exercise 2: Summarizing
page 31

1. (5) This is the best summary. Choices (1) and (4) are too narrow; each covers only one of the facts given. Choice (3) is too broad, and (2) is not even mentioned.
2. (3) This is the best summary. Choices (1) and (4) are too narrow; each covers only one of the facts. Choice (2) is not mentioned. Choice (5) is not a true statement.

Exercise 3: Finding the Main Idea of a Paragraph
pages 33–34

1. The main idea is "Cactuses are remarkable plants, made to live in one of nature's harshest environments." The rest of the paragraph gives you details on how they are made specially to survive harsh conditions.
2. The main idea is "Cars just seem to get more and more complicated." The rest of the paragraph tells you how simple the first cars were and how they got more and more complicated as time went on.
3. The main idea is "Even though it is only a reaction of your own body, an allergy can really make you miserable." The rest of the paragraph explains how an allergy is a reaction and just how miserable it can be.

Exercise 4: Finding the Main Idea of a Passage
page 36

1. (4) The passage describes safety features a crib should have. Choices (2), (3), and (5) are details.
2. (3) The passage is about a crib's safety features. Choice (1) is too broad, choice (2) is too narrow, and choice (4) is not mentioned in the passage.

Exercise 5: Cells
pages 38–39

1. f
2. i
3. g
4. a
5. h
6. c
7. b
8. d
9. e
10. (4) Choices (1), (2), and (3) are all too narrow, each covering only one detail from the passage.
11. (1) The paragraph under the heading "Plant Cells" mentions cell walls. There is no mention of cell walls in animal cells.

Exercise 6: Germs
pages 40–41

1. a. germs
   b. viruses
   c. bacteria
   d. protozoans
   e. immunity
   f. immunization
   g. vaccination
   h. babies
   i. protect
2. (1) Choices (2) and (4) each cover only one of the facts about bacteria. Choices (3) and (5) are not true according to the passage.
3. (4) The paragraph talks about how important it is to get immunized. Choices (1) and (2) are too narrow, covering only one part of the paragraph. Choice (5) is not true according to the passage.

Exercise 7: Food Factories
page 42

1. F Some fungi, like yeast, are helpful.
2. T Fungi have no chlorophyll.
3. F Fungi are plants without chlorophyll.
4. T This is stated in the second paragraph of the passage.
5. (1) Check the second paragraph of the passage.
6. (2) Choice (2) is the best summary. Choice (1) is only a detail. Choices (4) and (5) are not mentioned.

Exercise 8: Types of Animals
pages 45–46

1. a. (3)
   b. (6)
   c. (5)
   d. (2)
   e. (4)
   f. (7)
   g. (1)
2. a. (6) A cow gives milk.
   b. (4) A rattlesnake has scales, is cold-blooded, and lays eggs on land.
   c. (5) A robin has feathers.
   d. (2) A guppy has a backbone and breathes all its life with gills.
   e. (1) A bee has no backbone.
   f. (3) A bullfrog first lives in the water as a tadpole, then changes and lives on land.
3. (1) This is the main idea of the first section of this passage.
4. (4) Both birds and mammals are in the family called *vertebrates*, but birds are not mammals. Each of the other animals listed is a mammal.

Exercise 9: Animal Partners
page 47

Your answers should be a lot like these answers, but you may use different words. If you are not sure whether your answer is correct, check with your teacher.

1. Blind people, deaf people, people in wheelchairs, abused children, people in nursing homes, and prisoners are all types of people who can be helped by animals.

2. A hearing-ear dog can tell its master about many things, including doorbells, telephones, alarm clocks, fire alarms, crying babies, sirens, and train signals.
3. By riding horses, physically disabled people gain exercise, stronger muscles, and balance.
4. A dog in the children's ward would cheer up the sick children. It would help them express their feelings and deal with their problems and fears. It would comfort them by loving them.

Exercise 10: Genetics
page 50

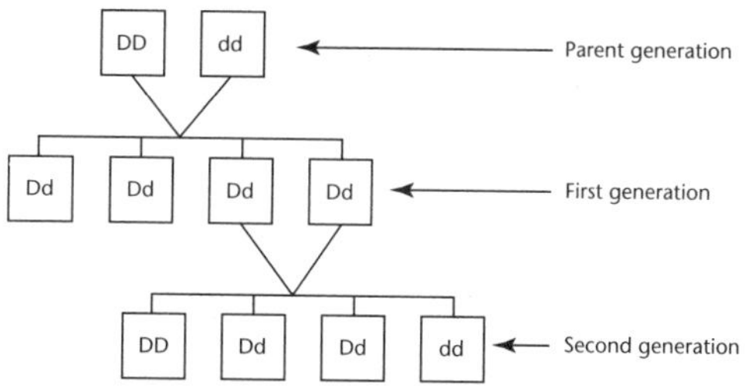

1. All the hamsters would have dark eyes because they all would inherit one dominant gene for dark eyes from one parent.
2. All of them would carry one recessive gene for light eyes from the other parent.
3. One hamster out of four would probably have light eyes; it would probably have gotten one recessive gene from each parent. Three would have dark eyes.
4. Two out of three of the dark-eyed second-generation offspring would carry a light-eye recessive gene.
5. (3) If any of the offspring are white, they must have inherited two recessive white genes, one from each parent. Therefore, the brown parent must have a recessive white gene.

Exercise 11: George Washington Carver
page 52

Your answers should be a lot like these answers, but you may use different words. If you are not sure whether your answer is correct, check with your teacher.

1. Being black made Carver's life more difficult in many ways. He didn't have a regular family life because his parents couldn't live together. His mother was stolen by slave raiders, and his voice was damaged by them. He had trouble getting an education because most schools would not admit black people.
2. Because Carver learned to read, he went on to become a college graduate and a famous scientist. If he had not learned to read, he probably would have been a field worker all his life.
3. Answers will vary; discuss them with your teacher.
4. Answers will vary; discuss them with your teacher.

Exercise 12: Chapter 2 Review
pages 53–56

1. (4) A statement about what someone *should* do is an opinion. Choices (1), (2), and (3) are facts, not opinions. Choice (5) is not mentioned in this passage.
2. (3) The risk of a bad reaction may be small compared to the risk of disease. Doctors would want to keep giving the vaccine. Choices (1) and (4) are too dangerous. Choices (2) and (5) are just ways of getting opinions, not scientific proof.
3. (2) This is stated in the last sentence of the passage.
4. (1) The size and weight of the apatosaurus are the largest given. The dinosaurs in choices (2) and (3) are both smaller. The pterosaur's size is not given, so (4) is wrong. Choice (5) is not mentioned in the passage.
5. (2) All of the animals discussed are dinosaurs. Choice (1) is too broad. Choices (3), (4), and (5) are all details, not the main idea.
6. (5) The passage mentions that some dinosaurs ate plants.
7. (1) See the second sentence of the passage for the definition of a mutation.
8. (5) A mutated animal usually does not survive to breed.
9. (4) See the last sentence of the passage for this definition.
10. (3) Children, teenagers, and adults can all enjoy gardening. Choice (1) is too broad. Choices (2) and (4) are too narrow. Choice (5) is false.
11. (3) Some people enjoy gardening, but others may not. Choices (1), (2), and (5) are facts, not opinions. Choice (4) disagrees with the passage.
12. (4) Small children, teenagers, parents, and elderly people were the age groups mentioned.

CHAPTER 3

Exercise 1: Diagrams
page 59

1. Parts of the Eye
2. No, it has a bump on the front.
3. the pupil
4. supporting fluids
5. the retina
6. the optic nerve
7. If the cornea clouds over, light cannot pass through it to the pupil and into the eye.

Exercise 2: Comparing Diagrams
page 61

1. It shows drawings of a fetus for the first 5 months of pregnancy.
2. It gets larger and more developed.
3. at four months

4. (4) Choices (1) and (3) are not right because the title says that this child hasn't been born yet. Choice (2) is wrong; the head looks different because it hasn't grown yet. Choice (5) has nothing to do with the diagram.

Exercise 3: Charts
page 63

1. It is about vitamins.
2. vitamins A, C, D, E, B_1, B_2, niacin, and B_{12}
3. scurvy
4. vitamins A and D
5. vitamins A, B_2, and niacin

Exercise 4: Line Graphs
pages 68–69

1. (3) Find the mark for two feet on the horizontal axis. Then follow an imaginary line straight up and over to 100 pounds.
2. (5) The heaviest rock (300 pounds) is the last one on the graph line and corresponds to 6 feet.
3. (4) The direction of the graph shows that longer crowbars move heavier rocks. Choice (2) is wrong because the length of the crowbar is important, not the thickness. Not enough information is given to conclude choice (1) or (3).
4. (1) The main idea of the graph is to show how long a crowbar must be to move rocks of different weights. Choice (3) is not true; some rocks over 300 pounds can be moved by other methods. Choice (4) is not told; other crowbars may be available. Choice (5) is not complete. The graph gives no information for rocks under 50 pounds, but that doesn't mean that there aren't any.
5. (2) Find the 4-foot mark on the horizontal axis. Look straight upward to find the right point on the graph line.

Exercise 5: Bar Graphs
pages 71–72

1. You expect to find information about the average temperatures in Vancouver.
2. It shows the months of the year.
3. It shows the average high temperatures in degrees Fahrenheit.
4. 5°F
5. 50°F
6. January
7. July and August
8. No, it probably doesn't get below freezing very often, because the lowest average temperature is only 42°F.
9. No, you probably could not grow tropical plants. They like very warm weather, which Vancouver does not have for over half the year, according to the graph.

Exercise 6: Bones and Muscles
page 75

1. T There are 206 bones.
2. T These are two of the main functions of bones.
3. F Most of your blood cells are made in your marrow.
4. F Cartilage is softer than bone.
5. T Ligaments are tough bands of tissue that hold bones together at the joints.
6. T One possible cause of osteoporosis is not getting enough calcium.
7. T See the paragraphs on the muscular system.
8. F Voluntary muscles are controlled by you.
9. F Only three types are listed.
10. T Cardiac muscles are found in the heart.
11. (4) See the diagram. Look at the skeleton's spine (backbone) and neck.

Exercise 7: Heart, Blood, and Lungs
page 78

1. **a.** lungs **b.** nose OR mouth **c.** mouth OR nose **d.** trachea **e.** bronchial tubes **f.** alveoli **g.** oxygen **h.** carbon dioxide **i.** Red blood cells **j.** White blood cells **k.** Platelets
2. (5) The white blood cells help the body fight disease.

Exercise 8: Nutrition
pages 80–82

1–3. Answers will vary. Check to make sure that your daily plan has the correct number of servings from each group.

4. (2) See the chart. Find carbohydrates in the "Nutrients" column. Then look to the right under "What It Does."
5. (4) A statement about what someone *should* do is usually an opinion. All the other choices are facts.

Exercise 9: Digestion
pages 83–84

1. h
2. f
3. d
4. b
5. i
6. c
7. e
8. a
9. g
10. (1) Your mouth, esophagus, stomach, and intestines are all part of the digestive tract. Numbers (2), (4), and (5) are not true. Choice (3) is not correct because the digestive tract contains more than one organ.
11. (4) See the last two paragraphs of the passage for the correct order.

Exercise 10: The Nervous System
page 85

1. **a.** skin **b.** sensory **c.** spinal cord **d.** brain **e.** brain **f.** motor **g.** hand
2. (5) If the sensory nerves are cut, that means he cannot feel anything at all from his foot. Since the motor nerves are all right, he can move the foot without any trouble.

Exercise 11: Stress
page 87

1. Answers will vary. One possible reason is that these events cause big changes in a person's way of life.
2. Answers will vary. One answer is that they all involve change.
3. Answers will vary.
4. (4) "Change in eating habits" is number 19 on the list. The other choices—pregnancy, trouble with the law, losing a job, and personal injury—are all rated as more stressful.

Exercise 12: Pregnancy Precautions
page 88

1–5. Answers should include five of these: German measles, some diseases, some medicines, illegal drugs, aspirin, alcohol, wine, beer, cigarettes.

Exercise 13: Dr. Elizabeth Blackwell
page 90

Answers will vary. Be sure that each opinion is backed up by a reason.

Exercise 14: Chapter 3 Review
pages 91–95

1. (4) See the definition in the passage.
2. (3) The diagram shows that these three bones are located in the middle ear.
3. (1) If the eardrum cannot vibrate, the person's hearing is affected. Choices (2) and (5) are wrong because we have no evidence about the effect of pain on hearing. Choice (3) is wrong because the fluid would be at body temperature, not cold. Choice (4) is wrong because, if the sound traveled better, the person would hear better, not worse.
4. (4) See the chart, across from "Males, 23–50."
5. (3) This is true for men and women of all ages. Choice (1) is not true because after 23, people need fewer calories. Choice (2) is wrong because a 19-to-22-year-old woman needs more calories than a 76-year-old man. Choices (4) and (5) are not right according to the chart.
6. (1) Women tend to need fewer calories as they get older. Choices (3) and (4) aren't good predictions because the trend (general direction) of the chart shows that people need fewer and fewer calories as they age.
7. (4) See the definition in the first paragraph.
8. (3) The passage talks about why STDs are dangerous and need a doctor's attention. Choices (2) and (4) are in the passage, but they are only details. Choice (1) is not in the passage. Choice (5) is false according to the passage.
9. (5) See the first paragraph. None of the other answers ever cure STDs.
10. (4) Look at the beginning of the middle graph line. It shows that a 25-year-old pack-a-day smoker can expect to live until about age 68, which is 43 more years.
11. (3) The graph shows that a 45-year-old nonsmoker can expect to live until age 75, while a two-packs-a-day smoker of the same age can expect to live only until age 68. The difference is 7 years.
12. (2) The graph shows that people who smoke less tend to live longer. This can be concluded by comparing the lifespans of smokers and nonsmokers.

CHAPTER 4

Exercise 1: Sequencing
page 99

1. c
2. d
3. e
4. a
5. b

Exercise 2: Logical Sequence
pages 100–101

1. Logical order: B, A. Steam engines must be invented before they can be put into locomotives.
2. Logical order: A, C, B. First the seeds are planted; then the plants come up; finally, the beans are picked.
3. Logical order: B, A, C. Before Franklin discovered what lightning really was, people could have believed it was a weapon of the gods. Franklin had to discover what lightning was before he could invent lightning rods.
4. Logical order: C, B, A, D. First you measure ingredients, then you mix them, then you put the raisins into the mixture, and finally you bake.

Exercise 3: Causes and Effects
pages 102–103

Your answers should be a lot like these answers, but you may use different words. If you are not sure, check with your teacher.

1. *Effect:* Uranium must be purified before use.
2. *Cause:* The chain reaction goes very fast.
3. *Cause:* The chain reaction goes too slowly.
4. *Effect:* The water boils.
5. *Cause:* The steam turns giant generators.
6. *Effect:* Atomic power plants have many safety devices.

Exercise 4: Finding Causes and Effects
pages 104–105

1. (3) Many people came to Bohr's home to talk about science, and that got him interested. Choices (l), (4), and (5) are true, but they did not cause Bohr to become interested in science. Choice (2) is not mentioned in the passage.
2. (2) The Nazis were interested in Bohr because he was well known and respected. All the other events did happen, but they were not caused by his fame.

Exercise 5: Making Inferences
page 106

Your answers should be a lot like these answers, but you may use different words. If you are not sure, check with your teacher.

1. People who don't use Saf-T have bad breath and shouldn't get close to anyone.
2. Smokeless tobacco can cause mouth cancer.
3. **a.** They are made of polyester.
   b. They were hard to take care of.
4. **a.** Too much fat and sugar can help cause heart attacks.
   b. A person should eat less fat and sugar to avoid heart attacks.
5. **a.** Many oranges are grown in southern Florida.
   b. Oranges need warm weather to grow.

Exercise 6: Simple Machines
page 109

1. **a.** simple machines
   b. work done
   c. force
   d. amount of push
   e. foot-pounds
2. (4) 2,000 pounds × 20 feet = 40,000 foot-pounds.
3. (2) Since 40,000 foot-pounds of work must be done, and the distance the car will travel is 100 feet, 40,000 ÷ 100 = 400 pounds of effort.

Exercise 7: Computers
pages 111–12

1. Any four of these are correct: telephones, accounting, banks, businesses, secretaries, writers, teaching, games. Also correct are any other true uses of computers.
2. Any five of these: keyboard, disks, tapes, paper cards, paper tapes, lights, modems, telephone lines.
3. Any five of these: screen, printer, disks, tapes, cards, telephone lines.
4. Answers will be different for each student.
5. (3) See the fourth paragraph of the article.
6. (2) Computers can do detailed, repeating tasks better than people can, but they have little or no creative ability.

Exercise 8: Atoms and Molecules
pages 113–14

1. c	**6.** a
2. h	**7.** b
3. d	**8.** f
4. g	**9.** e
5. i	

10. (4) You can infer this from the two statements that there are "only 108 different kinds of atoms" and that an element is "a material containing only one kind of atom." Choice (1) is untrue because many molecules contain more than two atoms. Choice (2) is incorrect because the article says that there are "millions of different ways" that atoms can combine to make molecules. Choices (3) and (5) are incorrect according to the article.
11. (2) A nuclear power plant worker would be exposed to radioactive substances like uranium.

Exercise 9: Electricity
page 116

1. ceiling light	**4.** dishwasher
2. counter lights	**5.** electric clock
3. outlet	

Check the diagram for this sequence.

6. (5) Nothing would work because there must be a complete circuit for the electricity to flow at all.
7. (3) See the sixth paragraph of the article.

Exercise 10: Nuclear Power
page 118

1. **B** Speaker B is worried about security not being able to stop terrorists.
2. **A** Speaker A feels that the safety record of nuclear power plants is very good.
3. **B** Speaker B asks, "How can they be sure?"
4. **A** Speaker A says the groups worried about nuclear power are "radical."
5. **A** Speaker A doesn't like being dependent on foreign countries.
6. (5) This fact is given in the second paragraph. Choice (1) is a fact from selection A, not B. Choice (3) is an opinion, not a fact, from A. Choice (2) is an opinion from B, not a fact.
7. (2) Obviously Speaker A is in favor of nuclear power. Utility companies are the companies that own and operate nuclear and other types of power plants. Choice (3) would be against nuclear power. Choices (1) and (4) would not necessarily be interested in nuclear power plants at all.

Exercise 11: Light and Sound
page 120

1. T
2. F Light is faster than sound.
3. F White light is a combination of all colors.
4. T
5. F A red dress reflects red light; it absorbs all other colors.
6. T
7. T
8. F Sound travels best through solid things.
9. (1) See the first paragraph of the article.
10. (3) See the third paragraph of the section on light.

Exercise 12: Marie and Pierre Curie
page 122

The correct order is 7, 3, 1, 6, 4, 2, 5.
Check paragraphs 8 through 11 for these facts in order.

Exercise 13: Chapter 4 Review
pages 123–28

1. (4) Only levers A and D are balanced. Check this by multiplying the force times the distance on each side.
2. (4) The work done is 300 pounds × 1 foot = 300 foot-pounds. The distance on the right arm is 4 feet. 300 divided by 4 is 75.
3. (5) Side A will go down because the heavier side always goes down, even if the difference is only a pound. It does not matter how *many* weights are on each side, but rather how *much* the total weight is on each.
4. (2) See the second paragraph of the passage.
5. (5) The passage tells you to look at the battery if you have trouble starting your car.
6. (4) This answer is implied because the author is clearly directing this at people who do not already know a lot about cars.
7. (3) This is implied in the sentence "The darker the object, the more light it will absorb and change to heat." Choice (2) is incorrect because of the same sentence. Choices (1), (4), and (5) are not mentioned at all in the passage.
8. (1) Solar heating systems cost less to run than regular heating systems do.
9. (2) Solar heat is defined in the passage as heat from sunlight. Choices (1), (3), and (5) are not indicated in any way in the article. Choice (4) is true, but it is not a problem; it is an advantage.
10. (4) As in the example in the passage, a sound twenty decibels higher is actually 100 times louder than the softer sound, because each 10-decibel jump means ten times as much sound. 10 × 10 = 100.
11. (5) See the second sentence in the passage.
12. (1) According to the chart, drills, shovels, and trucks put out the most decibels of sound, so a person working with them would have the greatest chance of job-related hearing damage.

CHAPTER 5

Exercise 1: Compound Words
page 130

1. horsepower
2. spaceship
3. sunspot
4. catfish
5. lifetime
6. earthquake
7. rattlesnake
8. wavelength

Exercise 2: Word Parts
pages 131–32

1. Hydrology
2. dermatology
3. Neurology
4. Biothermal
5. thermometer
6. thermonuclear
7. trimonthly
8. trifocals
9. tricycle
10. cardiac
11. cardiogram
12. cardiologist
13. microbiology
14. microfilm
15. micrometer

Exercise 3: Using the Context
page 134

Your answers should be a lot like these answers, but you may use different words. If you are not sure whether your answer is correct, check with your teacher.

1. An astrolabe might be **an instrument for looking at or measuring stars.**
2. Pasteurizing milk probably gets rid of **bacteria.**
3. Cyberspace might be **a kind of space that is controlled by computers.**
4. A piton is probably **a tool used by mountain climbers.**
5. Polychromatic probably means **many-colored.**
6. Carnivores are probably **animals that eat meat.**
7. Hydroponic farming is probably **farming without soil.**
8. A paleontologist might be a **scientist who studies ancient animals.**

Exercise 4: Translating Science to English
page 137

There are many ways to simplify these sentences. Here are some sample answers. If you are not sure whether your answer is correct, check with your teacher.

1. Air pollution can have very bad effects.
2. Experimental drugs often don't work and may have bad effects on people who don't know much about them.
3. Learning how to use water power to make electricity was necessary in order to make cheap electric power.
4. Children's toys should be educational as well as fun.

Exercise 5: Mixtures, Solutions, and Compounds
pages 140–41

1. M
2. C
3. S
4. M
5. C
6. S
7. S
8. M

Numbers 2 and 5 are compounds because two chemicals go together to make a completely different substance. Numbers 3, 6, and 7 are solutions because they could not be separated by sorting or filtering. The others are simple mixtures because they would be easy to separate into their original parts.

9. (2) If it could be filtered, the liquid would be an ordinary mixture. If it could not be separated by filtering, the liquid would be a solution.
10. (3) Salt is a compound, rather than a mixture or a solution, because it is an entirely different substance from its original parts. It can't be a poison, since people eat it every day.

Exercise 6: Chemical Names and Symbols
page 143

1. $CaCl_2$
2. CaO
3. H_2S
4. $NaSO_4$
5. CO
6. NaH
7. HNO_2
8. Fe_2O_3

Check with the chart in this article or your teacher if you missed some of these.

9. (5) It has four chlorine atoms and one carbon atom. Choice (3) has the wrong chemicals. Choices (1), (2), and (4) have the wrong number of chlorine atoms.

Exercise 7: Acids and Bases
page 145

1. a. Acids
   b. bases
   c–e. Choose three of these: vinegar, oranges, sour milk, lemons, grapefruit, canned goods
   f. drain cleaner
   g. washing soda
   h. ammonia
   i. sour
   j. bitter
   k. Bases
   l. acids
   m. litmus
   n. red
   o. blue
2. (1) It is the only compound given whose formula begins with H, as the passage said most acids do.
3. (5) The litmus paper test is a safe way to find out if a chemical is a base. Choices (1), (2), and (4) would be very dangerous. Choice (3) would not work because things other than bases also react with acids.

Exercise 8: Poisons
page 147

1–3. Answers will vary.
4. (2) The article says that telling children that medicine is candy is unsafe.

Exercise 9: Decisions About Chemicals
pages 149–50

1–3. Answers will vary.
4. (2) A statement that tells you what someone *should* do is an opinion. The other choices are facts from the article.
5. (5) This is discussed in the second half of the article. The other choices may be good reasons, but they are not mentioned at all in this article.

Exercise 10: Drug Abuse
page 152

1. c
2. e
3. g
4. f
5. a
6. h
7. d
8. b
9. (4) The answer can be found in the first paragraph.
10. (3) You can find this answer in the paragraph on barbiturates. Choices (1), (2), and (4) create psychological, but not physical, dependence.

Exercise 11: Early Scientists
page 154

Your answers should be a lot like these answers, but you may use different words. If you are not sure whether your answer is correct, check with your teacher.

1. People have always been interested in science because they wanted to understand nature and to control it.
2. Hippocrates is considered the Father of Medicine because he was the first doctor to say that diseases were caused by natural things. He also wrote many detailed descriptions of common diseases, and he composed the Hippocratic Oath.
3. Any three of these inventions will do: better ships, war machines, water pump, or block-and-tackle. Archimedes was the first scientist to apply science to everyday life.
4. Aristotle and many other Greeks believed that everything in the universe was made from only four elements: fire, water, air, and earth.
5. The alchemists were searching for the Philosopher's Stone. It was supposed to turn common metals into gold, heal sicknesses, and give eternal life.
6. Answers will vary.

Exercise 12: Chapter 5 Review
pages 155–59

1. (4) A molecule of SiO_2 contains one atom of silicon and two atoms of oxygen. None of the other choices contains both silicon and oxygen.
2. (3) Three of the listed compounds contain Ag, the symbol for silver.
3. (5) CuCl contains copper and chlorine. None of the other chemicals named has these two elements.
4. (4) All three body parts are listed as possible places of damage.
5. (2) See line 3 of the instructions.
6. (1) Children can't tell what is food and what is not. Choices (2), (3), and (5) are unimportant compared to the danger of poisoning. Choice (4) is irrelevant.
7. (2) Metal poisoning is the only choice given that is listed as causing problems with the nervous system.
8. (5) Dust is not listed as one of the causes of headaches and dizziness.
9. (3) Hardwood dust is the only choice given that is listed as a cause of cancer.
10. (4) The articles are about whether or not marijuana should be legal. Choices (2) and (3) are too narrow to cover the whole idea of the articles. Choices (1) and (5) are not mentioned in the articles.
11. (2) Speaker A would disagree with the other choices because he is arguing against the marijuana laws.

12. (1) You could prove how many people want marijuana legalized by taking a poll. Choices (2), (3), and (5) are opinions because no one can prove what could happen in the future. Choice (4) is an opinion because it talks about what people should do.

CHAPTER 6

Exercise 2: The Whole Story
page 164

Answers will vary. Here are some possibilities.

1. How hot or cold does it get in California? Is there much rain?
2. Which vitamins should be taken? How much? What specific health problems will each vitamin solve?
3. How much would taxes go up because of the park—closer to $2 or $200?
4. Is Bantex safe for people and animals? What insects does it kill?
5. Why are new roads needed? What does the speaker mean by "progress"?
6. Is there evidence that Chemical X causes cancer in humans? How many mice were tested in the study?
7. What are the benefits of space travel? What are the disadvantages?

Exercise 3: Information, Please
pages 165–66

1. Choices (2) and (3) are good sources. (1) is not a good source because the factory would be biased toward persuading you that it is not polluting the river. (4) is not the best source because the friend is probably not as knowledgeable as the health department or Citizens for a Better Environment.
2. Choices (1) and (4) are the best sources. Neither (2) nor (3) is as knowledgeable, unless one of them happens to be a doctor or nurse.
3. (3) and (4) are the best sources. Both NASA [source (1)] and the rocket parts maker [source (2)] are likely to be biased toward persuading you that the money is handled well.
4. (1) and (2) are the best sources. Your brother [source (3)] is probably not as knowledgeable, and source (4), the health food store clerk, may be biased, since her job depends on people buying health foods.

Exercise 4: Treasure from the Earth
page 168

Answers will vary. Here are some possibilities.

1. copper—electrical wires, kitchen pans, pennies, jewelry
2. iron—cars, stainless steel and cast-iron kitchen utensils, wood stoves, steel beams, wrought-iron railings, many tools
3. aluminum—kitchen utensils, foil, electrical wires
4. fossil fuels—gasoline, natural gas, heating oil, polyester clothes, draperies and upholstery
5. jewels—engagement rings, other jewelry, diamond saw blades, drills and files
6. (4) This is stated in the third paragraph.
7. (3) People will drive less because gas will be more expensive if fossil fuels, including oil, are scarce.

Exercise 5: Soil Conservation
pages 170–71

1. helps	7. helps
2. harms	8. helps
3. harms	9. helps
4. helps	10. harms
5. helps	11. helps
6. harms	12. harms

13. (2) The article says that manure is organic fertilizer. Organic fertilizer has humus, which is needed for healthy soil. Choice (5) is incorrect because soil needs more than just nitrogen. Choices (1) and (3) wouldn't help the soil. Choice (4) would cause erosion.
14. (1) Organic fertilizer is described as the remains of living things.

Exercise 6: A Forest Ecosystem
pages 174–75

1. The producers are green plants (the tree, the bush, and the grass). Only green plants can produce food.
2. The primary consumers are the squirrel, the insects, the deer, the raccoon, and the man because they all eat plants.
3. The secondary consumers are the fox, the wolf, the raccoon, and the man because they eat other animals.
4. The bacteria and the fungi are the decomposers.
5. The deer population would grow because none of the deer would be eaten by wolves.
6. (5) The squirrels are a main food source for the foxes. Wolves eat squirrels sometimes, but they also eat raccoons and deer.
7. (2) This is the main idea behind ecology. Choice (1) is not correct because people only *partly* control their environment. Choice (4) is wrong because all living things are needed; many plants couldn't survive without animals either. Choices (3) and (5) are in the article but are only details.

Exercise 7: Weather
pages 177–78

1. F The Earth is surrounded by a blanket of air called the **atmosphere**.
2. F **Air** pressure is also called barometric pressure.
3. T
4. F **Cumulus** clouds are soft-looking, puffy clouds.

5. T
6. T
7. F **Hail** is formed when frozen raindrops are blown up and down between layers of warm and cold air.
8. (4) Warm air rises. Choice (1) is wrong because the sun's gravity causes an equal (but very small) pull on *all* air on Earth. Choices (2) and (3) are not true according to the diagram.
9. (5) There is no indication on the diagram about how strong the wind is, so you can't tell whether it would be safe for a small sailboat.

Exercise 8: The Heavenly Bodies
pages 180–81

1. Jupiter
2. stars
3. universe
4. Saturn
5. asteroids
6. Mercury
7. galaxy
8. Venus
9. solar system
10. comet
11. (3) Some scientists believe that (3) is true, but it is not a proven fact. Choices (1), (4), and (5) are facts. Choice (2) is not in the article.
12. (4) The sun is the center of the solar system.

Exercise 9: An Eclipse
pages 182–83

1. Answers will vary.
2. (3) The article says people used to think an eclipse meant the sun had really stopped shining. Choices (2) and (4) are false. Choice (1) is incorrect: people aren't stupid just because they don't know something.
3. (1) Both the sun and the moon are on one side of the Earth, so people on the other side of the Earth can't see them.

Exercise 10: The Future in Space
page 185

1. gravity, air, and heat
2. Answers will vary.
3. Answers will vary.
4. (4) The final paragraph is all about things that cannot be proven.
5. (5) The last paragraph shows that the author thinks people need a challenge. Her opinions throughout the article show she would disagree with the other four statements.

Exercise 11: Galileo Galilei
page 187

1. The numbers, reading down, should be 4, 7, 1, 3, 6, 2, 5. Check back in the article for the correct order.
2. Answers will vary. Here are some possible conflicts to discuss:
   - Galileo's conflict as a student between studying medicine, as his family wanted, and studying science, which he preferred
   - his conflict between showing his pride and scorn for others and writing more tactfully, so more people would accept his writings
   - his final conflict between standing up for his beliefs and saving himself from torture

Exercise 12: Chapter 6 Review
pages 188–92

1. (4) Rocks that have been changed by heat and pressure are called *metamorphic rocks*.
2. (5) See the first paragraph of the passage.
3. (2) Since limestone contains small pieces of sea creatures, it must have formed under the ocean; therefore, it is sedimentary.
4. (3) Australia, labeled 6 on the diagram, is the smallest.
5. (3) This method would show whether or not the continents were shifting. Choices (1), (2), and (4) are not practical. Choice (5) is incorrect because ancient scientists weren't always right.
6. (4) The animal must have existed before the continents split in order to be found on both sides of the ocean. That eliminates answers (1), (2), and (3). Choice (5) is impossible; no animals lived on land before the crust cooled.
7. (2) The paragraph lists many examples of how the rain forests are valuable. Choices (1), (3), and (4) are all details. Choice (5) is untrue.
8. (1) All the author's statements show that he/she thinks that preserving nature is very important.
9. (4) The journal would be a good source of information on conservation issues. Sources (1) and (5) would probably be biased. Source (2) might have some information, but it would not be as complete as articles in a specialized journal.
10. (3) Lowest usage of both water and oxygen occur from midnight to 3:00 A.M., presumably because the crew members are all asleep. Choices (1), (2), and (5) are false according to the information on the graph. There is no information on the graph about Choice (4).
11. (5) This would account for the use of large amounts of water. Choices (1) and (4) are unlikely to be true. Choice (3) may be true, but it would not cause more water usage, since the graph indicates there is always plenty of water. Choice (2) is incorrect, because there is no "sunrise" in space. Sunrise is caused by the rotation of the Earth.
12. (2) There is nothing on the graph to show which crew members are using the water.